Praise for *Motivate Like a* CEO

"*Suzanne Bates argues convincingly that if nature abhors vacuums, CEOs must fill them. If the CEO is silent, the company will go dark. A great read.*"

—FRANK KEATING, governor of Oklahoma, 1995–2003

"*Once again Suzanne Bates delivers a must-read guide for all business leaders. With her innate talent to communicate, Suzanne offers sagely advice and shares the wisdom of high-powered motivators. She combines these with actionable suggestions, worksheets, and 'snackable' chunks of information to help business leaders to digest and master the art of motivating.*"

—SHERYL LINDSELL-ROBERTS, author of 22 books including *135 Tips: Writing Successful Business Documents*

"*Not every leader is born a natural motivator, but it's a critical management skill that can be learned, as Suzanne Bates effectively demonstrates in her new book. Executives seeking to motivate—not dictate—to achieve results will find a wealth of practical, helpful information here.*"

—MARGIE MYERS, SVP, Communications, Dunkin Brands, Inc.

"*Suzanne Bates gets it. This book will vastly improve the motivational skills of the reader and should become required reading for anyone who aspires to be a more effective leader.*"

—PETER ROLLINS, president, Chief Executive's Club of Boston

"*Suzanne Bates does for business what Viktor Frankl's* Man's Search for Meaning *(my all-time favorite book) did for psychology. Just as Frankl showed that people thrive when their lives have meaning, Suzanne demonstrates that companies thrive when they are designed around a shared purpose.*"

—STEPHEN SHAPIRO, author, *Goal-Free Living*

"*Unleash the power of your company's biggest asset—empowered and connected employees.* Motivate Like a CEO *provides practical methods to help leaders identify their personal passion and their company's purpose, including how to translate them in a manner that will truly inspire your entire team.*"

—MARK R. TOLOSKY, J.D., FACHE, president and
chief executive officer, Baystate Health

"Motivate Like a CEO *is a must-read for every executive and leader who wants their company to succeed in an ever-changing economy.*"

—SHELLEY ZALIS, founder and CEO, OTX

"Motivate Like a CEO *richly articulates the importance and nature of motivation. With this book, Suzanne Bates insightfully goes against the current models of business, based mainly on financial stimulus and behavioral response, and illustrates the importance of* people *rather than institutions. In a nutshell, this book is important, because it's about people connecting. Bates does a nice job of making that point—if not explicitly, then by example in every chapter.*"

—CHARLES H. GREEN, coauthor, *The Trusted Advisor*

"In a time when truly effective leaders are as rare as 40 mpg SUVs, along comes Suzanne Bates with powerful, practical advice on how to motivate people to achieve extraordinary outcomes."

—LYNN A. ROBINSON, author of *Trust Your Gut*

MOTIVATE LIKE A CEO

COMMUNICATE YOUR STRATEGIC VISION
AND INSPIRE PEOPLE TO ACT!

SUZANNE BATES

New York   Chicago   San Francisco   Lisbon   London
Madrid   Mexico City   Milan   New Delhi   San Juan
Seoul   Singapore   Sydney   Toronto

3 4 5 6 7 8 9 0   DOH   15 14 13 12 11

ISBN 978–0–07–160029–3
MHID   0–07–160029–9

McGraw-Hill books are available at special quantity discounts to use as premiums and sales promotions, or for use in corporate training programs. To contact a representative please visit the Contact Us pages at www.mhprofessional.com.

This book is printed on acid-free paper.

To Drew and Meghan
My purpose and passion

Contents

Acknowledgments

MANY FRIENDS, MENTORS, AND COLLEAGUES have supported, encouraged, and advised me on this project. They include Ken Lizotte, Meredith O'Connor, Donya Dickerson, Craig Bentley, Paula Lyons, Sarah Woods Bates, Alan Weiss, as well as Marcia Abbott, Mary Lou Andre, Vicki Donlan, Karen Friedman, Kasey Kaufman, Gayle Sierens, Annie Stevens, Chris Storr, Eleanor Uddo, and Kathy Venne. I also am grateful to my friends and colleagues in the Women Presidents Organization, the National Speakers Association, and The Boston Club.

With deepest gratitude, I acknowledge the people who graciously gave interviews and those who connected me with sources. All have helped me develop a greater understanding of the subject matter for this book. They include Steve Barron, Keith Blakely, Greg Case, Mike Curran, Mike Daly, Matt Davis, Kelly Drinkwine, John Fish, Archelle Georgiou, Robin Gundry, Deb Hicks, Brian Johnson, Paula Johnson, Ranch Kimball, Rich Krueger, Gloria Larson, Ken Liebler, Joanne Linhares, Andrew Liveris, Sean Martin, Ellyn McColgan, Maureen McGurl, Mike McNally, Evelyn Murphy, Jeff Neufeld, Laura Onessimo, Ellen Parker, Jennifer Parker, Dina Piran, Michelle Press, Vikki Pryor, Steve Rendle, Peter Roberts, Howard Schultz, Bill Swanson, Jeff Taylor, John Touchette, Kyle Warwick, Beth Webster, Rachel Whitehouse, Pam Wickham, and David Woods.

I would never have completed this project without the support and love of my family: my husband, Drew Yanno; my daughter, Meghan McGrath; my mother, Jane Bates; my sister, Mary Louise Gladden; my brothers, Richard Bates, and Charles Bates. Rosie, our faithful Jack Russel terrier, leaped out of bed at the crack of dawn each morning and kept me company as I wrote. Finally, I want to remember my father, Richard K. Bates, 1931–2008. He was my first and most important role model in business and in life, and will always be a source of tremendous inspiration.

1

What It Means to Motivate Like a CEO

I want to put a ding in the universe.

—STEVE JOBS

WHAT MOTIVATES US AS PEOPLE? This is a fascinating question because we are all different! How can there be one answer to such a question?

Yet I believe there is. As human beings, we all want to have a purpose. We want our lives to matter. We want to do something in the short time we have here to make a difference in the world.

The pursuit of purpose is so important to us as human beings that if we ignore it, we are not happy or fulfilled. Purpose is what allows us to discover who we really are. When we find purpose and meaning in our work, and we pursue that larger purpose, we discover our talents, skills, and sources of genuine satisfaction. We are happiest when we have the opportunity to apply our talents and skills to something meaningful. Purpose is necessary, critical really, to a healthy, happy, and successful life.

> *Purpose is necessary, critical really, to a healthy, happy, and successful life.*

In cultures where people live to be a hundred or more, research has found that individuals have a strong desire to fulfill their purpose. For example, in Costa Rica's "Blue Zone"—a place far from our business world—people live to a ripe old age; each individual creates a *plan de vida*. Costa Ricans believe that creating a plan for their lives is essential. They are taught that they must contribute to a greater good so they feel a compelling desire to be needed. And this drive for purpose that fulfills us isn't confined to any culture—it is universal. It is in all of us. We seek to find purpose and are happiest when we connect to a mission larger than ourselves.

Why begin a book on motivating people by talking about individual purpose? Because purpose is essential to motivation. Once we understand the role that purpose plays in our success and the success of our companies, we unlock the secret to achieving great things. As leaders, when we work with purpose and inspire others to purpose, we become a powerful force in the universe.

Regardless of where you are in your career, you can find purpose and meaning in your work. You can use this purpose to fuel your life and also become a great leader. When your work matters to you and you have a larger purpose that excites you, you inspire others. Making that kind of positive impact on the lives of other people, makes you an unstoppable force.

Your motivation and the motivation of your team will have a direct, undeniable impact on the bottom line of your business. A motivated, energized workforce is essential to accomplishing your goals. A good strategy and motivated people always accomplish amazing things. Motivated people will overcome the obstacles, defy the odds, and get more done.

> *Motivated people will overcome the obstacles, defy the odds, and accomplish more.*

Connecting people with a larger purpose is an exciting, worthy personal goal. As a leader, you have an opportunity to make those connections. Can there be anything more rewarding than helping other people to realize their own potential? When you embrace a purpose, they can't wait to get on board and work toward that common goal. As they discover their own connection to purpose, they look for ways to use their talents and, in the process, go the extra mile. They grow as people and professionals and achieve their own, personal goals. Therefore, one of the most effective things you can do as leader is to connect people with purpose for the good of every individual as well as the enterprise.

The *Oxford American Dictionary* says that motivation is "giving motive or incentive; to stimulate the interest of, to inspire." The person who *gives* motive or incentive is, by definition, a leader. The leader takes the lead in communicating motive and in the process *stimulates, develops, and nurtures* the talents and skills of other people engaged in the pursuit of the goal. As you will see in the pages of this book, leaders who provide motive and incentive align organizations and move them rapidly toward their goals. This could be the highest definition of leadership.

To write this book, I gave quite a bit of thought to what it means to *motivate* like a CEO. I finally decided that what it comes down to is this: *connecting people with purpose and passion toward a common goal.* Leaders help people to achieve a common goal and, in the process, realize their own potential. To motivate like a CEO is to be driven by purpose and passion and to connect other people to that purpose.

Over the years, working with hundreds of executives, I've always admired those who are purpose-driven. In writing this book, I've had a unique opportunity to interview leaders who exemplify living and working with purpose and helping others connect with purpose, too. A common theme among these leaders is articulated well by Greg Case of Aon Corporation, who says that motivating a workforce means "to create that connection between the people and the company, the people and the message, the people and the strategy."

Leaders who connect people with the company, the message, and the strategy find it a far simpler task to accomplish their goals. They have an entire organization of people who are working not just for a paycheck, but to achieve their own potential. They are energized by the possibilities and are connected to each other through a common purpose. These leaders harness energy and talent and drive their organizations forward. This is essential because, as a leader, you cannot do it alone. You need everyone. "In a nutshell," says Case, "that is what it means to motivate like a CEO, to make a connection between every single person and the fundamental mission of the organization."

Making a Difference

People want to make a difference. When they believe that what they are doing matters, it motivates them and stimulates their passion and creativity. Keith Blakely, CEO of NanoDynamics, a clean energy technology company, says, "One thing that can motivate people is the idea that they can make a *world of difference.* That phrase is the company's *tagline.*" From Nobel Prize–winning scientists to people on the production line, everyone is engaged by this mission. Blakely sees his role as getting "everyone in the boat pulling on the oars at the same time; to get them to understand where we are going and why."

> *People want to make a difference. When they believe that what they are doing matters, it motivates them and stimulates their passion and creativity.*

This is such an important aspect of leadership that it cannot be emphasized enough. To motivate and inspire others, you must help people to see what a difference they can make in the world. This means that you must not only feel a strong sense of purpose but also be able to communicate it to others. Your job as a leader is simply to communicate your passion and connect your people to that larger purpose.

Research shows that people work for a paycheck, but they live for a purpose. A 2006 Gallup poll of 540 adults employed full or part time found that the top three things that made people happy were "doing what suits me best/fulfilling," "interacting with the public/helping people," and "freedom/flexibility to do my job my own way." These were 41 percent of responses, and all these and a few others ranked significantly above good pay, flexible hours, and job security. Although college graduates were more likely to praise their job for being fulfilling, even non–college graduates cited fulfillment as the number one reason they enjoyed their work.

What is the leader's challenge in this? It is to *clearly communicate mission and purpose and do so with passion so that people are inspired.* In 2008, Bates Communications conducted a survey of 187 managers, leaders, and professionals, and the overwhelming message was how important it is to communicate mission and purpose. As we reviewed all these responses, it became crystal clear how universally people long for a purpose larger themselves. They also have a strong desire to work for leaders and companies that connect them with purpose.

A few examples:

- "I need my company's leadership to communicate to me and my colleagues to provide a context for our work and a purpose for our everyday contributions. I feel like I need that high-level, overarching vision to motivate me to do my best work and to focus my work toward what helps the company bottom line."
- "Employees are not mind readers. It's important that employees stay connected to a vision larger than their own to succeed personally and help their company succeed."
- "If employees understand why they are doing certain things and what the ultimate goal is, they will be more enthusiastic and take ownership."
- "People need to know that the efforts they give are on target, appreciated, and make a difference."
- "People enjoy being part of something bigger than themselves and particularly enjoy being asked to assist in working and participating in the growth strategy."

As a Leader, Do You Feel a Strong Purpose?

In our survey, the good news is that most *leaders* report that they *do* feel a sense of mission and purpose. Eighty-five percent of managers, directors, leaders, and business owners agreed or strongly agreed with the statement, "I feel fulfilled because I am doing work that matters to me and to my company." Eighty percent agreed or strongly agreed with the statement, "My job is important, and my boss communicates how it connects with our overall business goals." Of course, since most of them are the boss, one of the bosses, or a partner in or owner of the business, you would hope so!

> *In our survey, most leaders report that they do feel a sense of mission and purpose.*

Getting in touch with your own purpose is the first step to great leadership. The next step is to learn how to effectively communicate that purpose to others in a way that inspires them to do great things. This ability to communicate purpose is often what is missing in organizations.

In your company today, you may notice that motivation varies from division to division, team to team, site to site, office to office. It is common to have pockets of happy, productive people and pockets of unhappy, less productive people. Gallup found that in *every company* there are some groups that are highly productive and others that are not. According to Dennis Jacobe, Ph.D., Gallup's chief economist, these differences in work groups exist no matter how high or low a company's overall productivity.

Logic tells us that this inconsistency isn't for lack of a strategy, market, or customers. It probably is not because they don't like their benefits or the work environment. When all things are relatively equal it is more likely that the gap is a result of people not feeling connected or valued. Perhaps leaders in the organization are not equally effective in communicating with their teams in a way that motivates and inspires them. As you will discover in this book, your company must have leaders who consistently communicate mission and purpose and connect others to it.

Communicating, connecting, and inspiring people therefore are critical business skills; every leader must understand the power of purpose at a personal level and know how to communicate purpose with passion. "Many [leaders] come in and do their job and often forget they have *people* under them," said one person who participated in our study. "They haven't been properly mentored into their role; therefore, they can't mentor anyone else. Communication is key. Without sharing, people lack motivation and creativity."

A motivated workforce is your secret weapon in business—and it will allow your organization to overcome significant challenges. In talking with many leaders for this book, I heard over and over again how important they believe a motivated team is to their success. Rich Krueger, CEO of DynamicOps, a spin-off of Credit Suisse, told me that without a motivated workforce, he would sink. His company sells automation software to manage enterprise information technology (IT) organizations. As with most new companies, there's a long, long road between a great idea and customers who will pay for a product. Krueger says, "We don't have time or money enough to be successful without motivated people. If they treat it just like a job, we will fail." Every leader knows that you have to have people who are committed. When they are motivated they are committed to thinking about your problem as their problem.

Why don't leaders focus more of their own time and energy on communicating to inspire others? The simple answer is that they feel like they are too busy. Many are struggling to keep their heads above water. They feel trapped by their schedules of travel, meetings, and day-to-day activities. Yet, if leaders don't find a way to climb above the noise of the workday, to communicate a big inspiring message, they ultimately fail. Employees told us that their bosses are so distracted that they often forget to do the important things. "They are too busy 'doing' to lead," said one. "They are caught up in the day-to-day and neglect to communicate," said another. And then there was this: "They often say that they don't have time, but I think it is that they don't have a philosophy or plan about how they want to lead," said another.

What is the leader's challenge? *It is to clearly communicate mission and purpose with passion so that it inspires people and allows them to connect with their own sense of purpose.*

What If People Aren't Motivated?

When people start a new job, they are always enthusiastic as they anticipate where it will lead them in their careers. If you've hired even one person in your life, you know that he or she came in day one wanting to wow you. People genuinely want to do a great job, contribute in a significant way, and be acknowledged for their efforts. Yet sometimes, in a few weeks or a few months, their enthusiasm wanes. It seems that they've lost their motivation.

Is it their fault? Yes, they are ultimately responsible for their own success and happiness. Yet, more often than not, the problem really isn't the employee. The problem is that the leader and the organization have not made a strong connection with the individual and have not allowed him or her to see the excitement of being part of the organization.

If the employee does not find an opportunity to make a real contribution that is connected to a primary purpose of the organization, he or she doesn't feel important or valued. This is not a failure of the individual; it is a failure of leadership. Leaders must focus on connecting people to purpose, communicating with each individual directly and explicitly. Leaders need to talk out loud about the mission, purpose, and why the individual's work matters. If leaders don't do this, they have only themselves to blame when people are disengaged. It is the leader's job to communicate in a way that encourages each individual to explore his or her own connection to the larger purpose.

> If the employee does not find an opportunity to make a real contribution that is connected to a primary purpose of the organization, he or she doesn't feel important or valued.

"People love to feel important," said one respondent. This is why your ability to communicate and connect people with purpose really matters. The leader has to "allow people to see how their work fits in and why they are important to reaching the goal," said another. "We all need to be working toward common goals and need to know that what we do aligns with that strategy."

Ellyn McColgan, president and chief operating officer of Morgan Stanley's Global Wealth Management Group, says that leadership for her is about how the people who "pass through her life" feel valued. "It's not about controlling human energy; it's about expanding it. And if you expand it, you have to make sure it expands into the area that adds value. That's the art of leadership." McColgan explains, "Everyone comes to work wanting to do a good job. That sounds simple, but it is true. *Everyone* wants to do well. You can't be a good leader if you don't recognize that." She adds, "People will never disappoint you if that is how you come at them."

As a leader, you must believe in your heart that the people who work with you are truly in it for something bigger than themselves. When you believe this you are able to communicate in a way that respects their desire to make a difference. People don't just come to work for a paycheck. Once their basic needs are met, research shows that they seek opportunities for personal growth. Abraham Maslow, one of the founders of the humanistic school, theorized that there were five human needs and that self-actualization is the highest of those. In A *Theory of Human Motivation* (1943), he characterizes a person who is self-actualized as focused on problems external to himself or herself. If you accept that this is true, when you appeal to a person's desire to grow and develop, you are appealing to the highest level of that person's conscious needs.

When people have a reasonable degree of financial security, work in a safe, productive environment, and believe in what they do, they turn their focus to contributing and developing their talents and skills. Aon's Greg Case says that, in his experience, self-actualization is a driving force. "People want to maximize their ability to utilize whatever talents they have; that's what creates happiness and satisfaction." Case says consultants and brokers at Aon are especially driven by self-actualization. "A sense of individual accomplishment is paramount," Case says. "That lies at the heart of motivation."

To be successful communicating and connecting people to purpose, you have to get to know them and understand them. The results can be disastrous if you try to "dive in" from time to time with an inspirational message, whether for your own employees or your customers. One manager who responded to our survey told this story of a failure to take time to know the customer: "The CEO decided he wanted to join me as I called on people who had hired us. He had not been involved in the day-to-day activities of the company for a number of years, but a recent divorce changed his attitude toward being involved. He came to these meetings in a three-piece suit, black wing tips, and driving his sports car, even though the man who signed the contract to hire us typically wore blue jeans, a flannel shirt, and work boots, . . . and drove a pickup!

"Then my CEO proceeded to talk and talk . . . without listening to our client at all. I was told never to bring this CEO to our client's workplace again. If I did, our client would not take the meeting, and I would lose the account." The CEO's gaffe not only alienated a client, but it also had a profoundly negative impact on the employee. This is why it is so important to be consistently in touch with employees as well as customers. You cannot communicate and connect with people you don't know and understand.

Can You Motivate Everyone?

The truth is no. You will not be successful in motivating everyone. One might argue that you cannot motivate anyone! You can only inspire them to discover their own motivation. Motivation springs from within the individual when the right conditions exist. I believe, however, that you can *inspire* people to discover their own motivation. If you communicate effectively and connect people with purpose, they will feel the spark that motivates *them.* When you lead and communicate with purpose and passion, you give people the opportunity to discover how they fit in and what level of engagement they want.

Vikki Pryor, president and CEO of SBLI USA Mutual Life Insurance Company, said that she had an epiphany when she realized that once you've done your best to connect people with purpose and passion, it's their choice to participate, not yours. "Sometimes I had people I made all kinds of accommodations for because I could see their talent, but what I was missing was that they weren't interested in expressing it," she says.

By communicating purpose with passion, therefore, you attract the right people. Those who don't feel connected will leave and find a different place to exercise their talents, and those who do connect will look around and see the fit. You don't have to work so hard to manage them because they already want to make a difference in your organization. By consistently communicating purpose with passion, you attract the right people with the right talent, skills, and motivation. The right people come into your orbit; those who aren't right will move on. This is the law of

> By consistently communicating purpose with passion, you attract the right people with the right talent, skills, and motivation.

attraction at work. "When someone expresses an unwillingness to grow, then we move on to someone who wants to," says Pryor.

The question of whether you can truly motivate other people actually comes down to this: You can *inspire* other people to discover their own connection to purpose and what motivates them. The way you communicate purpose with passion will attract the right people and help those who are in your orbit make a strong commitment. When they feel the purpose and passion they are energized by it. This condition virtually guarantees that you will be more successful in overcoming obstacles, achieving milestones, and reaching your goals.

Powerful Purpose Requires a Committed Team

The more powerful your purpose, the more you will find clarity about which people to bring on board the organization. You must always be reviewing talent not only in terms of skill and experience, but also in motivation and commitment to the purpose. Mike Daly found that to be true when he took over a complex hospital system. Baystate Medical Center in Massachusetts had just been through a disastrous merger. When Daly took over, he found a demoralized, dysfunctional three-hospital staff. "As I assessed the top ten management people in the organization at that time, some of them were really good, while some were not so good," he said. "However, it was clear to me that regardless of their individual talents in respective fields, most carried so much baggage that anything we did would be suspect when the time came to execute the plan."

In fact, Daly ultimately determined that the entire organization was so demoralized and the leadership so crippled that he had to start anew. In the first 18 months, he replaced nine of his top ten executives. "You cannot motivate an entire organization if you are damaged at the top." This move had a profound, immediate, and positive effect on the rest of the organization—things were going to change! Daly was now able to communicate effectively with this new team and get them engaged to drive toward a new vision for the hospital. Ten years later, Baystate was an award-winning teaching hospital with morale so high that it was off the charts.

As you powerfully communicate purpose, you will attract the right people to execute the vision. But you must evaluate and reward them beyond their technical capabilities; look at whether they are able to embrace the vision. Your leaders must embrace purpose and communicate it to their teams. Often I have worked with organizations in which only one leader has the ability to communicate like this. This puts tremendous strain on one person and the result for the business is never what it could be. Everyone on your team must be attuned to purpose and be able to communicate it with passion. Later in this book I will talk about how to develop a team of people who can help you grow and prosper by communicating purpose with passion.

Your Job—Chief Motivational Officer

Think of your job as a leader as CMO—*chief motivational officer*. What does this mean? It means you decide that every day one of your primary roles is inspiring people and connecting them with purpose. Of course this means that you need to get clear about your own purpose. In Chapter 2 I'll give you many examples of how leaders have done just that. Great leaders understand what motivates them and then take it on themselves to drive that message down through the organization. Leaders who don't are not only less effective, but they also can do real damage to the organization.

> *Think of your job as a leader as CMO—chief motivational officer.*

"I was taking over a new team several years ago," said one participant in our survey. "The team's direction had changed several times through the years as the leaders changed or changed their focus, without employees being told. At the end of the year, I was asked to look at their incentive bonuses and keep from paying out 100 percent because no one had met the requisite goals. Yet I could not do that because it seemed to me they didn't have a clear picture of their goals all year, so how could they apply focus to them? In the end, I won out, but (if it were up to my bosses) the employees could have suffered unfairly."

Failing to communicate mission and goals is deadly to motivation. "During reorganization," said one participant, "many members of our staff were kept in the dark about the transformation that the department was going through; as a result, there was a lot of anxiety, [and] many started looking for jobs because of fear." "One . . . leader spoke to a large group of senior managers about what he wanted to achieve," said another participant, "but failed to mention at all how his audience connected to that vision. While some made the connection themselves, most left feeling that the leader talked right past them and didn't care whether or not they remained at the company. A simple sentence or two starting with, 'All of you are important to this vision because . . .' would have gone a long way."

As a leader, you have to learn how to communicate mission and purpose so that it makes sense to every single person in the organization. This can be challenging. You really have to get to know the individual and the group so you understand how to make the purpose relevant, exciting, and motivating for them. People need to see how they fit into the larger mission of the organization. Later in this book you'll see how Andrew Liveris, chairman and CEO of The Dow Chemical Company, a $54 billion company with 46,000 employees and customers in 160 countries, learned to communicate with a wide variety of audiences in a simple, powerful way. Liveris says, "Strategy is a very theoretical thing, the type of stuff you learn in business school. You [have to] take the concept and give it *content.*"

> *People need to see how they fit into the larger mission of the organization.*

We will look at how you, too, can target and make your message relevant and exciting for each audience. We will explore how to develop an exceptionally high level of skill in making people with many different backgrounds, interests, and motivations see and embrace a greater purpose. The art of motivation is communicating with people on *their* terms, in *their* language about what matters *to them.* From the factory floor to C-suite, from the lunchroom to the boardroom, you need to think about how best to get your message across to each individual and group. The best CEOs spend considerable time thinking about how they will communicate mission and purpose. "When that is well done, the company executes flawlessly because leaders and individuals know their roles," says Liveris.

How Important Is Talking with People about Purpose? Don't They Work to Make a Living?

As we have already discussed, people want more than a job. Of course they work to fulfill their basic life needs. They also hope to improve their lives by owning a home, sending their children to college, and taking nice vacations. For many, money is one way of keeping score and measuring success. Yet in spite of this, money is still not the strongest motivator for *most* people. Once they meet their needs and feel reasonably secure, they look for work that defines them and fulfills them.

What this means to leaders is that they need to understand at a deeper level what motivates people and to communicate with them about it. Many leaders make the mistake of assuming that most employees are primarily driven by financial concerns. Leaders have to learn how to get people excited about and engaged in the mission, because most people have this strong desire to connect to purpose.

> *It's a mistake to assume that anyone in your organization is motivated only by money.*

The CEO of a boutique consulting firm hired a consultant from a large, well-known, and respected national firm. She lured him to the smaller environment with the opportunity to run his own group and be paid very well for new business. She was mystified after two years when he was not delivering; he was lagging significantly in new business development and seemed listless and discouraged.

When she sat down to talk with him about what was going on, he stunned her. "I don't enjoy selling," he said. "I'm just not motivated by money." She left the meeting thinking, "How could a brilliant guy who could earn hundreds of thousands of dollars if he brings in more clients not want to work to give his family the best?" The consultant had a beautiful home in the suburbs with three young children and a wife who liked the finer things. The encounter forced the CEO to reconsider how she was trying to motivate him. She realized that people who *should be motivated by money* were not!

She valued this consultant, so she hired a coach to help him learn how to develop new business leads and close sales. However, it became clear that he was excited about working on certain *types* of projects. Unlocking this secret was really the key to getting him engaged and helping him to become far more successful. He brought in more business, and the CEO acquired a powerful insight into how to motivate people by understanding what makes them tick.

If money is the primary focus of your conversations with individuals and groups, then you will not attract motivated people, keep them, or make them happy. They will leave when they discover a job that helps them connect with purpose and apply their talents. It is a mistake to *assume* that *anyone* in your organization is motivated *only* by money.

Going on the Journey—Connecting People to Purpose

Communicating and connecting people with purpose is one of the most rewarding things you can do. Many leaders talked with me about how fulfilled they felt when they aligned others with purpose and saw measurable business results. As you go through the chapters of this book, you will discover how to measure the impact of your message.

> *Communicating and connecting people with purpose is one of the most rewarding things you can do.*

Greg Case spoke with passion about visiting over 500 Aon offices across the globe, working to connect people with the mission of becoming one global company. Aon had grown by acquisition and had many brokers and consultants who didn't want to be one company; they liked operating independently. Case felt energized by the mission to change how they saw themselves and their company. His is just one story; many leaders become animated when they discuss the rewards of connecting people to a purpose.

Of course, the ultimate goal is to achieve business results, and there is no doubt that aligning people with purpose is the way to do it. How do you know that you are succeeding? The financial results are real and measurable. For Greg Case, getting offices to work together increased profitability by leaps and bounds. "A global client is worth eight or nine times what a regional client is worth. The economics are staggering; a $1 million client becomes a $10 million client."

Motivation equals energy, productivity, and profitability. Motivating people is an integral part of your business strategy. A motivated team aligned around a common goal will take your business to the next level. And even better—it's fun! A motivated team equals a happy organization. You can't underestimate the significance of this. To motivate like a CEO is to connect people with purpose and passion and achieve great results. It is to expand human energy. This is an exciting way to look at leadership.

In Chapter 2 we'll talk about some of the principles that guide leaders who are successful in motivating others. In the chapters that follow we'll get more tactical in talking about what works (and what doesn't) in motivating others. You can use this book in a number of ways: You can skip around to the chapters that interest you, or you can read it all the way through. Although it is written as a step-by-step guide, the goal of *Motivate Like a CEO* is to provide you with what you need right now to meet the challenges of motivating your team like a CEO.

Summary

- Purpose is necessary, critical really, to a healthy, happy, and successful life.
- When we are connected to purpose, we are able to achieve great things.
- To motivate like a CEO is to connect people with purpose and passion toward a common goal.
- Think of your job as a leader as CMO—*chief motivational officer*; find ways to communicate and connect people to a larger purpose.

- A leader who communicates purpose with passion attracts the right people with focused energy that allows the organization to achieve spectacular results.
- This is why motivating people is a business strategy that leads to higher revenues, greater profits, and a happier, more productive organization.

2

Eight Principles for Motivating Others Through Communication

It takes time to persuade men to do even what is
for their own good.

—THOMAS JEFFERSON

THINKING BACK ON YOUR career—have you ever had a boss you loved? Perhaps this person was a mentor, role model, or driving force in your success. This leader communicated how much he or she respected your work, believed in you, and cared about your success. Leaders like this energize and motivate people. When you are in the same room with him you feel good about your work and more satisfied with your life. You go home and brag to your friends and family about what a great job you have. How lucky you are to work for someone who believes in you! I had a boss like this once, and he became the standard by which I judged all others. While his expectations were extraordinarily high, no one complained; we wanted to give 100 percent every day because we knew in our hearts that he believed in us. Our work mattered.

Imagine what the business world would be like today if there were more bosses like this. The tangible and intangible value of leaders who motivate and inspire others is incalculable. Imagine your company, only better—a place where every team, group, or division was engaged; morale was exceptional, turnover low, productivity off the charts. Improving in this area is not only desirable, it is essential to competing and winning. And the good news is that it all starts with you. You have the opportunity every day to mentor, encourage, and inspire. The principles discussed in this chapter on motivating through communication will help you to get in touch with the kind of leader you want to be. Whatever the competitive pressures of your business or the demands of your job, you can apply these principles daily. The result is happier, more motivated employees who get things done. While no leader is perfect, and we all have bad days, by keeping these principles in mind you will discover what a powerful impact you can make. These simple principles are the common threads that I've found by talking to and observing very effective leaders. You are not born with these skills—you learn how to communicate and motivate people and organizations.

Each one of us, no matter what our profession, has the opportunity to communicate purpose and inspire others if we so desire. I would argue that as leaders, we have an obligation to discover our own sense of purpose and to share it with others. You can make a significant impact on your organization and the lives of many people, and find tremendous satisfaction as a result. It is well worth the effort to make work exciting again and to help others to discover the personal and professional rewards.

It is always interesting to discover more about the people who work with you—what it is that motivates and inspires them. When you find it you have something like a window on their soul, and the connection is powerful.

My colleague Craig Bentley talks about his time at Citibank Amsterdam years ago. He ran treasury operations such as foreign exchange and bond trading. One evening after work, over a few good Dutch beers, his team got to talking about why they loved their jobs. They enjoyed the fast-paced environment, the thrill of trading hundreds of millions of dollars a day, and of course, the intellectual stimulation.

To Bentley, all of this was important, but he felt a higher purpose. What thrilled him wasn't the activity, but rather the *mission* of moving capital and goods between countries around the world. Without foreign-exchange trade, no one would be able to buy products globally; countries would not be able to raise living standards and pay for health care, education, and infrastructure development. He saw his purpose as helping to fuel a global economy and to elevate standards of living. Not surprisingly, he rose to executive positions in financial services because of this mission-driven view on his work. Today he brings that same mission-driven attitude to his coaching work with CEOs and senior leaders. In coaching, you must be committed to helping other people succeed; a great coach has to have a strong connection to that purpose.

Likewise, successful leaders work with a sense of purpose, and find it relatively simple to communicate that purpose to others. Not only are they excited by their jobs and opportunities in business, but they also see that through purpose, they can make a lasting impact and leave a legacy. After talking with many leaders and developing these eight principles for motivating through communication, one thing has become obvious to me. The process starts with *you*. The way you think about yourself and your purpose makes you a better, more purposeful, effective leader. Before you can communicate anything to anyone, you must start by looking inward to discover your own purpose and passion.

Principle 1: It Begins with You—Your Purpose and Passion

Jeff Taylor was the creator of Monster.com. His big idea to put ads for jobs online and make it a global market changed an industry. Prior to the launch of Monster.com, people had only one source—the newspaper. Today, Monster.com has millions of customers and 5,200 employees in 36 countries.

Taylor later launched a second company, Eons, an online community for baby boomers. He epitomizes the high-energy, curious, passionate entrepreneur. I asked him where he found his purpose. He said, "Your own interests have so much to do with your success. It's about your outlook, passions, and voice. I didn't realize this until I was pretty far into building my new company, Eons. The motto, 'Loving life flip side of fifty,' is *me!*"

An entrepreneur with a great business idea like Taylor's is bound to be passionate. But there are lessons for all of us in Taylor's story. Passionate leaders who live and work with purpose are in touch with what moves them and gets them excited. They see

> "Your own interests have so much to do with your success. It's about your outlook, passions, and voice."

work as an opportunity to express themselves and their talents. They just can't help sharing it, communicating with others. They feel so enthusiastic about their goals that they radiate a sense of purpose. Other people are attracted like magnets to this kind of leader.

How do you go about discovering this strong sense of purpose? I've found that you have to get to know yourself, sometimes again and again. Early in his career, Jeff Taylor had this idea that he wanted to do something big, so naturally an idea that involved two big things, the Internet and job searches, was interesting. He didn't want to do anything that wasn't a big, scary, "impossible" idea. It was just how he was wired. He wanted to make an impact, to do something global. It may have seemed kind of crazy, but it worked. Then, with Eons, he wanted to connect baby boomers around the world with the concept that they could "live to 100 or die trying." Again, he was driven by the idea of doing something big. "A small idea gets in trouble and runs out of steam," he says. "If you have fundamentally communicated the big message, the big idea; you can align people with the mission."

What Is Your Mission?

Getting to know what excites you is important to this process of becoming a leader who inspires. People will be inspired by people who *are* inspired. It's never too late in your career to start discovering what really excites you. It may start out as an ember, but if you fan the ember into a flame, you often will discover a larger mission and motivation. What you hope to find is the intersection between what interests you and the mission of your organization. While you can be rewarded by running a good business and achieving financial results, this probably won't feel like enough. Such achievements are far more fulfilling when they are connected with a larger purpose. What interests you in the mission of your company? How does it fit with your own interests? And how can you develop an even stronger connection between the two?

An executive in the insurance industry might find it rewarding to help people create peace of mind and economic security. A technology executive might find a strong sense of purpose in inventing better ways to do things. A hospital executive might find fulfillment in his or her role in improving the health and well-being of the community. For each of us, it is important to ask and answer the questions, "What interests me in this work? How am I connected to the mission of this company? Why does what we do matter?" This is the first step in the process of becoming a passionate, engaged leader who inspires others.

Your sense of purpose and mission can evolve over time. Over the course of your career, you may discover several missions. Or you may carry the same mission to different organizations. Jeff Taylor found a second big mission. He speaks passionately about what got him excited about Eons. "Drying up like a raisin was okay for our grandparents' generation, but we're going to live 20 years longer," says Taylor, "so we have a lot more time to live. The big idea is to show people how they can choose exercise, eating well, [and] taking care of themselves so [that] they live to 100 or die trying."

> *Your sense of purpose and mission can evolve over time. Over the course of your career, you may discover several missions.*

If you don't feel clear about your purpose, you may want to answer the questions below. This may help you to think through what excites you right now and why. It is not uncommon to feel a sense of purpose in your work and then to lose sight of it. These questions may help you to get back in touch with the things that matter to you.

How Does My Purpose Connect with the Purpose of the Organization?

- What do I really enjoy about the work that I do?
- Why does this work matter to me?
- What are the outcomes or impact of this work on others?
- When do I feel the greatest sense of satisfaction?
- If I were talking to my best friend about what I love about my job, what would I say?
- What would our customers, clients, and others say is the best thing about our company?

Don't Look for a Bolt from the Blue

What struck me about many of the passionate, purposeful leaders I interviewed is that their mission didn't come as a bolt from the blue. Jeff Taylor and others describe the process as an evolution that becomes more intense the further you go. You often discover purpose by first paying attention to an experience or insight. You might encounter a challenging problem or obstacle and decide it is important to solve it. You immerse yourself in learning about it and figuring out how to do it better. In Chapter 3 I'll talk more about how this passion develops.

At this point you may be thinking—*but this isn't me. I'm in business because I like business. I have family, friends, and interests that fulfill my life.* However, fulfillment in work is important for many reasons, not the least of which is the amount of time you devote to it. If you find yourself feeling something is missing, perhaps taking time to connect to a larger purpose and helping others to connect with it is the missing link. When you pay attention to your interests and take time to discover what really connects you with your work, you will feel a far higher sense of satisfaction and also become a better leader able to achieve greater levels of success. Being a leader is fun when you feel connected to purpose and can help others do the same.

> *When you pay attention to your interests and take time to discover what really connects you with your work, you will feel a far higher sense of satisfaction and also become a better leader able to achieve greater levels of success.*

Once you've started thinking about your own connection to mission, it's time to consider the many ways you can now communicate that purpose to others.

Principle 2: Communicate a Clear, Powerful Mission

People long to work for leaders who inspire them with passion and energy around a purpose. In our survey, 85 percent of respondents said, "Work is not just something I do to make a living; I enjoy it because people make me

feel like I'm making a genuine, important contribution." Everyone wants to
feel that they are doing something that
matters. The work of the leader is to
communicate that mission so that people get excited and want to apply their
talents and skills to the enterprise.

*People long to work for lead-
ers who inspire them with
passion and energy around a
purpose.*

Several CEOs I interviewed talked about how they strive to communicate purpose to everyone in their organizations, both as a matter of
respect for each individual, and also as a principle of good business. One
CEO said he makes a habit of thanking the people who clean the building at night and addressing them by name. Why? He appreciates what
they do, and he believes that their contribution is essential to the company's professional image. I noted that the company's conference rooms
and public areas are spotless, comfortable, and welcoming. This CEO
communicates how he values professionalism by sharing its importance
with everyone from the senior leadership team to those on the nightshift.

Alignment with your business objectives only happens when you
share purpose, goals, and ideals with everyone. You never know who will
step up and make a major contribution. If you don't move the message
down through the organization you put the entire company at risk. One
survey participant told us, "The CEO of a large company where I worked
in the Silicon Valley had the leading edge in the early dot-com era but
had to shut down an entire group because we were not gaining sales. We
had no clue that we needed to sell while producing client work, and I
was a senior director. I was not in sales or business development, but I
should have been educated on our business needs. Then I would have
been inspired to go beyond finishing projects—to generating ideas that
clients would get excited about and would lead to more new and profitable projects."

Imagine a different scenario, in which the CEO of the company
mentioned above had gone to the entire organization and communicated
what was happening and why. Imagine that this CEO had understood
that everyone needed to know the goals and challenges of the organization. Would this individual have gone home at night and thought about
how to solve a problem for the company? Would he have been motivated
to brainstorm with his team and come up with a big idea? We'll never

know. The only thing certain is that the CEO missed an opportunity to engage people and it's very likely that division of the company might have survived and thrived.

When you talk with people about purpose and share what is really going on you have an opportunity to make a connection at two levels; intellectual and emotional. People are far more motivated when they understand what is happening and feel a connection. Ken Leibler, former president and CEO of Liberty Financial Companies, Inc., says that he was fortunate to discover this early in his career. At age 36, he became the youngest person ever to be president and chief operating officer of the American Stock Exchange, and he attributes his success in part to connecting with people emotionally. "I always start from the premise that people want to *feel something*," says Leibler. "They want to know why they are there and feel good about it. It is beyond financial success and the logic." Once you do that, Leibler says that you can "get them excited about changing the industry, changing the world."

When communicating with your team, you don't have to be the world's most polished speaker, but you do need to speak from the heart. You will only be successful if people believe in you both as a business person and as a *person*. Emotional connections are important whether the news is good or bad. Share your high spirits when you have something to celebrate; let them see a little disappointment when the chips are down—balanced of course, with a sense of optimism about the future. Often I have coached leaders when they have great news to share and noted they didn't express any emotion. Feel the joy inside and express it. Don't be afraid to allow the emotional side of you to show—it's how great leaders communicate and motivate people.

Principle 3: Learn What Motivates Your People

You cannot assume that what gets *you* out of bed in the morning is the same thing that motivates others. Greg Case, CEO of Aon Corporation, says, "People have very different motivations. You have to be careful not to be confused that they are motivated by the same things that motivate you."

He continues, "Motivation is maybe two parts universal and one part very individual; highly tailored to each person. . . . A lot of people are motivated by economics, but a lot of people aren't. No matter how strong that motivation is for you, it may not motivate others."

"People have very different motivations. You have to be careful not to be confused that they are motivated by the same things that motivate you."

Take your company's stock price, for example. Employees who own company stock may follow its ups and downs and still not be motivated by its value. Meanwhile, as a leader in the company, you spend many waking hours thinking about shareholder value. Your employees are happy if the price is up, but they aren't *motivated* by it. "Even if employees own company stock in their retirement portfolios," Case observes, "most employees don't give it much thought." It is essential as a leader to understand, appreciate, and embrace what gets other people "up" for a task and excited about their work. "One lesson for me has been never to underestimate how important that is," says Case.

Here's how Rich Krueger, CEO of DynamicOps, a technology solutions company, explains motivating his people: "When you tell engineers that what you are doing is going to change how people do things, it really motivates them. Engineers have to be working on new and interesting things; they want to feel valued and that what they are doing is significant. They are inventing; they want to create something, and you want to give them an environment where they can express their creativity. They are the hardest people to manage. You have to manage them one on one."

Krueger's sales team is wired very differently. Team members believe that what the company is selling will find a huge market. "Salespeople want to make money, so you just say you're going to make money, show them how, make your case, and if they believe that, it's very easy to motivate them," he says. "They will work hard if they believe they will make money."

Be jazzed by what motivates you while still respecting what interests others. Krueger says, "I just love growing businesses, building things. It isn't even the money. Hand me a basketball and a pair of high tops, and I'm happy. If I make a lot of money, I'll just start another business. I don't need a house on Nantucket. The journey is the reward." Still, Krueger makes it a point to understand what makes other people tick. "I will invest a lot of time in understanding what motivates someone or how to motivate them if I'm not sure how to connect with them."

Principle 4: Make a Personal Connection with Others

In their *New York Times* best seller *Me to We: Finding Meaning in a Material World,* Craig and Marc Kielburger, founders of the nonprofit organization Free The Children, tell a compelling story of their journey to help children and families in poverty around the world. They cite countless examples of how they and others discovered a path to true personal happiness by moving from "me-centered" pursuits and carving out time to connect with and serve others.

Their remarkable story shows how one person can make a difference. They are exceptionally gifted at making personal connections with people all over the world. Everywhere they go, they win friends and create lasting relationships with people who want to work for their organization. These personal connections have been a huge factor in building an organization started by a teenager in his living room into a global movement.

You don't have to work for a nonprofit organization helping children to make personal connections. The opportunity to make connections is there every day in every kind of business. In fact, you will surprise and delight people when you do the unexpected, as Bill Swanson learned. As chairman and CEO of Raytheon, Swanson went to visit one of his company's manufacturing facilities. "A woman raised her hand," said Swanson. "'You don't want to know what our problems are. If you did, you would come to the factory floor and see how bad it is.' I said, 'Let me have someone come down and look.' She replied, 'I told them you wouldn't come down.' After a couple of other questions, she raised her hand again and said, 'Can you tell me why you won't come down and look?' I said, 'Because I'm getting on an airplane and I don't have time, but I'll come back.' 'A likely story,' she replied."

Swanson still had no plans to visit, but fate gave him an opportunity. A midwinter blizzard rolled into New England, delaying his flight back to Boston. So, at dinner with the plant manager, he said, "We're going on a site visit first thing in the morning. I don't want anyone to know we are coming, no announcement, because I know what will happen if they expect me."

The next morning when he arrived, the floor started buzzing. "I inquired about the woman in the meeting, and she was on the morning shift. My last stop was her station. She looked up and said, 'What are you doing here?' I said, 'Well, you asked me to come. Can you show me the problem?'" The woman explained that she couldn't put the circuit card into the radio. Since he had spent time working in a plant and being an engineer, he knew how to fix it. She then showed him how she was struggling with a harness on the assembly line, and he rolled up his sleeves and worked that out for her, too. By the time they finished, many workers in the plant were standing around watching. They started to clap and then to cheer.

> He rolled up his sleeves and worked that out for her, too. By the time they finished, many workers in the plant were standing around watching. They started to clap and then to cheer.

This story became somewhat of an urban legend at Raytheon. Because Swanson made a personal connection, problems were addressed, and morale started to improve dramatically. The factory became exceptionally productive as team members addressed their issues. It still has the highest on-time delivery and some of the highest quality statistics in the company. "That visit changed the attitude of the entire plant," says Swanson. By making the personal connection, Swanson demonstrated that leaders really do listen and care about people. "At Raytheon, if you have a problem, raise your hand, and we'll fix it."

Even the smallest connections can bring about major changes in people's attitudes. When you reach out and touch someone, it sets a powerful force in motion. When people come to expect this from their leaders, they feel a sense of pride in and loyalty to the organization.

People long for human-to-human interactions in their work, especially with their leaders.

Making personal connections isn't just good for other people—it is very good for you, too. Reaching out and extending yourself to others every day is the path to greater professional fulfillment. There is nothing as satisfying as a genuine conversation with a colleague about something that matters. You often discover that while your intention was to give, that you have, in fact, received something of greater value. As Ralph Waldo Emerson said, "It is one of the beautiful compensations of this life that no one can sincerely try to help another without helping himself."

There are so many ways that you can make a personal connection with employees and customers. You can pick up the phone, stop and talk to them, send notes, e-mail or small gifts, make time for breakfast, lunch or coffee. One interaction like that can have an impact for years. A simple acknowledgment is one of the most powerful motivators in the world.

Principle 5: Make the Conversation about Them

The CEO was dashing, worldly, brilliant, beautifully dressed, and obviously successful. We met at a business reception. He knew nothing about my company or me. For more than 30 minutes, the CEO held court, a glass of single-malt scotch in hand, discussing *his* favorite topics, the best golf courses, the finest restaurants, the virtues of private jet travel, and where to get a custom-made suit. I would like to say I made this up but it's true—he was almost a caricature of the "fat cat" boss. He also joked inappropriately about his wife's prodigious shopping habits. Throughout this half hour, he did not ask a single question of anyone in the conversation group.

While we've all found ourselves in a one-way conversation at one time or another, it is remarkable when a person like this makes it to the top. I can only imagine what kind of reputation he had with his employees and customers. Perhaps he didn't think any of us mattered. How would he have known? He never took a moment to find out much about who we were.

You can't choose when to connect with others. You never know who is standing next to you at a party or two seats down at the dinner table.

What if I had been friends with someone who was a potential customer? What if I knew someone that the company might want to recruit? If you're talking about yourself, you'll never know. If you don't make a real effort to get to know other people and turn the conversation to them, you are virtually guaranteed to miss an opportunity.

> *When you don't make a real effort to get to know other people and turn the conversation to them, you are virtually guaranteed to miss an opportunity.*

When speaking with your employees, customers, and other important audiences, it's not about you — it's about *them*. When you are a leader in the company, you may notice that people crowd around to speak with you because of your position. Naturally, they are going to ask you questions, and before you know it, you're talking about yourself. Make conversation a two-way street, show genuine interest, and make real connections.

People will go out of their way for any boss who treats them with respect and gets to know them as individuals. It's no more work to ask a few additional questions to get to know them better. People love to talk not just about the things that tend to arise in social conversation, but also about the work that they are doing. It gives them an opportunity to get direct feedback and also to shine. Taking a few extra minutes to go deeper into a conversation will also provide you with insights that you will never find by reviewing professional development assessments and evaluations. There is nothing like a good conversation to help you get perspective on a person.

Think of Motivation as a Political Campaign

Evelyn Murphy, the first woman to win statewide or constitutional office in Massachusetts, learned the value of making personal connections during her campaign for lieutenant governor. When she first hit the campaign trail, she focused on communicating to the voters why she was "qualified" for the job. "I spoke incessantly about policy and emphasized why I was the most qualified candidate." Murphy knew she had an uphill battle in a state where few women had been elected to any office.

After hearing her stump speech, however, one of Murphy's advisors, Ron Asner (actor Ed Asner's brother), told her something that surprised her. He said, "Lighten up, Ev. They know you're qualified. This is really about whether they *like you* enough to *vote* for you." It was the best advice Murphy says she ever got. She stopped worrying about how other people perceived *her* and starting focusing her conversations on *them*. Out went the policy wonk—and in came a woman who wanted to connect with people.

Murphy began to enjoy campaigning, growing more confident by the day. "I sat down and ate at a picnic instead of dashing around shaking hands; I had no agenda except to enjoy people and learn what was going on there. I wore casual clothes instead of suits. I watched people's responses; they would put their arms around me and hug me. They found out that I'm not a stiff. I was more physically present and at ease and laughing at myself. That, more than anything else, was a turning point in my career."

She won the election.

Principle 6: Praise, Recognize, and Reward

What is better than making someone else's day? Most of us try hard to remember to thank and congratulate people, and do most of the time, but would probably admit that we sometimes forget. Life gets busy and that note we intended to send never gets written. If we set aside time to think about who we should acknowledge, the list quickly grows. If we do this regularly it becomes a habit.

I always thought I was fairly good at this until our firm took a customer survey—we found there was deep and wide satisfaction with our services, however, several people interviewed mentioned that they had not been thanked for their business, or for giving a referral. That was a wake-up call. Developing the habit of acknowledging people is usually easier if you do it in the moment, rather than wait. Leaders who are good at motivating others make it a regular practice to stop and think about who they need to recognize.

Praise is a *precision tool* in leadership. It allows you to reinforce the exact behaviors and values that will make your organization successful. Praise is also a *power tool*; it reverberates around the organization, and people remember it for years. I bet that you can remember every boss who supported you, congratulated you, and sang your praises. They won you over. This is why it's important every single day to take the time to tell people how much you appreciate their efforts. Is this Management 101? Yes.

> Praise is a precision tool in leadership. It allows you to reinforce the exact behaviors and values that will make your organization successful.

However, if more people practiced it, there would be a greater number of high achieving companies with happier employees.

The simplest methods of recognition are often the most effective. Vikki Pryor, president and CEO of SBLI USA Mutual Life Insurance Company, a $1.5 billion insurance company doing business in 49 states, has made a point of holding regular recognition events. As the company grew, she scheduled them every quarter. She didn't leave praise and recognition to chance.

How does she do it? "It starts with getting people together on a regular basis," she explains. "We have associate celebrations once a quarter, and in that meeting we post everyone who has a birthday on the intranet and on the wall in every break room." SBLI also gets people together to sing happy birthday to everyone in the company once a quarter; they have cake and fruit, and we announce important life events such as engagements, weddings, and babies.

"We also talk about our sales and how the company is doing in a more informal way than in our regular quarterly associate meetings," says Pryor. These meetings are separate from quarterly business associate meetings or offsite meetings with all officers and managers; those happen four times a year at SBLI. In addition, SBLI has many company social events. "This allows us to continue to get our mission out there and to demonstrate that we *live* the mission," says Pryor.

Recently, one of my clients received a big promotion. I wrote him an e-mail to congratulate him. He replied immediately, "You are a big part of my success." We have had these types of exchanges many times. While he would most certainly have achieved everything in his career without me, this practice of giving credit to others is a major contributor to his success. It's really true; you can never say thank you often enough. We all must remember that we didn't get here on our own. Acknowledge people. Appreciate them. Don't allow your busy schedule to keep you from taking a few minutes to give credit. Write a memo, an e-mail, a personal note; stop by someone's office; send a gift; give a plaque, a dinner, or a gift certificate. Such small gestures mean a great deal to anyone, and I mean anyone.

Don't Assume They Know

An executive tells the story of how shocked he was when one of his direct reports, a brilliant guy, walked into his office one day and said, "If you're going to fire me, why don't you just get it over with?" The executive had just awarded this direct report preferred stock options, reserved for a few select, outstanding employees. He was pleased with the man's performance and couldn't understand how he had come to this conclusion.

What happened here? The direct report had been hearing through the grapevine that some of his colleagues, other direct reports of the executive, were opposed to his initiative. Since he hadn't heard any support from the boss, he assumed that the boss was allowing these colleagues to undermine him. The boss, meanwhile, was unaware of what was going on and thought the project was on track. The employee actually ignored the stock options "message" and assumed that his boss was secretly trying to get rid of him. What a miscommunication!

When they sat down to talk, the man was quite distraught. He had been working very hard on many projects and had been stung by his colleagues' criticism. He assumed that the boss's silence also indicated his lack of support. The boss, however, had assumed that by giving the direct report the stock options, he would know how important he was to the company's success. The boss saw this as the highest level of recognition, yet the direct report had disregarded it completely. In truth, the vote of confidence he was most looking for was a word from the boss, privately or publicly, that he recognized and supported his worker's efforts.

Principle 7: Walk the Talk

When you walk the talk, people believe in you and your organization. Acting in a way that is consistent with your words is essential to your success as a leader. A leadership team that acts with integrity generates confidence and enthusiasm, and ultimately results in a motivated workforce that gets things done. When people see you mean what you say and that they can count on you to act in concert with your principles, they tend to behave the same way. You win their trust, and can also trust them. You

> *When you walk the talk, people believe in you and your organization. Acting in a way that is consistent with your words is essential to your success as a leader.*

cannot have a motivated workforce or a successful company if there isn't a reasonably high level of trust between management and employees.

Integrity is money in the bank when things aren't going well; a team still will work hard even if things aren't going well if they know you're a stand-up person. If you have to make a tough decision, you can draw on your integrity bank without damaging the organization. Act with integrity, and you show your entire organization how to be.

Walking the talk can make even a "mission impossible" possible. Mike Daly, whom you met in Chapter 1, discovered this when he became CEO of Baystate Medical Center. Daly, you'll recall, was brought in after the disastrous forced marriage of three hospitals in Massachusetts. He inherited an organization in financial disarray, with low morale and dismal support from the community. Over a period of a decade, Daly turned it around. Baystate today is recognized year after year as one of the top 100 hospital systems in the United States.

How did Daly and his team achieve this? In the simplest terms, they walked the talk. Daly insisted on a culture of open, honest collaboration. He set out to eliminate the carping, infighting, and distrust among the hospital's medical and administrative staffs and to get people working together. "What it meant was [that] we had to commit to each other's success by helping each other succeed," he explained. He told the leadership team that they had to support each other's individual decisions if they were consistent with the strategic plan.

Still, Daly needed to make sure that his own team was walking the talk. He couldn't allow them to say one thing to each other in a meeting and then walk out and undermine each other in the highly political, back-stabbing atmosphere that had existed before. Therefore, they had rules: "If you disagreed with a colleague on the team, it was absolutely required that you register that disagreement openly and honestly. It had to be resolved before we went a step further." You can imagine the issues this approach created. Most people at the hospital weren't used to working in this manner. Daly required them to "red light" an issue if they disagreed, go work it out, and then come back with a yellow or green light to continue. "We lost a few leaders along the way," he recalls. "There were executives on the team initially who couldn't tolerate that kind of openness."

Although it didn't happen overnight, Baystate was transformed. Decades later it is recognized in the health care world and by its community as a model for merged hospital systems. Daly says that if he had to point to one thing that was responsible for the ongoing success of Baystate, it was walking the talk. By communicating through his actions, he created a shared value system. In later chapters we'll look at ways that Daly and others walk their talk and motivate people to adopt and share the mission and values of the organization.

Why Should They Listen?

If you are not walking the talk, the repercussions down through the organization will grow from a ripple to a tidal wave. A CEO who was hired to run a medical device company noted that meetings were not well managed. Employees were chronically late to meetings by ten or fifteen minutes; every meeting ran long. They were afraid to commit knowing the meeting might run into another or that it would keep them from their work; so when the Microsoft Outlook invitation came out, they often checked "tentative" and then didn't show up. There were other problems. Most meeting participants openly worked on their BlackBerries and ignored the conversation even if it was relevant to their area. There were side conversations; few meetings had formal agendas, and even when they did, people tended to ignore them. The CEO asked the human resources team to post meeting guidelines on the walls of all the conference rooms. The human resources team dutifully obliged; but the words on the wall simply were ignored. It turns out that the CEO and the executive team were among the worst offenders of the guidelines. Prior to developing the guidelines, the executive team never discussed this issue at their level. They offered no training to help people unlearn bad habits and to institute new practices. But the biggest problem was the fact that the leadership wasn't walking the talk.

Meetings continued to run as poorly as they always had, and productivity did not improve. More importantly, because the problem had now been highlighted, employees grew cynical and even more resentful of meetings. Now, they had a constant reminder of the hypocrisy. The guidelines became a joke—the company limped along, and it stands to reason that low morale and productivity were a major factor.

Principle 8: Empower People

People are highly motivated when you empower them and trust them to go out and do their jobs. They won't do it the way you would, nor should they. Nearly every leader I interviewed for this book mentioned the importance of empowering employees to the success of their organizations. Giving people the latitude and flexibility to use their judgment and apply their talents rapidly accelerates progress. You send a message of respect and inspire people to be creative and use their individual talents toward the goals of the enterprise. Empower people by letting them know that you believe in them and allowing them to take action.

> *People are highly motivated when you empower them and trust them to go out and do their jobs.*

Trusting people and empowering them also allows you to focus on the things you need to accomplish. Ellyn McColgan of Morgan Stanley says that she felt free to do her best work when she realized that she needed to let other people go do theirs. "I used to say to people all the time, 'I can help you figure out just about any problem you throw at me, but is that really what you want from me?' They would look at me funny, and they would say, 'Not really.' I would say, 'I think what you would like is to do a great job and then give me an opportunity to say, 'Great job!' Then they would respond, 'Yes, that's true, although I never would have thought of it that way.'"

Micromanaging is a demotivator. This issue came up frequently in our survey. "Many years ago," said one person who wrote to us, "I helped launch a new initiative that was supposed to make everyone rethink how we did business. My boss's boss was calling me at all times of the day and night, changing minor details at the last minute (even about where we would take clients to dinner that evening). She kept on saying that we had complete flexibility, but every time we made a decision, she would just change it."

Are You an Empowering, Motivating Leader?

Yes, No, Not Sure

- I enjoy finding ways to help people demonstrate their talents.
- I prefer that people on my team figure it out for themselves.
- I ask questions before providing direct tactical advice.
- I am willing to let people take risks and fail.
- When people fail, I spend time helping them learn from it.
- I feel very happy when I see people on my team succeed.
- I always give credit to the people who got the job done well.
- People who work for me have gone on to do great things.

You may find it challenging to avoid jumping in to save the day or giving advice rather than coaching someone to find the answers. Most leaders I have observed stumble on this from time to time. It is difficult to let go when you feel so much riding on the decisions and actions of your key people. However, if you are aware of this tendency and stop to ask the right questions rather than give the answers, you'll be amazed. If an individual doesn't rise to meet the challenge, you will have information to make decisions about them. Don't be hard on yourself if you "catch yourself" micromanaging, just take a step back, provide direction, and let people do it.

Now that we have looked at the eight principles of motivating through communication, in Chapter 3 we will look more deeply at a central theme: how leaders discover and develop a strong sense of purpose that drives their success and motivates and inspires others. We'll look at how ordinary people have become outstanding leaders by discovering their purpose and communicating that purpose to accomplish great things.

Summary

- Leaders who motivate others have a unique ability to see a larger picture, the broader view, and the real value of the work.
- Having a mission is the difference between working and working *with purpose*. If you're going to motivate others, you need to understand what motivates you.
- The eight principles of motivating like a CEO will help you to connect other people with purpose and move them toward a common goal.
- Understanding what motivates other people is not the same as understanding what motivates you. People want to make money, but they have many other hopes and desires that work can fulfill.
- Make it about them; use praise, recognition, and reward; and empower people to do their best work.

3

Discovering Your Purpose and Communicating It to Others

We must have a theme, a goal, a purpose in our lives. If you don't know where you're aiming, you don't have a goal.

—Mary Kay Ash

Working with purpose and passion brings joy to our lives. With a goal and a purpose, we have a far more fulfilling career. If we have a vision for our company, team, or organization, and we know exactly how we are personally aligned with it, time flies—we are completely absorbed by activities that take us in that direction. Thus, if purpose is the secret to fulfillment in our work, then we need to understand how to tap into the energy and thinking that fuels it. We need to use a process that helps us to find our purpose and communicate it to others.

In this chapter we'll look at how leaders like you have found purpose and how that purpose has defined their careers. If you are looking to discover or rekindle your mission and purpose, I hope that these leaders' stories will inspire you. None of us is born with purpose; we discover it. You don't wait for it; you find it. The question is how you unlock the interests that allow you to define purpose. It isn't as great a challenge as you might think—it is a natural evolution, not a moment in time. You may wake up one morning and say, "I've got it!" but the process is more of a journey than an epiphany. Later I'll provide some questions that you can ask yourself as you seek to define or redefine your purpose.

For most of us, work is a significant expression of who we are in the world. It is not, however, *all* that we are, but instead, it is one significant way we discover ourselves, create value, and even leave a legacy. Purpose in our work allows us to create and fulfill a vision for our lives. Purpose makes work exciting and rewarding. If you don't feel that sense of purpose, going through the process these leaders have used may help you to reconnect with your current work or find something that does fulfill you. Either way, this is a conscious process. Learning about your own interests will motivate you and allow you to grow as a person and a leader.

> *None of us is born with purpose; we discover it. You don't wait for it; you find it.*

How One CEO Discovered Purpose

The process of discovering purpose is a journey. Vikki Pryor, president and CEO of SBLI USA Mutual Life Insurance Company, grew up in humble circumstances. Married at age 19 with no college education, she took a job selling coats at minimum wage. "I had zero money," she says. Pryor struggled to make ends meet, and lacking a plan, she had no idea how she would improve her financial situation. However, those tough times taught her a most valuable lesson: If she wanted a prosperous life, she would have to carve it out for herself.

Pryor was so determined to increase her paycheck that at the end of every workday, she stopped into the company's human resources department to ask for a job that paid more. Each day, the staff there told her the same thing: "No other jobs are available." Then, one day, Pryor stopped in on her lunch hour, and another woman was already there, standing at the receptionist's desk requesting a job application. While Pryor stood there, the receptionist told the woman that there were a number of good positions open.

When it was her turn, Pryor asked the receptionist to call the woman from human resources who had claimed that there were no jobs. Suspecting now that the company may have been discriminating against her because of her race, she decided to quietly confront the woman and ask to see a list of available positions. After the human resources representative blushed, she brought out the list and then offered Pryor a job that doubled her pay overnight! But this isn't the end of the story. Pryor went in and tackled a six-month backlog of work in two weeks, getting her noticed by a new boss. When she decided that she must then go to college to move ahead faster, the boss enthusiastically not only agreed to give her time off to go to school but also "offered to pay [her] . . . 40 hours for 30 hours of work during that time because he said [she] . . . was doing 60 hours worth of work anyway."

Discovering Purpose

Pryor eventually earned a law degree and an MBA and also became a CPA. Today, as the president and CEO of SBLI, she feels a strong connection to the company's mission to "empower people to improve their finances so they can have a stronger, better, and more prosperous life." Pryor has led expansion of the company from a single base in New York to 49 states with more than 330,000 people insured, $1.5 billion in assets, and $16 billion of insurance in force.

"I realized back then that there was a direct connection between resources, education, and freedom of expression of my talents," she says. This is why she took the job at SBLI. Pryor maintains that alignment with purpose and passion is "very fundamental to success." She says, "So many leaders aren't aligned with what drives them. You need to take your skill and ability and translate it into something that works for you. What drives me is that if you have financial freedom, it frees you to do the things you are here in this life to do."

> "So many leaders aren't aligned with what drives them. You need to take your skill and ability and translate it into something that works for you."

A Process of Discovery

Over a lifetime, if we are fortunate, most of us will discover a purpose that drives us, some of us several times. When you're paying attention, you may feel that you are going down a path that really excites you.

Not every interest will become a driving purpose, but some can take your career in an exciting direction. Many leaders say that they didn't go out to "find" a purpose so much as they stumbled onto it, paid attention, and then pursued it with vigor.

CEO Howard Schultz discovered a passion for coffee that drove him to build the iconic Starbucks brand. Where did his journey begin? An executive in New York City for another firm, he stumbled onto dark roast coffee in a small shop in Seattle and fell in love. It wasn't in his career plan; he discovered this passion by accident, and then he pursued it. His personal journey immersed him in the world of coffee until he felt certain that his mission was to bring great coffee to the United States. Under his leadership, the tiny Seattle waterfront operation expanded into 1,600 cafés nationwide.

In the book where he tells this story, *Pour Your Heart Into It*, Schultz says, "It took years before I found my passion in life." On a trip to Europe, he stumbled onto the romantic ritual and romance of the Italian coffee bars. He visited 500 espresso shops in Milan and Verona, sitting elbow to elbow with Italians and listening to the ubiquitous opera music, mesmerized by the artistry the baristas put into every tiny porcelain demitasse of espresso and each and every cup of foamy cappuccino. He returned to the United States to advocate that Starbucks open similar cafés and sell single cups of coffee, an idea the founders could not embrace. But Schultz was certain that his idea was a good one. What kept him going? "The key is heart," Schultz says in his book. "I pour my heart into every cup of coffee, and so do my partners at Starbucks."

Why is it important to follow your interests this way? Because you don't know until you pursue them what the possibilities are. If you feel a tingle of intellectual and emotional connection, it will drive you and help you to find your way. Of course, once you discover your mission, your purpose and passion become contagious. Vikki Pryor says, "You can't help [to] align someone with the mission if you're not aligned personally." Leaders who connect strongly to purpose use such words as *passion* because the connection is emotional. It goes beyond the desire to run a successful company or make more money. "A lot of times leaders have money or power goals, but they are not connecting with the mission with heart and soul," says Pryor.

As you pursue your passion, you become a very powerful person in your sphere of influence. You will notice that others gravitate to you. This can be affirming on the journey to self-discovery. People can see that you believe in your mission, and they can't help but pay attention to or be influenced by your commitment. When the passion is real, people respond. Pryor explains, "People know whether you're genuinely passionate about something."

To inspire others, you have to feel passionate and communicate that passion.

Ask yourself these questions: What's my personal mission? What is the mission of my organization? How do the two connect? Try the following Personal Mission Questionnaire to get you thinking.

Personal Mission Questionnaire

Question	Answer
What issues do I care about?	
What should change or improve?	
How does what I'm doing now connect with other things I've cared about in my career?	
What activities do I enjoy most in my work and why?	
What projects, when completed, give me the greatest satisfaction and why?	
What purpose have those activities and projects filled?	
If I am working for an organization that is out of sync with my own mission and purpose, where do they diverge?	
If I could do anything, what would it be?	

The Journey: Total Immersion

> *Your journey to finding and clarifying your passion is not so much about having a sudden epiphany as it is about immersing yourself in an experience.*

Your journey to finding and clarifying your passion is not so much about having a sudden epiphany as it is about immersing yourself in an experience. It is a growing sense that you are going in the right direction. As you completed the preceding questionnaire, you may have found that you have several interests that have not yet developed into what you'd truly call purpose or passion.

Even though Howard Schultz fell in love with dark roast coffee in an instant, it took him years to learn the art and science of coffee, and as he did, his passion grew. Leaders like Schultz spend very significant amounts of time observing, questioning, reading, analyzing, and thinking about how something is—and how it could be. They don't just look *at* a problem; they *bury* themselves in it. They devote themselves to learning. They are deeply curious. They absorb everything they learn. "When I start something," says Schultz in his book, "I immerse myself totally in it."

Another example of this type of immersion experience is the story of Ellen Parker, executive director of Project Bread. When Parker went to work for the organization, its role was largely to raise money for food pantries. Parker immersed herself in the topic of hunger. She went into the field and spent time with all kinds of people—not just the usual hunger advocates or her own staff, but many others who were on the front lines—teachers in Head Start programs, school nurses, families, children, and other people who had different perspectives from hers. The more she heard, the more she wanted to understand how the system had gotten so broken.

During her immersion experience, Parker was struck by something. The "experts" talked about food, not people. A successful food drive was measured in tons. "I'm not a good tonnage person," she says, "so I was struck by that, as well my feelings when I visited food pantries and saw people standing in line with two kids." As a former social worker, Parker had worked with people in need. But this immersion experience brought to her an exciting new idea: Why not address hunger before children could be hungry and improve nutrition so that they did better in school?

"It was so clear to me that people who got emergency food were paying a real psychological and emotional price for it," she observed. "A food pantry . . . seemed like an emergency room. You could get crisis help, but . . . long term it was a very poor way to address hunger." As a result of what she learned, she transformed her organization and created a new national model for addressing hunger.

Likewise, Schultz's immersion started with hundreds of hours behind a counter brewing coffee at Starbucks. He loved being there; he tasted coffee the way a connoisseur would taste wine. His immersion experience was so intense that he couldn't keep it to himself; he felt passionate about the fact that great coffee was meant to be shared, enjoyed with friends, and not just taken home in a bag. Schultz now became utterly convinced that the original one-store Starbucks was missing a point. He felt a burning desire to open cozy, attractive bistro-type coffee shops. It wasn't just a thought; it was a powerful drive fueled by strong feelings. "It was so immediate and physical that I was shaking," he writes.

All three of these leaders' stories have this in common: The mission didn't strike from the blue. Each pursued his or her interests and allowed them to take root. Curiosity got them started on a journey; they immersed themselves in learning so that they could understand and develop a viewpoint and an emotional connection to the work. Ultimately, they were driven to do something—to communicate the purpose so that they could connect other people to it.

Developing a Unique Perspective

Parker developed her unique perspective and didn't back away. While most "experts" she talked with saw hunger as an enduring, unchangeable facet of poverty, her research convinced her it was a problem that could be solved. She could do something before kids got hungry. She researched some more and ultimately persuaded educators that breakfast can be linked to improving test scores. She won support for a universal free breakfast program in Massachusetts schools that now reaches 100,000 low-income school children. As a result, Project Bread evolved; while continuing to raise money for 400 emergency food programs in 132 communities, Project Bread also was creating a new national model of integrating direct assistance with strategic programs for preventing hunger.

Parker's plan and passion were born out of her unique perspective. She had a new insight: Families could be fed where they work and play, not just in a place where they have to publicly acknowledge that there's an emergency. By investing time and effort in developing this new, contrarian viewpoint, she was able to realign her own organization and make a plan that had a dramatic impact. The lesson in her story is seen in other leaders' stories as well.

Tapping into "Collective Wisdom"

Leaders who discover passion tap not only into their own interests but also into the collective interests and wisdom of others. They are curious about getting many perspectives. Almost every single leader interviewed for this book, and many others I have known during my years of coaching and consulting, have described this phenomenon. As they get interested in something, they talk to people and find that getting each viewpoint only fuels their passion and interest. As they gather collective knowledge and wisdom, they are able to synthesize it and develop a viewpoint that leads to a plan or purpose for their work.

> *Leaders who discover passion tap not only into their own interests but also into the collective interests and wisdom of others.*

An example of tapping into collective wisdom came up in my conversation with Ellyn McColgan, who prior to joining Morgan Stanley spent 17 years working her way up to one of the top three jobs at Fidelity Investments. Each time she was promoted to run a new division, she started the same way: never putting a business plan on paper or creating a central theme for her work until she completed an intensive 90-day listening tour. "There is a system to it," she says. "The first thing I did when I got there was listen to every constituency that had a vested interest in the success of the business: clients, employees, colleagues, management . . . anyone who had something to tell me about the business."

During that period, McColgan said nothing to anyone about what she thought should be done. She just listened. "I might test a hypothesis, but I didn't say anything. I compiled the information, and at the end of 90 days, I put together a business plan that reflected 80 percent of what people told me." The other 20 percent of the business plan came from her experience and analysis "because people in the organization may miss something, and that's my role." The business plan was more than a roadmap to increasing revenues and profits; it was a mission for the organization.

Ellen Parker of Project Bread described a similar process, refraining from going into the inquiry process with too many preconceived ideas. One of Parker's philosophies is that you need to begin your inquiry with "an open mind and a willingness to look at things differently." Collecting intelligence from many sources, analyzing it, and turning it inside out and upside down helps her to develop a new point of view, the seed for the purpose and plan. The key to this process is collective wisdom—the more you learn from many sources, the more you begin to see a pattern.

Collective wisdom is magical in a way. The more people you talk to, the more you see, the more patterns emerge, and the more you are inspired. Ideas bubble up, you sort through clutter, things become clear, and what emerges is often a big, exciting idea. And even if you've been doing what you do for a long time, this immersion process really works. The magic is that you are tapping into the universe of experience, insight, perception, and intelligence. When you penetrate this universe and look

> *Collective wisdom is magical in a way. The more people you talk to, the more you see, the more patterns emerge, and the more you are inspired.*

around, you are often amazed at what you see. The more curious you are, the more robust is the process and the richer are the insights.

So you aren't born with this sense of mission and purpose; you discover it through a process of inquiry. Sometimes you find it by looking at ways to solve problems or challenges with which you are presented. Greg Case, CEO of Aon Corporation, whom you met in Chapter 1, became a globe-trotting ambassador when he took over his firm. He went out to learn. He met, on average, 100 clients a month and presided over employee meetings at over 500 locations around the world. This wasn't a haphazard plan, however. "I went about it in an efficient way to get their input and guidance. I would codify the information; summarize it on the fly, and keep track of it," he recalls. "The fundamental messages that would drive our success were developed along the way in those meetings."

Is it worth it for you to invest so much time in gathering collective wisdom and developing a plan connected to purpose? The experiences of each of these leaders suggest that intense curiosity and a devotion to learning are what kindles real passion and makes their work rewarding. This purpose is one they can communicate effectively because they believe in it. They can now powerfully convey the message and align their teams around it. Greg Case says, "If you define good communication as changing behavior and changing attitudes, then sitting down on a Saturday and writing about strategy and sending it out to employees will not change any attitudes or behaviors." The only successful plans are developed out of a rigorous investigative process, he says.

When you gather collective wisdom, you gain a torrent of "bottom up" insights, more ideas than you probably can ever even use. Case says that for him, "there was a groundswell of information about what our clients were telling us to do." Aon decided that to become a global organization, it needed to establish centers of excellence to improve client service, so it rolled out a single worldwide sales and marketing system. In 2007, the company received high praise for client service through the 2007 *Business Insurance* magazine's "Reader's Choice Award."

"It sounds trivial," says Case, "but those lessons gave us credibility because they came bottom up from the clients. I summarized what they said. That was quite powerful and helped shape our strategy." Aon also got bottom-up data from employees through surveys. The surveys with employees and clients create what Case describes as a "virtual dialogue." Now, Case says, "We are talking about it all the time with each other. That's the power of this method. We're having an ongoing conversation."

One of the important lessons from these leaders is that you will discover mission and purpose simply by gathering the information and being committed to learning.

Out of the conversations and connections you have, you come away with a strong sense of mission and purpose and a plan for moving your organization forward. One of the important lessons from these leaders is that you will discover mission and purpose simply by gathering the information and being committed to learning.

Now, Write Your Mission/Plan

If you enter into a process of gathering collective wisdom and analyze what you have learned, what often emerges almost without effort is a mission and purpose. The insights you gain show you the way to go forward and drive results, and then it is simply a matter of putting it on paper. Now you have what you need to write your mission and plan. "When you have an extensive data collection like that," says Ellyn McColgan, "the top five issues rise to the top. These issues are generally well understood by everyone." She continues, "If you take those five or six things and reflect them back to the audience in a business plan, people start listening, and they believe you are brilliant because you put together a plan that they gave you."

It's not just that people believe that you're smarter—you *are* smarter! You have a mission, goal, and plan based on facts and collective wisdom. The more that others contribute to the thinking and formation of the plan, the more compelling a case you can write and communicate. The information you gather from different constituencies is ammunition in selling your ideas. When stakeholders have contributed and helped you to shape the plan, they will have a hard time refuting it. They may disagree with some aspects, but you'll win points for asking. At the end of the process, you'll have what I like to call the "big idea."

Mission and Purpose: What's the Big Idea?

Figure 3–1 illustrates how you might use a 144-day period to gather collective wisdom and develop a "big idea." Ninety days of observation, a

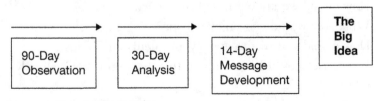

Figure 3–1 90 Days to the Big Idea

month of analysis, a couple of weeks writing and editing, and voilà: mission, analysis, and a plan. You don't have to *wait around* praying for inspiration. At the end of a 90-day period of investigation, you can practically guarantee that you will have some insights that could lead to a big idea. After this period of listening, you'll find yourself waking up in the morning with new inspiration that you can't wait to put into a plan and share. This is how it happens.

> *After [a] . . . period of listening, you'll find yourself waking up in the morning with new insight that you can't wait to put into a plan and share. This is how it happens.*

The big idea for Ellen Parker was to start seeing hunger as a problem that could be solved. The big idea for Vikki Pryor was that anyone, absolutely anyone can take control of their own financial future. The big idea for Howard Schultz was that Americans would enjoy great coffee in cafés and make it a social experience.

There is no limit to the big ideas you might pursue. It's a matter of using this "curiosity" muscle, looking at problems as challenges, immersing yourself in gathering collective wisdom, analyzing it, and developing a mission and purpose that drives you and your organization.

Some questions you might ask as you gather collective wisdom include

- What's going well? Why?
- What's not going well? Why?
- What would you change if you could?
- What would be the impact of that?
- How would you go about that?
- What other ideas do you have?
- Why would we do that?
- What would be the impact?
- How would we know we had succeeded?
- What role would you enjoy playing?
- How would you like to apply your talents and skills?
- What else should I know about this that you haven't already told me?

When to Start

When should you begin? Why not start today? If you want to develop a big, exciting idea, mission, or purpose, the first step is simply to assess at a closer level what is going on around you and in your organization.

Here are some questions to consider:

- Is there a significant problem or challenge that you would like to solve or meet?
- Why does it interest you?
- Who knows a lot about it, and how can you talk with them?
- Is it interesting enough to immerse yourself in learning about it?
- What would you hope to learn or resolve as a result of this process?

Once you have answered these questions, the next step is to start the process of gathering information, tapping into collective wisdom. You may find that you are not as interested in the problem or issue as you expected. In other words, you may lose interest. However, if your interest grows as you learn more, keep pursuing it, keep asking questions, and develop a viewpoint. If it is interesting enough, you may find yourself immersed in it, which is a sure sign that you are moving in the right direction toward purpose.

People Want to Know: What Are Your Big Ideas?

When you take on a leadership role, people want to know what your big ideas are. It can be intimidating to think you need to have a big idea to succeed; yet, if you want to make a difference, it is important. A few years ago I worked with a newly promoted senior vice president of technology in an organization of 13,000 people. He had a stellar reputation as a superb technologist but was having trouble establishing himself as a leader. He stayed quiet in meetings and didn't have a plan for where to take his organization.

Finally, his boss sat him down and said, "I need to know something. What are your big ideas? I never hear from you." The senior vice president was stunned. He had not thought that he would be judged or expected to have big ideas. Since he had "grown up" in the company, he had plenty of knowledge about what was going well and what wasn't. He simply hadn't analyzed it and allowed it to guide him to mission and purpose.

He and I started with stories—stories of success and failure. It was amazing how clearly some big ideas emerged as he went through this process. Now he had several big ideas that excited him and gave him purpose. He decided on a plan to revise how the plethora of new technology ideas that bubbled up every day should be evaluated for "go or no-go." The result was an innovative approach that saved a lot of money. The boss was very impressed.

If you're not sure where to start, gather stories and analyze what they are telling you. Trust the process. You will be amazed how these big ideas can emerge. By looking at your own organization and reviewing successes and failures, you will make all kinds of discoveries. Not only will it give you some big ideas, but you'll also learn a lot about the values and behaviors that make your organization successful.

> *If you're not sure where to start, gather stories and analyze what they are telling you. Trust the process. You will be amazed how these big ideas can emerge.*

What Constitutes a Big Idea?

- It solves an important problem.
- It meets a critical need.
- It has potential to make a significant impact.
- People see it as transformational.
- It challenges typical ways of thinking or approaches.
- There is a clear, compelling benefit to resolving it.
- It improves a situation or organization.
- It meets a high-priority goal.
- You are excited and enthusiastic about doing it.
- Other people are excited about it and want to be part of it.

Big Ideas Challenge Conventional Thinking

Big ideas often challenge conventional thinking. They usually spring from a thorough immersion process and a close analysis of data gathered in many places. You can't just go to the same sources or talk to the "usual suspects." If you do, you'll just get the same answers. You have to move into new circles, talk to new people, and ask questions no one else will.

Ellen Parker at Project Bread asked how many hungry people actually took advantage of emergency food pantries and was shocked to learn that the figure was only 25 *percent*. "That meant [that] around 75 percent of people who are judged to need service were *not* making use of food pantries and soup kitchens." The revelation led to a new solution that required Project Bread to debunk old assumptions. "We could either dismiss them by saying, 'What's wrong with these people who are hungry?' or we could ask the question: 'What's wrong with *us*?'"

Challenging conventional thinking requires you to pay attention to the obvious. Parker says "zillions of dollars" were thrown at a problem that never seemed to get better, yet no one examined why. "Antihunger organizations every year are reporting that there is *more hunger*. To report [that] there is more hunger and to continue to do the same thing to address it, you have to ask yourself whether that is the definition of insanity," she says.

One of the secrets of leaders who lead from a strong sense of mission and purpose is that they investigate and challenge assumptions. It is exciting and invigorating to do this and then to communicate from a position of deep knowledge. And remember, these aren't just your ideas; they are the product of collective wisdom. You have a network of employees, clients, customers, and stakeholders who have contributed to the creation of this mission and plan.

> *One of the secrets of leaders who lead from a strong sense of mission and purpose is that they investigate and challenge assumptions.*

Rediscovering Purpose and Passion

Even if you have a great job and work for a great company, you can lose that spark. From time to time we all feel a little overwhelmed by everything we have to do. We may need to focus on family or the personal and not be able to devote as much energy as we would like to our jobs. Ultimately, however, it is important to be able to rediscover purpose and passion in our work.

If you lose that sense of purpose and passion, you can rediscover it. But it doesn't just happen. You have to make it a conscious journey. As a leader, refueling purpose and passion should be part of your job. Vikki Pryor, CEO of SBLI, says that it's a lot like a marriage or a relationship: "You have to keep recommitting. Once you're conscious and you know you feel this challenge, you have to do the work of recommitting."

If you find that your sense of purpose and passion is waning, it is important to stop, think about what you're doing and why, and consider what would get you excited again. This is how, over time, you become the kind of leader you want to be—one who is purpose-driven and able to connect others to purpose. "I periodically do my self-test—asking myself if I still love this," says Pryor. "You can't go blindly in saying I took this on without periodically reexamining your own heart."

Guard against burnout professionally and personally by moving around, connecting, meeting new people, asking questions, and becoming a lifelong learner. Work is so much more fulfilling when you keep the fire burning and periodically renew your sense of purpose. If you are too insulated or mired in routine, you can lose the energy and the spark. Go out, listen, and learn. When you talk to other people, you acquire fresh ideas, a new frame of reference, or a new perspective. It also can renew your faith that the path you're on is the right one.

> *If you are too insulated or mired in routine, you can lose the energy and the spark. Go out, listen, and learn.*

"When I go outside the company," says Pryor, "I see [that] we're making a difference. When I talk with my customers, my employees, and the world, it renews me." On the other hand, Pryor admits that when she gets wrapped up in the company's day-to-day issues, she quickly moves toward the burnout zone. "It really is like a relationship, and a relationship is hard work. But if you travel and have interactions with other human beings, you start to value the person you're with."

When the Big Idea Doesn't Win Friends

As you pursue your mission and purpose, especially when you challenge conventional ways of thinking, you won't always win friends or accolades. "I've probably had more resistance from people who are my peers across the country," says Ellen Parker. "There is a huge investment in this country in feeding people through emergency food programs. There's a whole infrastructure, people who see themselves as hunger leaders defining their mission in that way. And I think that this is a more complicated way to look at it."

People may think you've lost your mind when you start shaking things up. This is why it is so important to do the work, get grounded in the analysis, and develop a strong, passionate point of view. When people question your plan and test your resolve, you will know that you have the facts on your side, and you will believe in what you are doing.

Don't allow delays or length of time to discourage you from your growing sense of purpose. Naysayers often expect overnight results, and you cannot always accomplish big things on their schedule. It takes time to realize a vision, to turn a big idea into action. As Greg Case at Aon knows, leading an organization to realize a big vision is "always a work in progress."

> *It takes time to realize a vision, to turn a big idea into action.*

What If the Big Idea Isn't Your Idea?

Often your job as a leader is to execute a big idea that isn't your own. How do you connect with that mission and develop passion about it? The answer is not an easy one, but I believe that it is really about knowing yourself. You need to know what motivates you. You need to analyze how closely you are aligned with the

> *Why work for a company that isn't aligned with your own mission and values? If you look at your work as a powerful expression of who you are in the world, you need to honor that.*

organization's big idea or mission. Why work for a company that isn't aligned with your own mission and values? If you look at your work as a powerful expression of who you are in the world, you need to honor that.

If you find yourself in the wrong place, working for the wrong company, consider how you might make a change that would reinvigorate you and help you to become the best leader you can be. It is impossible over the long term to fake your interest in or commitment to a mission that doesn't match your own. People know when you are genuinely engaged and when you are not. In our survey, many respondents brought up the desire to work for a leader who could articulate purpose with passion. "If a leader isn't passionate about the strategy he or she wants others to follow, then the results will be marginal and difficult to measure. Good communication skills and passion create something intangible that drives an organization forward," said one participant.

Developing a closer alignment with the mission of the organization will make you a far more effective leader, influencer, and advocate. You'll find new energy and excitement about going to work every day. You'll find it easier to get things done. You'll find that it greatly enhances your ability to communicate, influence others, and get the outcomes you want. You'll also feel greater confidence, courage, and conviction about what you are doing and why. This is an elixir for the people who work with you and who look to you as their leader.

Once you have done the work of defining your purpose and developing a plan, the next step is to consider how you will bring others along. In the next few chapters we'll look at how to do that, beginning with the critical link people need to see between what and why.

Summary

- It's a privilege and an opportunity to be in a position of leadership, to have the opportunity to pull people together and work toward a common goal.
- When you know what drives you, and when you share that purpose with others, the result is very powerful.

- You can use the process of inquiry and gathering collective wisdom to develop a mission and plan.
- When you connect with the mission of your company in a very real way, other people see it and are excited by it.
- The process of making personal connections, asking questions, immersing yourself in a topic, learning more, and developing the big ideas can renew your energy and passion.

4

Connecting People to Purpose: Link *What* and *Why*

I believe that if you show people the problems and you show
them the solutions, they will be moved to act.

—BILL GATES

THE LIFE INSURANCE INDUSTRY was facing a major challenge—a series
of highly publicized alleged and real scandals had severely damaged public confidence in the integrity and value of the industry. Despite much
hand-wringing within the industry, no one had stepped forward to solve
the problem.

The Life and Health Insurance Foundation was created with
the express purpose of redeeming the industry's reputation and helping
people to understand the value of life and health insurance in their financial lives. CEO David Woods now had to rally the industry behind this
mission and raise a huge amount of money to mount a counteroffensive.

Woods created a dramatic chart to demonstrate what had happened
to the industry. "Public appreciation of the life insurance industry and
the value of its products was in a freefall; slipping from a healthy 73 percent to a sickly 47 percent—and was continuing to decline," Woods says.

However, establishing the problem was only the beginning. Why did
it matter? Who should care? Woods needed to show his own industry the
link between poor image, slumping sales, and shrinking business profits.

Woods and his board created an ambitious multiyear, multi-million-dollar plan to rebuild public confidence and prepared a presentation to demonstrate to industry leaders why it mattered to their businesses.

The leadership of the Life and Health Insurance Foundation was able first to establish the link—creating in the minds of industry leaders a sense of a clear and present danger to all segments of the industry, most especially their own organizations. Then and only then did Woods and his team roll out the bold plan for solving the problem. And the money poured in.

In motivating people to get behind a plan, it's imperative to connect the *what* with the *why*. People have to understand the reasons it matters to them, and you have to communicate those reasons effectively so that they see for themselves the logic and truth of it. People will carefully consider any plan and support you if you present them with a compelling reason and benefit to them. Whether you're selling your idea to colleagues, your boss, your employees, or your customers, you have to take the time to explain it.

People are motivated to take action when they reach their own conclusions. As a leader who must influence others and motivate many people, you have to be adept at communicating with each audience the link between *what* and *why*. Motivation and logic go together like a hand in a glove. Your job is to help people see the logic of something before asking them to buy in.

You might be surprised at how many leaders don't adequately explain why they are advocating a plan. Perhaps their own analysis is incomplete; they may not understand their audience's motivations; or they may not have a robust communication plan or the skills to sell it. For whatever reason, during our survey, when we asked, "Why do leaders fail to motivate people to action?" we found that people seem disappointed and impatient with leaders on this score. One respondent told us, "Many leaders just assume that people will be satisfied taking direction without understanding why. I saw a 'change management' initiative fail miserably because the case for change was glossed over, and leaders gave *direction*

> *Motivation and logic go together like a hand in a glove. Your job is to help people see the logic of something before they buy in.*

instead of *motivation*. People never understood *why* they should do something different, and it probably took five times longer to get the change accomplished, which was twice as long as was needed. The leader didn't get the lesson and attributed it to 'Change is hard.'"

In the case of the Life and Health Insurance Foundation, David Woods and his board realized that if industry leaders saw it simply as an industry problem, they would not buy in. Woods had to help these business executives see that they "owned" the problem; they controlled the money—they had to "buy into" the solution. No problem, no money. In driving forward with your purpose and plan, you must do the same thing. You may see heads nodding, but you cannot motivate people to act until they understand why. There is a difference between agreement and action. What prompts action is when people see that it matters to them.

There are three reasons why people don't act: They don't know *what* to do, they don't know *how* to do it, or they don't know *why* they should do it. If you present a plan and people fail to move forward and take action, chances are that it's the third reason— you haven't explained *why*. Why it matters to *them* is the question you need to answer before they act.

> *There are three reasons why people don't move forward with a plan: They don't know what to do, they don't know how to do it, or they don't know why they should do it.*

For example, let's say that your company has just purchased new customer relationship management (CRM) software. You send out an e-mail that everyone will be scheduled for a training program. But people are complaining. They hate training. They are busy. They don't see the need. What is so wrong with the current CRM system? They don't understand why you're making them miserable by requiring them to learn the new one. The complaints escalate as people imagine what a stupid waste of time and money this is; they are already predicting that it will fail. Long-time employees are especially vocal; they have been through these so-called upgrades before, and they can tell you that they were nothing but a pain in the neck.

At this point, as a leader, you have a choice: You can issue a directive, expect cooperation, and ignore the complaints, or you can reach out, understand their concerns, and look at it from their point of view. Once you understand their interests, you can explain why the initiative is so important not only to the company but also to them. This may seem obvious, yet most leaders tell us that after they do this careful analysis, they realize that they had previously failed to see it from the other side. The fact that leaders often fail in this regard is confirmed by our survey. Scores of employees noted that their bosses don't take the time to put a plan in terms that everyone understands. Taking the time to analyze your audience not only helps you to make a better case, but it also demonstrates respect, one of the most important elements of a persuasive transaction.

Start By Sharing the Facts

Jeff Neufeld, the former chief information officer and executive vice president of the Fidelity Brokerage Company, was facing a particularly difficult "sell" to his team. Fidelity was extremely profitable — but Neufeld believed that sooner or later the company's leadership would demand more accountability and efficiency from its technology team. New technology solutions often took too long to develop and were abandoned after significant investments. Duplicate solutions in various parts of the organization also were creating unnecessary costs. Fidelity was experiencing spectacular growth year after year, and there was little pressure to tighten things up at the time, but Neufeld still believed that the technology team eventually would get hammered to institute more discipline and closely monitor and manage the cost of development.

As he prepared for his all-hands technology team meeting, he realized that it was going to be hard to persuade his own team to become more diligent when top management had not insisted that the team do so. Neufeld was going to ask his team to raise the bar on its own performance when team members already believed that they were top performers. "To say we weren't good enough seemed out of sync with the reality they had been living," he explains.

Neufeld's professional background might suggest that he would not be the kind of leader who understood as he did how essential it was to win buy-in. Neufeld began his career as an officer in the United States

Marine Corps responsible for communications software and hardware in military command and control. He later directed a huge satellite program at Lockheed Martin and then went on to serve as chief information officer and manager of GEO Aerospace Telecommunications. Thus one might assume that a long-time military guy working on classified projects would be more inclined to issue directives. Yet Neufeld is a leader who fully appreciates how to motivate his team and persuade them to take action. His approach, confirmed by every member of his team, was to engage in open, honest communication. He respected his team's intellect and knew that team members needed to analyze the facts. He set out to explain the *why* of the plan.

Neufeld presented a careful analysis and made a rock-solid case for why his group needed to bring its standards closer to those of technology groups in public companies. He showed team members exactly how the facts pointed to a pending issue that, even if the rest of the company didn't see it yet, indicated that they would not remain competitive with current practices. The team bought into his analysis and adopted new approaches. Team members got behind the idea of making every technology project efficient and cost-effective. And their timing was perfect. Only a few months later, when new leaders joined Fidelity, their first order of business was to cut costs and look at how to become—guess what?—more efficient!

The Truth Is a Powerful, Motivating Ally

The truth is always the best road to persuading people to act. If the facts point to a solution, reasonable minds may disagree on the tactics, but people will be on the same page that something must be done. Neufeld enjoyed a remarkably high level of respect from his team. When I asked him why, he told me that he believes it is the result of a commitment to telling the truth and respecting other people's intellects. "The mistake many leaders make in communicating strategy is that they tend to underestimate how much people can take at once," he says. "With all the right intentions, they parse it out and try to protect their teams." Neufeld's experience taught him that if you don't explain everything, you end up "robbing people of the opportunity to hear the whole argument." In other words, full disclosure of the facts allows rational people to come to the same place on an issue and deal with it.

Not only is the truth persuasive, but it is also a powerful motivator for action. People really want to know the "up and up," and when they do, they want to do something about it. While it can be difficult to open up to your own team about some aspects of your business, resist the urge to report selectively, and give it to them straight. Whether the news is good or bad, people will respect you and be more inclined to act as you recommend if they know it all and don't believe that there are hidden agendas. In our survey, one respondent said, "I believe leaders don't feel that people can handle the truth, which reminds me of Jack Nicholson's famous outburst in the film A *Few Good Men*. They don't give people enough credit for being mature and able to handle potentially unpleasant news."

> "I believe leaders don't feel that people can handle the truth. . . . They don't give people enough credit for being mature and able to handle potentially unpleasant news."

Explain It as Many Times as Necessary to Win Buy-in

You may think that you've communicated enough, but when an issue is difficult, people need to hear it and have an opportunity to discuss it, often many times. You may need to set up a system of communicating through many forums. While you may get tired of repeating the message, that's part of your job as the leader. Don't assume that if people hear it once, they get it.

The value of repetition in communicating any message has been widely documented. People can take in a lot of information, but they usually cannot do so all at once. Through repetition, you create opportunities for people to really "hear" different aspects of a plan or strategy; it can take six or seven repetitions for the average person to fully comprehend a complex issue. In addition, as you communicate the same message, you can roll out specifics and use examples that make it clear.

As the preceding respondent told us, "I think leaders sometimes feel that the strategy is self-evident, so why do they need to say it over and over. Often, however, the reality is any-

People can take in a lot of information, but they usually cannot do so all at once.

thing but obvious. It may be self-evident to the person saying it, but frequently it's not so obvious to employees. I can think of many projects where the team was not on the same page due to scanty communication, and the project suffered."

People can only be part of the solution if they truly, completely understand the problem. When preparing to introduce a plan, initiative, or project, plan on using many forums for discussion—presentations, e-mail, blogs, online discussion groups, and informal conversations are all opportunities to repeat your message. When you do this effectively, you turn employees into partners in the mission or project. They fully understand and thank you for taking every opportunity to engage them in a conversation about the challenge. People are highly motivated to work in an organization where leaders communicate with them often about the things that matter.

The *Why* Has to Make Sense

I'll never forget a personal experience I had while working in television that illustrates how leaders fail to connect a decision with logic and common sense. The general manager of the television station called a rare meeting of the entire news department. The station's news ratings were slipping precipitously after it switched network affiliation, and people were worried. The decision we were told was made because the new network would provide a much-needed infusion of cash; the owners of the company believed that while the network's programs were not highly rated, they would trend upward. Meanwhile, the network shows were providing pathetic lead-in numbers, which, in turn, caused our local news ratings to tank.

I supposed that this general manager (effectively the CEO of the station) had the best of intentions when he started the meeting with a positive spin. He assured us that the station was still profitable, that it had a good fall lineup of programs, and that the network wasn't unhappy (yet) with our local sales because we were still profitable. Then he said something that simply mystified us. "Our goal is not to be number one in the ratings," he said. "We can be number two or three as long as we are making money. Being number one just isn't that important."

The entire room sat there in stunned silence. We couldn't believe what we had just heard. For our entire careers we had been about *striving to be number one in the market!* News people get up in the morning and look at the ratings before they brush their teeth. Every reporter, photographer, anchor, writer, producer, and editor lives to be the top-rated station. Needless to say, we were dumbstruck. It made no sense to us. We wanted to be the best and be recognized as the best in the market.

We adjourned and went back to the newsroom. People went from stunned to outraged and then to demoralized. We couldn't believe that the leader of our organization didn't care about being recognized by viewers as the best. Clearly, he either didn't understand our business, or he wasn't facing the truth. Of course, we cared about being profitable, but we were smart enough to know that profits would soon disappear as we had to negotiate commercial rates with lower ratings. His message just didn't make sense. It may not surprise you to learn that many years later the station remained stuck in fourth place.

If things aren't going well, you have to tell the truth. People will figure it out anyway. They have radar for spin. You are not protecting people with spin; therefore, be sure to tell the truth, and don't twist the facts to fit a hopeful outcome. We would have preferred to hear the truth and learn that the station's leadership had a plan to turn things around. We wouldn't have minded a positive message, but the facts can't be sugar coated or distorted. Your explanation must make sense. Have faith that your people can handle it.

> *The mission has to make sense to people. They have to understand why.*

Give Them a GREAT Reason to Buy In

In thinking about how to communicate your case, you might remember this acronym: GREAT. Give people a GREAT reason, and they will usually buy in. Here's what GREAT stands for:

- **G**rounded in fact
- **R**elevant to the audience
- **E**xplanation makes sense
- **A**pparently, obviously logical
- **T**ruth about the situation

Every single person who works with you or buys your products and services is a thinking, reasoning human being. They all want to simply understand the facts and reasons why you are making your proposal.

A great plan, project, or goal is grounded in fact. Remember our discussion in Chapter 3 about collective wisdom. If you've done your homework, you have gathered the appropriate amount of accurate data. Now you simply have to communicate these data in a way that is relevant and clear to your audience. The facts have to be correct, and the explanation has to make sense. You have to give people the opportunity to digest the information, ask questions, and draw their own conclusions. This is what a GREAT reason does.

If you ground it in fact, make it relevant, take time to explain it clearly, make it logical, and speak the truth, you also demonstrate respect for your audience. Leaders who issue directives are not going to get a positive response because they are subtly telling people not to think, just to act. People resent this. Instead of issuing a directive, if you give your people the opportunity to evaluate the situation for themselves, you will get the result you want. When people feel empowered in the process and they see that the logic and reasoning are sound, they will support you and even share your enthusiasm. They will become advocates instead of adversaries.

When people disagree (and some will), they are still likely to give you the benefit of the doubt if you have made a genuine effort to give them a GREAT reason. They will respect your process and willingness to work with them, and they will at least appreciate how you've arrived at your plan or decision. They also will be grateful that you've made a genuine effort to talk with them and learn how they see it. The fact that you have taken the time to engage in a dialogue, sharing the *what* and the *why*, shows that, above all, you respect them. Even if the decision is not the one they prefer, you will encounter far less resistance when its time to act.

> *People don't want to be sold; they want to buy. If what their boss says fails to jive with logic or fails to make sense, they won't be buying. If what they hear does make sense, they are likely to conclude for themselves that it's a good idea.*

People don't want to be *sold*; they want to *buy*. A GREAT reason is how you start the process of getting people to buy. Try to sell an idea without a GREAT reason, and you may see heads nod, but you won't see action. Sometimes you even may have a mutiny on your hands. People may smile at you as you walk down the hall, but they will be less productive, less motivated, and less efficient.

Make a GREAT Case

To develop your GREAT case for any plan or project, you need to take the time to analyze it and make it highly relevant to your audience. Proceed this way: After gathering sufficient data and information, get into the mind-set of your audience. Imagine that you are sitting across the table or in their seats. Think about what would matter most to them. Then complete the phrases in column 1 in Table 4–1 by filling in the blanks in columns 2, 3, and 4 (as needed).

As you complete the questions in the table, you will know whether you have a GREAT case. Remember, it has to be relevant to *each audience*. Take the time to consider what makes sense to each individual, team, or group, and then communicate this on their terms.

You often may believe that you have a persuasive case, but when you engage in this exercise, you'll see that it is hard work to capture other people's thinking and connect with their interests. Many times I've seen

Table 4–1 Great Case Questions

The facts of this situation are			
This affects you because			
My analysis of the impact of this is			
If we were to do this or not do this, what it would mean to you			
The outcome of this plan or action for you should be that			

well-meaning leaders fail at this. If you aren't sure, talk to people you want to persuade or people who know them, and get their viewpoint so that you understand how they see it. Start informally with conversations and ask questions that help you to understand. Find out how other people see it before you prepare your GREAT case and present your plan. The only way to win buy-in is to establish relevance to their interests.

So What?

You know you've made your case when you can answer the question, "So what?" for each audience. The "So what?" factor may be significantly different for each. In proposing an action or plan, you need to ask yourself as if you were the other person or group, "So what?" This question allows you to probe more deeply what the real issues are and why your audience would buy in. Don't be satisfied with the answer to the first "So what?" question; keep asking until you have identified a clear, powerful benefit to them.

Let's return to our earlier CRM software example to demonstrate how the "So what?" question can help you to persuade others. Your company is insisting that people be trained on how to use new software they don't believe is necessary. You might say, "This will increase efficiencies in our operation." But imagine your audience; put yourself in their shoes. Do they really care about the efficiency of the operation? "So what?" they might ask. "Efficiencies in the operation will save all of us time, which we can spend with our customers." Another "So what?" Is that really going to convince them? No. "Well, if we can spend more time with customers up front, we will have fewer complaints to handle." Not bad. But I'm still thinking, "So what?" "Fewer complaints mean higher bonuses because you have time to create happy customers." Now you're talking. Don't stop until you have carried the "So what?" exercise to a point that really resonates for your audience.

The "So what?" tool will transform and improve your persuasive presentations, reducing the time and energy required to drive change and motivate people to act. Think of your audience first, imagine what really matters to them, and keep asking the question "So what?" until you hit on the nugget—a persuasive set of reasons why they should embrace a plan or go in a particular direction. If you can simply and clearly articulate the GREAT reasons and answer all the "So what?" questions, you will become a very influential, motivational leader. You will find it far easier to move your organization forward and achieve your objectives.

> *The "So what?" tool will transform and improve your persuasive presentations dramatically, reducing the time and energy required to drive change and motivate people to act.*

Get Input

One participant in our survey said, "If the communication style is one that 'crams down' information without first seeking the input of key members of the team, even if the message is delivered clearly and routinely, the strategy lacks individual buy-in . . . because people there weren't included on the front end."

As I mentioned earlier, before you go out to make your case, you need to get input. This is that collective wisdom process we discussed in

Chapter 3. Gathering collective wisdom is a powerful tool. Give people a chance to tell you exactly what you need to know to put together a GREAT plan.

The obvious sources of information are employees, clients, customers, and other groups affected by your decision. You also should ask people who know them, understand how they think, and interact with them. Gathering input even if you think you know the answer is important because conditions in your business are always changing. What you knew a few years, months, or even weeks ago could be different now.

You would think that more leaders would ask, but they don't. They are busy, they make assumptions, and sometimes they are arrogant and don't know what they don't know or don't care. The failure to get input is fatal to many business plans and ideas. Think back to a time when you were not the boss, and you may recall that you were one of those people who had to execute a plan, when no one asked your opinion. Had they done so, you might have saved them a lot of trouble. You probably had very useful information and would have been happy to share.

If your company conducts employee and client surveys, you know that responses really can surprise you sometimes. What's interesting is that employees and customers love to be asked. They are happy to share information and opinions, and in the right forum, they will always tell you the truth. I have found that even very busy executives and clients are quite willing to spend as much as 45 minutes or an hour providing feedback to our firm. If you have good relationships, you will get thorough responses; even if you have a problem, people respond because they want to help. They appreciate that you ask and want to help you to get it right.

> *If your company conducts employee and client surveys, you know that responses really can surprise you sometimes. What's interesting is that employees and customers love to be asked. They are happy to share information and opinions, and in the right forum, they will always tell you the truth.*

Save Yourself from Making a Big Mistake

Gathering input may take resources and time upfront, but it will save you from making costly mistakes and doing harm to your business that takes months or even years to undo. You simply must gather input before you try to persuade people or institute any significant plan. One survey participant told this story: "A new CEO came into the company from a venture capital buyout. This CEO did not have industry-specific experience in the company. Instead of becoming acclimated to the environment and market, he turned things upside down. He altered internal documents and procedures, and he unnecessarily shuffled personnel."

By failing to start by gathering input, the executive squandered his "honeymoon period" with the company and never recovered. He didn't have enough information to start shaking things up. Had he listened and learned, he would have created a solid plan and won buy-in. "But it became clear that he didn't walk the talk of listening," said our respondent. "He spent thousands of dollars revising the vision, mission, values, all of which felt like a joke. He demoted executive management and brought in his team to make things worse. Morale tanked, as did any momentum that was present before the buyout. He was eventually let go after making a total mess of things."

I wish stories like this were less common. Too often a failure to seek the views of others and to capitalize on their experiences leads to precipitous actions and career-ending moves. You cannot devise an effective plan or motivate people if you don't listen. People will throw themselves into helping you to understand if you do this well. Your questions may confirm your viewpoint or change it, so you need to be open to both. And remember, your staunchest critics can become your greatest supporters in this process because you include their ideas and views. Ask, listen, listen some more—and then make your plan and communicate it.

> You cannot devise an effective plan or motivate people to buy in if you don't ask questions and listen.

Remember that great ideas still will encounter resistance, especially at the senior leadership level; difficult challenges mean that people don't always agree. If you don't have initial agreement, you may need to go back and gather more input until you have enough evidence to create a tipping point where a decision or action seems obvious. Even if you are absolutely convinced that your way is the right way, go back and solicit other people's views until your case is made. "I have seen many Fortune 500 companies that we do work for where the leader's strategy is brilliant," one survey respondent told us. "However, . . . ego and attitudes often get in the way. It takes communication in both directions and a lot of input to create follow-through on a new strategy."

The Benefit of Engaging People

As the CEO of my firm, I am not immune to the temptation to plow ahead without input. At times, I have had to be convinced of the benefits of engaging everyone in solving a problem or developing a plan. I find this a challenge because I am a person who believes in action and have had to acquire patience with process. Here's an example of a situation that taught me how important it is to engage people: I attended a strategy mapping workshop where I had some breakthroughs in my own thinking about how to move our business forward. I was so excited by these tools and the new revelations that all I could think about was how quickly I could write up the plan and announce it to the team. I was so focused on getting it done and "checking that box" that I didn't stop to consider what they might be able to add. I assumed that since I had been the only one to attend the workshop, I should charge forward and make it happen.

Fortunately, one wise member of my team prevented me from charging ahead and undermining my own good intentions. After hearing what I had planned, he walked into my office and said (diplomatically of course), "You know, I think we need to take our time with this. It would be better if we all took part in formulating it. Everyone needs to talk about what we're doing and why. We need to agree on what each of these strategic initiatives means to us." Although I was still itching to get moving on *my* plan, I also knew deep down that he was right. So I scheduled eight half-day meetings, a huge amount of time, but what I believed would be required to go through the process and develop a plan for our firm.

The result of taking the time to step back and engage people was amazing. They threw themselves into the project; after the first meeting, the mood in our office was upbeat. Although the strategy work was difficult, everyone was engaged. The more we worked, the more energized we all became. As the plan came together, we shared a sense of excitement about what this could do for us. We agreed on goals, created projects, set up accountability, and most important, understood *why* we were undertaking each and every project. And since all of us were engaged, I didn't end up with a solo to-do list—everyone had a significant role. We also now agreed on measurements, timetables, and desired outcomes.

> *This defining experience demonstrated to me the power and impact of engaging everyone in the process. It wasn't just a plan on paper; we were living and breathing the plan.*

This defining experience demonstrated to me the power and impact of engaging *everyone* in the process. It wasn't just a plan on paper; we were living and breathing the plan. Even when things didn't get done or didn't get done when we had hoped, we were able to get back on track because we had all agreed that it was important and knew why. This is how I learned how absolutely vital it is to engage everyone. This is the secret to alignment and motivation. When people are involved in the planning, they become part of the process and invested in the outcome.

So engage people. Even if you think that you can make a decision yourself, invite them to participate. Let them in, ask their opinion, encourage them to take ownership, and get them working together toward a common purpose. This approach powers people up!

Case Studies, Examples, and Stories Make Powerful Points

An excellent way to engage people and win buy-in is to provide real-world case studies and examples. You can wow your audience when you present relevant facts in a story form. Jeff Neufeld used this technique when he persuaded his team that it needed to address efficiency in its operation. Neufeld took situations from his own organization that highlighted inefficiency and presented them as stories, or case studies. This was a very effective way to allow his team to "see" in their minds eyes what happened. As they followed the story, they made the link to other, similar situations. Case studies, examples, and stories help people to relate and remember. They also show people that you know them, understand the situation, and took the time to do your homework, building your credibility. Neufeld says, "What made it powerful was that these were actually examples they lived every day."

With stories and examples, Neufeld said, "I could talk about the way we did our testing processes. The handoffs, the wait times, and the lack of automation that resulted in additional time and cost." Neufeld saw the value of presenting "on the ground" evidence, that is, vignettes from the organization, situations that everybody lived. "All I had to do was provide a few of these relevant situations," he recalls, "and they seemed to immediately understand why."

Stories are very powerful emotional tools in winning buy-in. They allow you to appeal not only to the logical side of people's brains but also to their emotions. People are usually not persuaded to take action by mere fact—they must feel something about a situation, too. What motivates them? Sometimes it's fear; sometimes it's desire; and sometimes it's hope. In Chapter 9 we will look more closely at how to develop and incorporate stories into your communications.

Speaking of emotion, when Neufeld presented these case studies, he asked his audience questions that contained both *feeling* and *logic* words. He would say, "Does this *feel right* to you? Would you *like* to do this better? Are you *satisfied* with this?" Each time he spoke, he made it a point to use both logical and emotional words. He says that this made it stick. "They quickly grasped the reasons. You could see that they were thinking that while some things looked good, we were not yet a wow technology organization that others would want to emulate." Being a "wow" technology organization appealed to their emotions—tapping their desire to be the best.

Logic Words

How can you appeal to both logic and emotion? Certain words evoke logical or emotional responses. Logic words are important because they trigger the logical side of the brain to analyze and process facts. You actually can use language to trigger a logical thought with words that guide how you would like your audience to think about something. This is a critical factor in buy-in. When making a case, choose words that signal to people that you are about to provide a logical statement. Here are some *logic* words:

- Research
- Study
- Investigate or investigation
- Inquiry
- Quantify or quantifiable
- Measure or measurable
- Verify or verifiable
- True or truth
- Specific
- Evidence
- Data
- Facts
- Tangible
- Actual
- Concrete
- Detectable
- Objective
- Conclusive
- Decisive
- Definitive
- Proof or prove
- Substantiate
- Substantive
- Result
- Finding
- Performance

Appeal to Emotion

Of course, as human beings, we certainly do not live by logic alone. We also need to connect with an idea on an emotional level. If you return to

Jeff Neufeld's case studies, you see how he was able to crystallize the logic of tightening up his group's technology operation while also making an emotional appeal.

Speaking to a highly technical audience does not alter the need for both a logical and an emotional appeal. No matter how technical your audience, they are human beings. Some audiences may by nature be more logical, but don't presume that they won't respond to emotion as well. If you present only the logical side of your argument, you miss out on an opportunity to connect and also inspire. With logic, you help people to understand, but with emotion, you move them to act.

> *Speaking to a highly technical audience does not alter the need for both a logical and an emotional appeal.*

Here is a list of words to keep in mind that could be used to appeal to the emotional side of the brain:

- Feel or feeling
- Hunch or gut
- Inclination or inkling
- Instinct or notion
- Thoughts
- Reaction or sense
- Suspicion
- Sentiment
- Surprise or surprised
- Positive or negative
- Fear, concern, or worry
- Apprehensive or apprehension
- Strength or weakness
- Impression or sense
- Motive or motivation
- Appetite, will, or urge
- Hope, wish, or desire
- Attitude or disposition
- Outlook or mind-set
- Love or hate

- Like or dislike
- Trust or distrust
- Confident or confidence
- Intention
- Appeal

Communicate a Picture of the Future

Once you get people on board with a logical explanation and an appeal to their emotions, the next step in the process is to provide an answer—to focus on a future state. This is where you can tell them how things could and should be. I call this *future focus*, and it is a critical step in persuasive communication. The leader who can help people see the future becomes influential. Future focus is motivating because when people see this shared vision, they start moving together toward that end.

As you look at your organization, you may see a lot of people who "know" what's wrong and complain about it. When you move into a leadership role and it is your responsibility to fix it, you must paint a picture of future success. A leader sees what's wrong and asks, "How are things now, how could they be better, and what will it look like when we get there?" A leader paints a vivid picture of the future that motivates and inspires others.

Returning to the example of how Jeff Neufeld won people over—he shared a clear *future focus.* "Our business partners will tell us when we are successful—their costs will go down, our cash flow will be up, and they will give us credit. They will say—it's thanks to our technology organization." He also predicted that customers and trade journals would talk about how Fidelity technology is at the heart of its success. These specific descriptions of successful outcomes were highly motivating to his team.

In my first book, *Speak Like a CEO,* I discussed in greater detail how to develop a future focus and communicate it. I highly recommend this as an approach with every audience—employees, clients, prospects, the public, and the media. People need to see it as you see it and imagine it as you imagine it. A leader who is able to focus people on the future and then achieve that future is regarded as a visionary. I encourage you to look at each persuasive presentation you make and consider whether you are clearly painting that vision for the future.

Last But Not Least, Don't "Bury the Lead"

A common issue in many presentations is that people deliver the message sequentially without putting the most important, relevant message and call to action at the top. Few audiences, especially senior leaders, have the patience to sit through this kind of step-by-step presentation, which is why they usually interrupt or lose interest. There is an expression in the news business: "Don't bury the lead." In communicating your case and motivating people to take action, this means to always put your big idea, the linchpin, and your most relevant information at the top. Don't bury the *what* and the *why* way down inside the rest of the story. Put it right up front, and preview deeper-level analysis. If you don't grab your audience right up front with the *what* and the *why*, you will lose them.

A rising star in a financial services organization was chosen to be on a team to formulate the company's next five-year strategy. This young leader was smart, had done impressive research, and had come up with a great idea for building the company's brand in a market where it was a distant number three. He carefully prepared a presentation for the company's senior leaders. But 20 minutes into the rehearsal of his presentation, the coach working with him still didn't get it. He hadn't yet heard the "big idea," and he knew that this young leader would only have about three minutes to grab his audience.

"What's the big news that you want to be sure no one misses?" the consultant asked him.

"That this is a $700 million market!" he replied, somewhat shocked that the consultant wasn't already getting it. "I thought it was obvious," he said.

"It's not," said the consultant. "And you need to make it your opening statement." On the day of his presentation, the rising star opened with a bold line: "Make no mistake, this is a $700 million market. We cannot afford to miss this opportunity." The rising star not only won approval, but he also won a big promotion within six months.

Put the big news up front—then you can make your case. You can influence people only when they are really listening. In Chapter 5 we'll examine how once you have developed your persuasive case, you can align the entire organization and inspire people to act.

Summary

- In motivating people to get behind a plan, you have to connect the *what* with the *why*.
- People will carefully consider any plan and support you if you present them with a compelling reason and benefit to them.
- People don't want to be sold; they want to buy.
- You know you've made your case when you can answer the question, "So what?" for each and every audience. The "So what?" factor will be different for various audiences.
- Human beings do not live by logic alone. We also need to connect with an idea on an emotional level.
- Don't bury the lead. Get the big idea and compelling reasons right up front so that you grab your audience from the beginning.

5

At the Helm: Align the Organization with Mission, Values, and Strategy

Conviction is worthless unless it is converted into conduct.

—THOMAS CARLYLE

As IT GREW TO become the third largest construction company in the United States with $20 billion in projects worldwide, Skanska faced a significant challenge in moving forward as one company. Since it had grown largely by acquisition, the operations, processes, and cultures of these firms had to come together. The corporate decisions had been made to centralize management, eliminate the local company names, and adopt the Skanska logo internationally. Yet each local construction company continued to adhere to its own rules.

Mike McNally, president of Skanska Building USA, says that it finally came together for reasons that were unexpected but logical. One issue that everyone in all the global offices cared about was safety. It was how the company defined safety that created synergy. "Historically, safety meant wearing hard hats and fining people who didn't follow the rules," says McNally. "Those practices weren't improving safety at all, however." The Skanska leadership team broadened the definition to mean creating an injury-free environment. "We started to focus not on rules, but on the *human side* of safety. We emphasized how important it was to take care of yourself and the people around you on site." Skanska employees enthusiastically embraced it because it was about getting home at night, not about following the rules. They got on board with safety standards because it was personal for them.

Aligning an organization with mission, strategy, and values is essential to your success. The result for Skanska was a dramatic improvement in safety as people started to embrace the culture and act differently. An additional benefit was that employees now saw Skanska as a company that cared about its employees. Safety became not just a goal, but a value that defined the company.

The act of redefining safety and aligning people with that value unified the company. McNally says that it did what many companies that grow by acquisition find impossible—it consolidated the culture. "IFE [injury-free environment] is communicated constantly. When people walk on job sites, the leader always talks about safety. It's on our Web site, in all our publications, even in our proposals. It's the first thing you hear when you become a new employee. IFE is required training," he says. The message is everywhere; people hear it over and over again.

When you communicate a powerful message that resonates, you align your organization and motivate people to act in concert. The value of communicating and aligning your company around a shared vision and values is inestimable. What is the culture of safety worth to Skanska every year? "Alignment around that is everything for us," says McNally. "If we don't have a motivated, aligned workforce, there is no other asset."

> *Aligning an organization with mission, strategy, and values is essential to your success.*

In this chapter we'll look at how to communicate and align the organization with the mission, purpose, and values. As a leader, you are responsible for aligning people by driving the message home and creating accountability. As you will see, you can overcome tremendous odds and bring organizations together if you develop the skill to focus people and motivate them with a powerful message.

Against the Odds

Sometimes, aligning an organization can seem like "mission impossible." When Mike Daly, whom you met in Chapter 1, took over Baystate Medical Center in 1981, the three-hospital system was reeling. How had this happened? A year prior to Daly's arrival, the previous CEO had made a quick handshake deal to merge; the shotgun marriage was never planned, and people were unprepared. It was a disaster. Instead of streamlining operations and creating efficiencies, the three hospitals clung to their separate identities and went to war.

So the odds appeared to be stacked against Mike Daly when he walked in the door. Alignment looked impossible. People were unmotivated and discouraged. Not many executives would have even taken the job, but Daly loved the challenge. He had worked for another company that had been through a successful merger, so he had some experience, and he believed that it could be done at Baystate. In fact, the organization did come together under his leadership and eventually was named one of America's best hospitals by *US News and World Report*. In the following sidebar, Daly describes in his own words how he managed to align these organizations with a mission, make the hospital profitable, and make people feel good about working there again.

In His Own Words: Mike Daly's Story

I was in communication 24 hours a day—staying on message—being visible, responding to criticism, accepting criticism. The messages were: This place has the ingredients to be really great. No one believed it at first. But I had worked in a great hospital, and now at Baystate I could recognize all the ingredients—I could see the right stuff in every employee throughout the medical staff and every member of the board. They had become used to being the Avis of the hospital industry, second rate in comparison with all the other hospitals in New England. My message was that it didn't have to be like that. The ingredients of greatness are here, I told them, and we just had to work together to realize it.

The first thing to do was get rid of this feeling of three identities. We had to create one, single institution. That message, more than anything, was critical to getting everyone, including the medical staff, to believe it. These people were openly fighting with each other. I had to get rid of that. I had to bring everyone together and eliminate that conflict. I had to develop an atmosphere of teamwork and cooperation.

As you know, any good organization must begin with a vision that is absolutely bought into by everyone in the organization. Then, once you get alignment on that, you have to next draft a strategic plan that allows you to fulfill that vision. I brought in essentially a new management team who bought into what I was trying to do—that was part of the secret to our success. As you'll encounter in any large organization, you can bring in lots of superstars with their own agendas, but that won't align the organization around the goals.

When I went to one of my first medical staff meetings, they had 60 people in the room representing the three hospitals. The meeting started at 6 p.m. and went on until midnight, what with all the constant bickering and infighting. I went to two or three other similar meetings and then called in the heads of the medical staffs. "I'm not going to attend these anymore," I told them. "You're just flailing around here, and you have no agenda. Unless you change this, I want no part of it."

One of the three said, "Okay, I'll follow your lead." So I helped him design meetings with agendas—no more than two hours, with times set on each agenda item. People soon started enjoying the meetings because now they felt they weren't wasting their time. They eventually agreed to downsize and become an effective working body.

Daly's success in aligning the newly merged hospital organization did not happen overnight. There was no quick fix. And there's a lesson in this. With morale low and resistance to cooperation high, he had to communicate with various factions again and again to keep them on track. He needed to align the medical staff, management, patients, business partners, and contributors, and he was able to do it with a shared vision that resonated for all. One common trait of leaders like Daly is that they enjoy the challenge of communicating and driving the message about the "big idea" home. It took a decade, but ultimately, Daly succeeded, and the result was one very fine hospital system.

> *It took a decade, but ultimately, Daly succeeded, and the result was one very fine hospital system.*

Align with Action

Aligning an organization requires more than words. It takes action. Daly quickly discovered how he would have to show people what he meant. "Our town halls were wide-open forums; people could ask anything, and they often did," he says. He describes how he would field the questions and stress the vision and values. In the beginning, staff pointed out all the inconsistencies. They talked openly about hospital managers who were not adhering to the five values that Baystate lived by—collaboration, communication, trust, integrity, and respect. Many times they told Daly to his face that he was hypocritical for tolerating behaviors from managers and clinicians that did not reflect these values.

Daly was determined to act in a way that was consistent with his statements. "We would investigate first to determine whether the criticism was founded, and if it was, we removed those people from the organization," says Daly. Employees noticed. "They said, 'Wow, he means what he says.'" Physicians and managers who didn't support the new strategy left the hospital or were asked to leave.

You Need the Right Team

Alignment requires not only the right message but also the right team to carry it out. Your team must be perfectly aligned with the purpose and be as capable of communicating as you are. Sometimes this means that changes may be required in your leadership team. Every leader must be engaged in aligning the organization by communicating the big idea in a persuasive way and acting in a way that is consistent with those words.

John Fish, CEO of Suffolk Construction, found this out—and made major changes to the company that he had founded. He graduated from college and got an $80,000 loan from his dad, building a company from scratch with sheer drive and determination. Severely dyslexic, Fish worked hard to compensate for his condition by working extremely long hours and devoting himself to the company. His incredible work ethic drove the company's success in the beginning. "We had no plan, no clear direction, but the thirst to learn and the energy to achieve helped me take the company to a level people never expected it to go," he recalls.

However, as the company hit a plateau, Fish says that he realized one problem was that the culture was "more brawn than brains." He says, "I thought I could do it all working 6 days a week, 18 hours a day. I was obsessed with succeeding." The result of this approach was that Suffolk had poor customer relationships. The company was regarded as the "skunk at the lawn party," according to Fish. "We would push a job, but it would be like a war zone at the end because there was no finesse. After the first ten years, I realized that wasn't what I wanted this company to be when we grew up."

Fish decided that to change the culture, he had to bring in new people. As he looked around, he discovered that some people in his organization could walk that talk, and others could not. He began to recruit leaders who could help him to build a different kind of company and mentors who could help him to change his own habits. The new culture they began striving for was to put customer relationships first.

> *Fish decided that to change the culture, he had to bring in new people. As he looked around, he discovered that some people in his organization could walk that talk, and others could not.*

As the right team came together and agreed on the importance of this culture, it was easy to communicate it to the rest of the organization. In fact, the company began to attract people in the construction business who naturally understood and appreciated the importance of putting customer relationships first. "The company had unique personality characteristics. The employees who had those characteristics worked well in the organization, and those who didn't just didn't match up. We found [that] they were leaving after a few months." Over the next decade, Fish rapidly accelerated growth and built Suffolk into a very profitable $2 billion business.

Aligning the organization requires a clear picture of what you want it to be. When you have this, you tend to attract similar people who resonate with the purpose and values of the organization. Good people seek out companies where they resonate with the vision and values. You can bring those people into your sphere only if you are crystal clear about who you want to be and what you stand for. As you determine this and communicate your vision and values, you align the organization. You will lose some people, and that's okay. You'll wind up with a more aligned team that is on the same page working with purpose and energy toward a common end.

> *Good people seek out companies where they resonate with the vision and values. You can bring those people into your sphere only if you are crystal clear about who you want to be and what you stand for.*

Many companies are out of alignment because they tolerate people who do not fit in. Often these are high performers who get results but ride roughshod over people and cut corners. In the end, these high performers may contribute to short-term success but undermine morale and create dissonance. When a company hasn't defined its vision and values clearly, with the goal of alignment, then hiring, managing, and keeping talent are difficult. One key person who is out of sync is like having a wheel out of alignment on your car—initially, the ride will be bumpy; eventually, you'll get a flat and have to pull off to the side of the road.

Mike Daly confronted this alignment challenge when he took over at Baystate Medical Center. "If I were to assess the top ten people in management at the time I started, some of them were really good, some not so good, but it was clear to me that regardless of their individual talents in their respective fields, most of them carried so much baggage [from the infighting] that anything we did would be suspect if they had to be the ones to execute the plan." While some of those managers might have been able to change their ways, collaborate, and work as a team, Daly said they were too damaged. "We quietly and properly replaced nine of the ten. We had to have the right people on the bus," he says.

The right team, aligned with your vision and values, will know what to say and what to do. As you get clear and then communicate clearly, a good team will pick up and run with that message and help you to bring the organization into alignment. They will talk about it with their teams. The vision and values attract the people who care about what you care about and act in ways that are consistent with the best interests of the company.

The vision and values for your company aren't just words; they should spring from your experiences as an organization. It is easy to discover your mission and values when you look at what is working and what isn't and seek to discover what makes your organization work. John Fish says, "We found our core values. We didn't *define* them; we *found* them." By talking about what was working and what wasn't, it became clear to everyone at Suffolk, from management on down, that the culture of the organization had become far more professional. Fish says, "What we had grown up to be was fascinating."

Suffolk came away from this process with a set of values by which Fish says it operates today: passion, integrity, hard work, and professionalism. These aren't just words they post on the walls of conference rooms; they spring from the stories of the company's successes and failures. Once the Suffolk team examined what worked and what didn't, it was easy to see the values that were already driving their success. And once they wrote up and agreed to live by those values, the logical next step was to create the business practices, recruiting, training, and development that supported this vision for the company.

The impact on the business was significant, apparent not just in increased revenues but also in other ways. For example, "Once we realized that and stressed the importance of aligning and developing our people against these values," says Fish, "our turnover dropped dramatically. We went from 24 to 4 percent over a ten-year period in a competitive industry where turnover is notoriously high."

Finding Your Values

If you have not yet gone through the process of identifying values, now is the time. As Fish notes, you must discover them; you can't make them up. They are found in the successes and failures that have taught you who you are as an organization. You may not be sure what they are right now, but if you go through a discovery process, you will have something that is real.

We found in working with companies as well as in looking at our own firm that stories were an easy way to identify values and also a good way to communicate them to others. When we work with other leaders, we encourage them to get specific and look more deeply at successes and failures. If you take time as a team to look back, examine significant events, write them down, and discuss them, it is amazing what emerges. The behaviors and values that drive your success become clear.

This process of discovering your values is as important as, if not more important than, formulating your business plan. When you think about it, the vision and business plan tell you where you want to go; the values tell people how you are going to get there. It is impossible to be there when every decision is made or every action is taken; people must have a set of values to live by. Values are the core DNA of your organization. They teach people how to act, and if you communicate them well, you create a highly efficient, effective, and satisfied organization.

> *When you think about it, the vision and business plan tell you where you want to go; the values tell people how you are going to get there.*

You may think that you already know what values are important to your business, but I still would encourage you and your team to go through this process of discovery. Otherwise, you won't know for sure, and it won't be grounded in what is real and unique to your company. You can put a lot of pretty words on paper, but your leadership team and entire organization will recognize the real, driving values when they see them. When you gather stories and data from your employees and your customers, they will tell you what behaviors and values make you who you are. The more clarity you have about those values and the more real they are, the easier it is to align the organization.

Team Exercises: Determine the Values that Drive Success

Exercise 1: Success Stories
- Get the team together.
- Ask each person on the team to relate the story of a recent success.
- Appoint someone to take careful notes that can be transcribed for everyone.
- As each person tells his or her story, ask questions to draw out the details.
- Leave nothing out—your goal is to search for precisely what you learned.
- Discuss and agree on what the behavior was that led to the success.
- Don't depend on one person; everyone should agree on the behavior to determine the value that this lesson illustrates.
- Decide whether this is universal—in other words, does the value drive success?

Exercise 2: Lessons from Failures
- Get the team together.
- Each person brings in the story of a recent failure.
- Repeat the steps above.
- Determine the lesson.
- Identify the behavior you want to discourage or avoid.

Now You Can Put the Message "On the Wall"

After you go through this process, you are ready to post the values "on the wall." Many organizations have made the mistake of posting vision and values without involving enough people in the process of discovery. Both Daly and Fish went deep into their organizations to engage many

people in the process. Once they'd
done that, they had something real.
They could post their values on the
wall, and people would understand.
Then they could go about communicating and reinforcing those values in
all their business interactions.

> *Many organizations have made the mistake of posting vision and values without involving enough people in the process of discovery.*

It is a good idea once you have agreement on values to remind people of them. Some companies post them on the wall, put them on
employees' key cards, or make them a part of quarterly reviews. These
and other visual reminders are powerful communication tools. The Suffolk "Pyramid of Values, Mission, and Vision" is posted in every conference room. Fish believes strongly in the power of the visual. But it doesn't
stop with posting a pyramid. You need to see evidence of the values at
every turn. For example, when you walk into the Suffolk building, you
encounter a beautifully designed space with glass, brick, nice furnishings,
clean bathrooms, and artwork. Conference rooms are spotless, and the
greeter at the front desk has excellent manners.

Fish also insists that on all the company job sites, Suffolk management must be dressed in uniform: white shirts with logos and khaki pants.
Even carpenters and laborers dress this way. Members of senior management wear suits and ties. This is a visual reminder of the professionalism Suffolk wants to project. "It's a differentiator for our business," says
Fish. "When you walk into a meeting with a client, and the client can't
tell the lawyer from the Suffolk management representative, it instantly
communicates how serious we are about professionalism."

Alignment comes not only through visual reminders but also
through consistent, positive action. There are countless opportunities to
demonstrate what you stand for. Baystate Medical Center, for example,
had a policy of requiring patients in hospital beds to "reactivate" their
TVs every 24 hours, paying $10 for
the privilege of being interrupted
each day. Nurses wanted it changed—
the practice seemed severely out of
sync with the value of respect promoted by the company. At first, Daly

> *Alignment comes not only through visual reminders but also through consistent, positive action.*

resisted because this policy generated $1 million in much-needed revenue per year. Once he understood the nurses' view that they had to walk their talk on respect, however, he changed the policy. Daly says that the decision was worth every penny. To parody the famous MasterCard commercial: "$1 million to show people that you mean what you say; living your values—priceless."

What are other ways to align people and live your values? Sometimes the actions are simple. For example, Fish demonstrates professionalism with prompt responses. "I try to return a phone call in an hour, and I return all calls. It doesn't matter who calls me. When I do this, it tells clients, and our own people, that we're professionals, and we're never too busy. I try to set an example for the rest of the organization. It's about respect for our colleagues and our business partners."

Stay Aligned as You Grow

As you grow, it becomes harder to stay aligned. Even if your company has previously worked hard on vision and values, as new people join, they have not been part of the process. This is one of the challenges that successful companies face—growth requires you to constantly focus on alignment. You need to work hard to keep communicating vision and values. Many executives I know have struggled with this as they find themselves busy just trying to keep up with a fast-growing business. Sometimes they wake up and realize that there are a lot of people there who weren't around when the company's core vision and values were formed.

It is an irony that success can threaten the very identity that was a driver in your success. How do you address it? Never assume that people know. Make communication of your vision and values a routine part of your work. Regularly talk about the vision and values, and don't leave it to chance. As you bring new people on board, make sure that they have opportunities to be trained not just in new skills but also in the behaviors and values that are your core DNA. You have to be vigilant about this. Keep communicating the message through words and actions to keep your organization aligned.

Here are some of the principles that are important to staying aligned as you grow:

Consistency and Repetition

If you set forward fundamental principles and you repeat them often enough, people know that you're keeping your eye on the ball, and they will too. New people may be hearing it for the first or second time, and even though you've said it many times, they may not be there yet.

Andrew Liveris, president and CEO of Dow Chemical, asserts that to have alignment, you must keep it simple and repeat it often. "We believe in having strategy on a page. If you can put your strategy on a single page, then you can circulate it, communicate it, and align your organization around that one page. We did that. It was laminated, and everyone carried it around with them."

If people hear something once, they undoubtedly will forget. (I am particularly guilty of this. Just ask my teenage daughter, who often says that she told me something when I have no memory of it!) When you hear it twice, it starts to register. After three times, you may remember it. With five or six or seven repetitions, you may finally be able to drive it home. A clear, consistent message repeated up to six or seven times makes an impact. Liveris explains, "I would advise anyone to distill, simplify, and communicate as fast as you can when you get into the job." Start early, and communicate often. Keep people engaged. Alignment requires repetition.

> *If people hear something once, they undoubtedly will forget. (I am particularly guilty of this. Just ask my teenage daughter, who often says that she told me something when I have no memory of it!)*

Repetition is only effective if your written words are also consistent with the message. What is in writing matters. People notice. For example, Baystate employees also complained to Daly that the company's newsletter never mentioned the company values; articles focused primarily on the business operations and financial reports. In response to this complaint, the communications team at the hospital began writing articles that illustrated the values. They also published stories about employees' achievements to promote the behaviors that everyone agreed were important. "Some of these things like the newsletter are no-brainers, but we had overlooked them," says Daly. As a result of this change, Daly noticed that employees started talking about what they read in the newsletter around the lunch table.

Passion and Enthusiasm

Another critical factor in keeping people aligned as you grow is your own passion and enthusiasm. Don't underestimate the importance of this. Your energy drives it forward. As your company grows and new people come on board, maintain the passion. New people need to be brought in to the fold, to feel the same excitement as did the original team. They need you

> As your company grows and new people come on board, maintain the passion.

as a role model to show them how genuinely enthusiastic you are about the mission, the people, and the values.

Your energy and enthusiasm in delivering the message day in and day out are so important. You may not feel high energy every day, and that's okay; it's a lot to expect of yourself. In general, though, you do need to consistently demonstrate your passion and communicate it to others. When you speak with enthusiasm, people feel it and believe it. A growing organization needs leaders who are energized and able to communicate their passion and enthusiasm.

There are many ways to keep your energy level high so that you exude the energy and passion that motivates others and inspires them. You need to take care of yourself physically, even if you are working long hours, by eating healthy foods, getting rest, exercising, and doing things you enjoy so that you feel renewed. Some executives work out in the morning, some midday, and some in the evening, which is especially important when you are traveling, eating meals away from home, and entertaining. I've seen executives purchase "standing" desks because staying on their feet invigorates them. Take brisk walks with employees, or play a sport instead of having a sit-down meeting. Schedule your day with time to reflect, not just to "do." By taking care of yourself, you will find it is easier to communicate your enthusiasm and passion. When you feel energized, people around you feel it, too.

Policies and Practices

Your vision and values need to be on display everywhere, not just in a statement. They need to live in your policies and practices, as well as in all your communications. Whether in your employee manual, training programs, employee workshops, individual professional development plans, or compensation plan, the values need to be evident. You can demonstrate your commitment to the values as well in your customer letters, communications, and loyalty programs. You can show that you are serious even in your recruitment process and exit interviews. If you communicate your values everywhere in a consistent, effective way, you will see results.

Bill Swanson, chairman and CEO of Raytheon, says, "When you look at strategy, success is the alignment of resources in pursuit of your goals. So, if people understand the overall goals, they can align resources to go with those goals, and those resources will be people, money, time, focus, or attention."

> *Your vision and values need to be on display everywhere, not just in a statement. They need to live in your policies and practices, as well as in all your communications.*

"To me, if all those things are aligned toward your goal, then your strategy is well thought out, and everyone gets it," says Swanson. "A good football analogy is that if you want everyone doing a 'sweep,' which means everyone moving in the same direction, you can't have someone going off in a different direction. Everyone has to execute the same play the best they can."

Alignment through Compensation

Peter Roberts, CEO of Jones Lang LaSalle, America's top real estate services and money management firm, with offices in 100 cities and

36 countries, says that one of the surest ways to align the organization is to tie compensation to the values. In the commercial real estate business, this is not the norm. "I am a big believer that the most effective organizations have the most alignment around the strategy, business model, and culture. I'm not saying one model or approach is good or bad, or better than another. But I am saying organizations that have the most alignment running through all those things are the most successful."

At Jones Lang LaSalle, a big chunk of bonuses is tied to values, not just results—values such as client satisfaction, employee engagement, teamwork, and collaboration. "There is no question that to be a successful business, you have to align compensation around growth and financial metrics, and we have that as well, but there's absolutely an element different from our competitors. It's the alignment around our reward structure and our business model, strategy, culture, and values."

> At Jones Lang LaSalle, a big chunk of bonuses is tied to values, not just results—values such as client satisfaction, employee engagement, teamwork, and collaboration.

Compensation is one of the ways the firm has achieved cultural alignment, which is one of its most important competitive advantages. "We are aggressively trying to use our culture as a competitive advantage. Culture is very important to us," Roberts says. The leadership team spent considerable time together defining their values, not for public consumption or marketing, but for internal purposes. "We didn't have any script writers, but we came up with a set of values we put under two headings: leadership and excellence."

Recruiting and Hiring

The exercise of defining cultural alignment at Jones Lang LaSalle became a springboard for recruiting and hiring, too. The values became a shared filter for recruiting and promoting talent. Beyond skills, the company looks to hire people who have similar values. "It is a great value for us to say to candidates, 'This is who we are and what we stand for, and what we believe in,'" Roberts says. If it's a fit, that's okay; if not, that's okay, too.

The values became a powerful management tool to find and develop the right people.

As noted earlier, once Mike Daly defined the mission, he started looking for the team of leaders and other contributors who shared the values that would make Baystate successful. "I was looking for a team that would share a single agenda," he recalls. "Over time, I removed individuals who didn't buy into the sense of teamwork that I was requiring. People who would get engaged in little firefights with one another over who was most powerful and all that baloney, they had to go. It was making sure we hired people after that who came in and shared the same values and lived and worked by those values," says Daly.

> "I was looking for a team that would share a single agenda."

One important factor in recruiting and hiring talent at Baystate was the concept that the senior team had to look out for each other. It wasn't enough to champion their own initiatives; they had to help others succeed. "If I'm feuding with you and undermining you on something that is critical to the forward movement of the organization," Daly says, "then I'm not helping the organization." Not only do the members of the team have to live by the company's values, but they also have to help each other to live them every day too.

The Impact of Alignment

What is the impact of alignment? It's almost impossible to overstate its value. In truth, it's everything. Perhaps most important, when you have alignment with purpose, people know what to do, how to do it, and why. This is highly motivating, reinforcing successful activities. And this dramatically increases productivity and profitability.

John Fish says that in the construction industry, many companies are driven by the profit margin of a project, whereas Suffolk employees are encouraged to focus first on *client satisfaction*. "If we satisfy a client, we make or exceed our profitability nine times out of ten," he explains. "When we don't exceed client satisfaction, we don't come close to profitability. We have to drive alignment around this concept."

By driving alignment around the appropriate values, you achieve consistent, predictable results. You know how people are going to behave, you can take action if they don't, and this means that you will have consistent results. "If we have everyone dancing the same dance, we have predictability in our business results," Fish says. "The concept of predictability is very important in the construction business. To the extent that you can introduce predictability into the process, it makes all the difference in the world to our clients. So we focus on it. That simple icon, our mission, vision, and values, is our strategic plan." He adds, "I'm proud to tell you that 100 percent of the people in this organization can recite it chapter and verse. And 75 percent of their spouses can as well."

Once you begin the process of aligning the organization, you will need to know how you are doing along the way. It's important to measure the impact of your communications and make sure that you are in close touch with the organization. In Chapter 6 we will look at how successful leaders create mechanisms for reviewing and evaluating success in communicating the message.

Summary

- The benefits of motivating and aligning your workforce are impossible to estimate.
- To motivate and inspire people, you need a theme or mission or value that resonates, and then you have to overcommunicate again and again and again.
- To align the organization and motivate people to execute the plan, you have to have the right people in place. When you have a clear vision and message, you tend to attract those people to the organization.
- You have to communicate not only through words but also by living the values—walking and talking what is important to the organization's success.
- When you have alignment with purpose, people know what to do, how to do it, and why. This is highly motivating, reinforcing successful activities. And this dramatically increases productivity and profitability.

6

Feedback Loop: Track and Measure the Impact of the Message

What the people believe is true.

—NATIVE AMERICAN PROVERB

BILL SWANSON, CHAIRMAN AND CEO of Raytheon, is a big believer in feedback. Raytheon conducts an all-employee survey every other year, and in off years it surveys a 15 percent sample of the employee population. This employee input has helped the company to align its people with its mission and values and track closely how it is doing against its goals.

There has been significant improvement since the company first started surveying several years ago on alignment, when about half the respondents indicated that they understood the direction of the company. Raytheon instituted new programs. By 2007, three-quarters of respondents indicated alignment, placing Raytheon in the 95th percentile compared with a national norm of employees, including many from Fortune 500 companies. Swanson attributes this significant improvement to getting feedback and doing something about it.

Moreover, in the 2007 Raytheon survey, nearly eight in ten Raytheon respondents answered favorably when asked about their seeing themselves working at the company 12 months from now, placing Raytheon in the 99th percentile compared with norms from a national sample of companies.

Swanson attributes this huge leap to seeking out feedback and doing something about it. He really wanted to know how they were doing—he knew they should never assume that the message was getting through.

> You need to know whether people are hearing what you say.

Measurement is important. It was especially heartening to see the change in how employees answered the question, "Do you see yourself working at Raytheon 12 months from now?" Because the company took action and didn't shirk from the initial findings, by 2008, the percentage of employees who said that they wanted to be working at Raytheon in another 12 months had skyrocketed to 95 percent.

As every leader knows, you must continually track and measure how your company is communicating its message. You need to know whether people are hearing what you say. Do they know where the company is going and why? Are they connected with the company's mission? Do they understand and live the values? Are they motivated and engaged? This chapter will explore some of the essential strategies companies use to track and measure the impact of their messages.

You can measure alignment in business results; in fact, sales and financial results are the ultimate measure. However, such measures may come too late. The profit and loss statement is a result, not a harbinger. You

> As every leader knows, you must continually track and measure how your company is doing.

need to be able to make corrections and adjustments along the way. This is why you need a system that puts you in the loop and brings you accurate insights about what people know and believe. You can do this by creating a feedback loop—a constant, reliable pipeline and source of information.

A feedback loop is just what it sounds like: a steady flow of dependable information coming to you and moving through and around the organization. It is communication input and output. The feedback loop will help you to monitor the important vital signs, as in a medical checkup. This feedback loop will monitor financial results but also should include much more. It consists of the data you collect from selected sources that reveal measurable, transactional changes in your business—from employee surveys, market surveys, client feedback forms, performance reviews, and exit interviews to e-mail, blog posts, and infor-

> *The feedback loop will help you to monitor the important vital signs, as in a medical checkup.*

mal information you receive. If you want to know whether your message is getting through, you need a reliable process, a feedback loop, to gather, analyze, and monitor these data. You can align and motivate people if you have this information and act on it.

The feedback loop provides you with information you can act on and also share with others. As you gather and analyze the communications data, you can convey in a timely way what's happening and why. The quality of the information you gather determines the quality of the decisions you make.

Keeping people in the loop is one of the biggest challenges for many organizations, and yet a failure to do so has a negative impact on people. Employees are always frustrated when they don't believe that they are "in the loop." One participant in our survey said, "I experienced this first hand with my previous employer. It was one of the largest companies in the world. My division was making some very big strategic moves with our product line. The changes were going to have a very positive impact on the entire organization. We [sales management] were *not* allowed to share the vision or strategy with our sales teams for a full year. We missed a *great* opportunity to get the team rallied around the goal and focused in on direction. We lost an incredible amount of momentum and great talent due to the uncertainty this unknown strategic shift created."

Leaders sometimes decide to withhold information for what they see as good business reasons. Certainly, some information must be confidential. However, overprotecting information is not a good strategy because you need to involve people in helping you to make good decisions. If there is bad news and you share it, people can help you. While you must be judicious, you will benefit greatly when you have all the appropriate people in the loop. You never know how or when people will step up and provide an amazing insight.

When a feedback loop is not working, it is often because the boss assumes that people already know what's going on. "Leaders assume that information flows downward," said another survey participant. "They don't have the metrics or processes to ensure an even/updated flow of information. Inevitably, this failure is demonstrated with the incongruity that can develop between long-term business strategies and tactical operations and budget expenditures." Without a well-defined, working feedback loop, you don't know what people don't know, and the result is that your people feel less motivated and inspired to work toward common goals.

Keeping people in the loop is one of the biggest challenges for many organizations, and yet a failure to do so has a negative impact on people.

People who are in the loop are far more motivated and engaged. The feeling that they are included can generate tremendous passion and keep them energized even through difficult challenges. The feedback loop that works prompts people to stay in it and think about how they can make their best contributions. When they know what's really going on, they are motivated to apply their talents to the right projects and activities.

The feedback loop (Figure 6–1) is extremely valuable in motivating people and sustaining momentum. When you have a big, important goal and you let people know where things stand, you can feel more assured that they will stay on track. It is important to give them information in a timely way so that they also can be responsive.

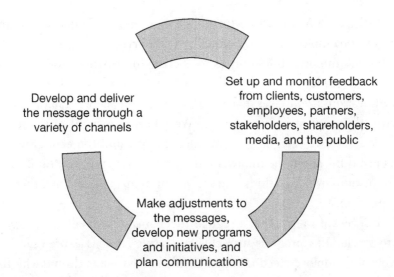

Figure 6–1 Feedback loop diagram.

Employee Surveys

Employee engagement surveys are an excellent way to gather a wealth of information. Most people enjoy sharing their responses, especially anonymously, if they believe that management will be responsive. Even if they have negative views, the fact that you are asking them their opinion sends a very positive signal about your intentions. People are looking for appropriate outlets to communicate with the top of the organization about what is working and what isn't. They see a survey as the first step toward improving their own work lives.

Bill Swanson says that a high level of participation in a voluntary survey is a key indicator that people are engaged. "It's been a blessing," he says. "We had 82 percent participation in our most recent employee survey. That's 12 percentage points higher than the average company. So when we get a survey back, I know it's accurate. With a survey, you see what you can fix, and you fix it, and then you see the needle moving."

People are looking for appropriate outlets to communicate with the top of the organization about what is working and what isn't.

SBLI USA Mutual Life Insurance Company conducts an anonymous online employee survey annually. Vikki Pryor, president and CEO, says that it's important not only for gathering information from employees but also for letting employees know how the leadership team thinks. "The questions themselves make an impression on people. That's why we rewrite those questions every year. We add and expand questions to include issues we see going on in the company and the economy. We don't just think about the information we want to *receive*. We think about what the employee will think and feel about management when they see the question."

Bill Swanson says that a regular mechanism for feedback is essential to accelerating progress and achieving results. If he is assured through surveys and employee feedback that people know what to do and why, the company can ask them to go the extra mile. There won't be a question of whether people know why they are doing what they are doing. "If we know that people understand," Swanson says, "we can ask for their support in the *execution*."

What Else Goes into the Feedback Loop?

There are many things you can track and measure, which is why it is important to make a conscious decision about what information is most valuable. What you measure, you act on. The data must track and tell you essential information that moves you toward specific goals.

For example, Jeff Neufeld, chief information officer at Fidelity Brokerage Company, whom you met in Chapter 4, created pillars of measurement as well as a plan to monitor and communicate the information. One of the pillars was "information technology (IT) excellence."

What you measure, you act on.

There were a few, specific ways that excellence was tracked and measured. One of them was the percentage of projects the company achieved on schedule and on budget. By creating and monitoring an accurate, specific measurement that reflected a specific goal, the team could communicate with each other in a common language. The results were dramatic. "We found that just by making it a goal and focusing on it, it went up over 30 percent in the course of three years," he says.

Neufeld's team of direct reports didn't just monitor results; they talked about it in every weekly meeting and then communicated with their own teams. Not a week went by when people didn't know where they stood against the goals. Since it was discussed so often, people got the message that it was a priority. They focused on it and worked hard to improve. "We were able to achieve over $100 million increase in output of the organization, or threefold, in five years, and we went from 70 to 80 percent completion of what we were asked to do each year to consistently completing 100 percent," Neufeld reports.

As you develop the criteria for information that goes into your feedback loop, agree in advance on what to measure, how often, and why that measurement works. You may need to spend time in the beginning to get it right. Prior to agreement on the IT excellence measurements, Neufeld says, "Everything was subjective." And after they agreed on a goal and accurate ways to measure it, the dynamic between the business units and the technology team was measurably better. "We no longer wasted time and energy," says Neufeld. Even when they didn't achieve their goals, they were no longer spending hours debating who was at fault or what defined success.

Gathering Client Information

One of the best elements to include in your feedback loop is information from your customers or clients. If you want to know how to improve your business, there is nothing more powerful than understanding at a deep level how your customers see your products and services. Most large companies conduct client surveys, but many do not share the information in a way that is useful to the people who need to act on it. And if you are not currently conducting client surveys, you probably know that they are important. It's nice to have anecdotal information through conversations with clients and prospects. However, an outside research team can gather independent data that provide richer, more accurate insights and can help you to see overall trends. It is dangerous to allow yourself to rely on only what you think you know from your own employees' interactions with customers. You won't hear it all, what you hear will be filtered, and it is impossible to evaluate it objectively.

Greg Case, CEO of Aon Corporation, whom you met in Chapter 1, says that his company has many ways to measure how it is doing with clients, beyond surveys. "As a service company, it is essential to have several ways to measure how clients perceive our value." Aon tracks new business opportunities, closing rates, and client retention. The company solicits client feedback directly through a device called the *net promoter score* (NPS). "We ask our clients roughly every quarter in a simple Web-based tool, 'Would you recommend Aon to one of your friends?' We don't ask whether they like us; we ask whether they would recommend us."

> *If you want to know how to improve your business, there is nothing more powerful than understanding at a deep level how your customers see your products and services.*

While over the first two years the company had not yet achieved the results it wanted to see in the surveys and measurements, Case says that he is now confident that the company can achieve success because it is tracking and communicating the right measurements. "We are on a journey. . . this is not about a destination. We're fortunate we've made progress; we are in the early stages and have a long way to go. At least now we have a way to track it."

All these methods for tracking client satisfaction are valuable only if you share the information widely with the organization. It is vital to get the information out there to the people in the field so that they can act on it. Let them know often how they are doing. Good news is highly motivating, and bad news gives them a chance to fix it. Consider whether you have lately related the information your people need to do their jobs well. Communicate and tell them how they can achieve success.

Sharing Financial Results

Your company is always gathering financial information, so in this section I would like to discuss how to share it. Financial results are a vital piece of information in motivating people and keeping them in the loop.

You need to communicate basic financial results to everyone in the organization. Giving people this information in a timely way not only provides them with context for business decisions, but it also demonstrates your respect for them. Even if you are not a public company, you still can and should share information about how the company is doing financially. People will guess anyway and often will be wrong, so you may as well make sure that they have the correct information. Even if the financial news isn't good, they may assume that it's worse than it is if you don't tell them. If you have good news to share, then you can congratulate them and celebrate success with them.

Make sure when you report financial results that you put them in terms that everyone can understand. Your words, graphics, and visuals should be easy to grasp, remember, and repeat. If the chief financial officer, treasurer, or other finance officer is delivering those reports, make sure that he or she develops a high level of skill in communication—he or she needs to say it in layperson's terms. Many chief financial officers I have worked with assume that their audiences can interpret the numbers, but they can't. Even a sophisticated audience does not have the full story or background. The business report should always tell the story behind the numbers. The CEO, chief financial officer, or treasurer always should incorporate stories and examples that explain what's happening and bring the numbers alive.

And as we discussed in Chapter 4, don't bury the lead, especially when it comes to financial reporting. Resist the temptation to start at the beginning and plow through to the end, with piles of graphs and charts. Don't make people wade through what they don't understand or wait for the big message. Even your board or senior team may lose sight of your big message if you don't put it up front. People usually assume that you don't have anything important to say if you don't get to it right away. Make sure that you tell the story up front and make it easy to understand so that people don't miss the point.

Performance Reviews

Performance reviews are an important opportunity to engage people. While organizations say that they do performance reviews, many acknowledge they don't do them consistently or well. Yet this is such an important part of your feedback loop—the opportunity to evaluate, review, listen, and offer advice. What you measure in performance reviews is, again, what people act on.

In evaluating performance, it is important to take a careful look at all the skills, values, and behaviors you want to drive through the organization. Many performance reviews focus primarily on skills and experiences and, of course, financial results. Andrew Liveris, chairman and CEO of Dow Chemical, says that it's a mistake to provide feedback only on financial results. "Financial results . . . have to do with your ability to execute against a strategic plan; to do that, the short term has to make sense with medium and long term so [that] we have *goal* alignment," he explains.

Performance reviews at Dow provide feedback on how leaders are doing against short-, medium-, and long-term goals. Liveris says that it is not just about whether the company made enough money for the quarter. "I hold senior leaders accountable for making the right decision for the long term so [that] they make good decisions in the short term."

Performance reviews can track anything that is important to the mission and values of the organization. In fact, the more aligned the performance indicators, the more people will focus on them. Baystate Medical Center tracked the growth of clinical programming, as well as the number of high-caliber employees and clinical leaders the organization was able to attract. As individuals applied themselves to these goals, the organization began to turn the corner and achieve collective results.

> *Performance reviews can track anything that is important to the mission and values of the organization. In fact, the more aligned the performance indicators, the more people will focus on them.*

Another good example of incorporating business goals into performance reviews was the way Dow Chemical handled recruiting of scientists for its China operation. The company determined that it was important to hire talented Chinese scientists; they didn't want to recruit just from the United States, even though in the short term it was more expedient. Executives at Dow were measured by how well they recruited from China, not how expediently they filled the positions. It was very effective. Andrew Liveris says, "We had to communicate all the way across the globe to our recruiting managers that our long-term goal is to have Chinese professionals working in our China operations."

E-mail in the Loop

While e-mail is now an integral part of our business lives, we are all trying to figure out how to make it a positive communication tool. Bill Swanson of Raytheon sees it as a way to both gather information and reinforce the messages about vision and values. He routinely receives e-mail from people at every level of the organization, including new employees, and is very faithful about answering his messages quickly. With tens of thousands of employees, this is no small feat. I personally experienced his responsiveness when I sent him an e-mail on a Sunday (not expecting a response) to tell him that I enjoyed meeting him and had sent him a copy of my first book, *Speak Like a CEO.*

To my surprise, he responded within 30 minutes, saying that he had received the book, was taking it on a flight, and looked forward to reading it. I must say that I was surprised and flattered that he got back to me so promptly. Little did I know that this is his standard practice. He has decided that responsiveness is a value he lives by and wants to drive down through the organization, and this is a way to send that message loud and clear.

I'm not suggesting that you need to invoke a 30-minute response time to e-mail, but you can institute practices that send the messages that are important.

Suffolk Construction Company CEO John Fish, whom you met in Chapter 5, is also keen on responsiveness, so he has several assistants working in his office who have the authority to answer phone and e-mail messages. Ken Leibler, former CEO of several companies, including Liberty Financial and the Boston Stock Exchange, whom you met in Chapter 2, waits and "batches" responses while flying and hits the "send" button when he lands. The value he wants to communicate is the importance of working efficiently and managing your time.

Every leader has to perfect the art of the pithy, content-rich response. You can communicate with many people if you keep it short and focused. Any communication that requires more than a paragraph or two often should be a phone call or a meeting. The exception to this rule is when you need to share written information in a timely way and want to have an electronic record. Preface lengthy messages by letting people know what is inside, and use underlines and bullet points to make it easy to read.

If you need to reduce the time you spend on e-mail, remember this rule: E-mail generates more e-mail. If you send out a note, you will get a response. If you copy people, you will get more responses. Your inbox will quickly fill up. Consider whether you need to send a note or respond to one, and put a stop to e-mails that become long conversations. Pick up the phone instead.

> *Every leader has to perfect the art of the pithy, content-rich response.*

Good News Should Travel Fast, Too

Bad news travels fast. Good news should travel faster. If you have good things going on in your organization, people should hear about them. The feedback loop can be a very effective tool in motivating and inspiring people if you use it to spread good news. Many organizations make the mistake of forgetting to communicate good news. People hear from the boss only when there is a problem. If you have something to celebrate, get the news out there; people will come to expect that they will hear from you when they've done well. "What I feel strongly about," said one survey participant, "is that whenever I finish a project or mission, I don't get prompt feedback no matter the result—good or not. I'd prefer to have some . . . advice directly from the leader so that I will be clear how to improve."

How to Make Sure that Good News Travels Fast

- Ask your management team to share a success story at the beginning of a meeting.
- Ask people what's going right.

- Tell people that you want to be the first to hear about wins, good public relations, recognition, and awards.
- On completion of a project, make sure that you are in the loop so that you can acknowledge the achievement.
- Ask your communications team to publish success stories in the company newsletter.
- Set up a blog and encourage people to share success stories electronically.
- When you hear good news, respond in a timely, appropriate way:
  - Keep stationery on your desk, and send handwritten notes.
  - E-mail thanks or congratulations every single day.
  - Call a meeting and spend a little money to celebrate.
  - Send flowers or do something unexpected as a token of your appreciation.
  - If you're in a large company, write the individual's boss a note of congratulations as well, and copy the person who achieved a positive outcome.
  - Send out a company-wide announcement on the intranet.
  - Walk into the person's office and shake his or her hand.
  - Congratulate the person's spouse at a family event.

Be Thankful for Bad News

Bad news is far better than no news. At least when you hear it, you can do something about it. The last thing you want is people to think that they need to hold back or be afraid of sharing bad news. If they make a mistake or something goes wrong, make it clear that you want to know right away. Treat them with respect, and thank them for sharing the information. Mistakes are going to happen, and as many leaders know, if people aren't failing, they aren't trying.

> *A good leader promotes risk-taking and communicates this to the entire organization.*

Let's look at an example of bad news that you definitely want to hear about: a complaint from a customer. Client relationships can sour in an instant if you don't respond. However, if you don't let employees know that it is vital to immediately share customer complaints, they may fear reprisal and cover them up. One survey participant told us that her own boss preferred trying to "sweet talk" a client rather than reporting a problem to his boss. "Instead of listening to why there was a problem and coming up with a solution to fix it, this manager would 'sales talk' the client and backtalk his employees." Since the feedback loop wasn't working, the CEO wasn't hearing about this. The manager ultimately ruined a number of important client relationships that led to lost sales.

Bad news provides learning opportunities. You can allow people to make a correction and learn from their experience. You also can appropriately share the bad news without placing blame and turn it into a lesson on values and behaviors for others. When you encourage people to share bad news, your feedback loop is really working; you create a culture of people who are less afraid to take risks or report mistakes. People will be innovative or try an approach and share the results, good or bad, if they know that they won't get in trouble for trying and failing. A good leader promotes risk-taking and communicates this to the entire organization.

How to Get Started Creating a Feedback Loop

Creating a robust feedback loop is, as we discussed, a matter of deciding what you want to measure, setting up a tracking mechanism, and then listening and communicating what you know. Start by determining the most valuable information you need in order to achieve your long-range goals. What will keep your organization on track and moving in the right direction? What are the best ways to measure employee alignment and customer satisfaction?

Once you know what you want to measure, create the expectation among your own team of leaders so that they will listen and respond. Make sure that everyone monitors and communicates what they learn. You can very quickly change the culture of an organization for the better by creating a robust feedback loop. You can turn around attitudes and motivate people when they know that you care about their opinions and want to keep them in the loop.

Determine the most important success factors to measure and the simplest, most accurate, and available way to track them. Invest time up front in determining this. Communicate on a daily, weekly, monthly, quarterly, and annual basis. The feedback loop works only if you have a dashboard of important things to measure and you keep the information flowing. There is no time like the present to start. If you sense that there is a problem, don't delay. What you don't know really can hurt you.

You can very quickly change the culture of an organization for the better by creating a robust feedback loop. You can turn around attitudes and motivate people when they know that you care about their opinions and want to keep them in the loop.

Don't Wait—Start Right Away

An insurance company that had grown by acquisition and had dozens of affiliates nationwide was sensing growing tension between the corporate office and organizations in the field. The organizations historically had operated independently, and it had always been difficult for the parent company to impose standards. The affiliates were complaining to low-level staff people about the lack of support from corporate headquarters. Still, the feedback was anecdotal; it had never been compiled or analyzed.

Yet there was a debate at corporate headquarters about whether to even ask the affiliates how they thought it was going. Managers weren't sure whether opening up a dialogue would stir up trouble they couldn't address. They also weren't sure what to ask. They were afraid that if they asked the wrong questions, they would create an expectation that they could change things that could not be addressed quickly. So inertia ruled. The indecision continued, and affiliate relations grew worse. All the while, the financial results were suffering, and it was hard to imagine how they would turn things around.

It is disheartening to watch a company collectively throw up its hands and do nothing about a problem such as this. You can't be afraid of learning the truth. Take the difficult steps, and ask. Determine what needs to be measured, measure it, take appropriate steps, and communicate every step of the way. The very act of asking people will begin to turn things around as they realize you are aware of a situation and care about their opinions. Motivating an organization is impossible without having the courage to get the information and act on it.

Walking Around: A Great Way to Gather Information

Walking around and staying connected is very important to motivational leadership. You will be successful motivating people if they perceive that you are in touch. You can stay in touch by visiting, going, and being there. Walking around isn't just a symbolic gesture; you actually learn a lot. While this is challenging for a business of any size, it is especially challenging as your company grows, opens new offices, and expands nationally or internationally. Still, if you can plan your schedule to be sure that you visit with clients and employees, you will learn things that you will never see in a survey or through second-hand reports.

When you're walking around, you'll not only learn more, but you'll also have more to share with others. Walking around and talking to people is a great way to gather stories and examples that you can share with others. I have been surprised many times when working with an executive that he or she does not have a story or example from a recent client interaction or employee project. You need to know what people are doing, and you need to share it; that's how you stay in touch and show people that you are connected. When it comes time to prepare your presentation, record a Web cast, do an interview, write an e-mail or blog; you'll have a great story to share. Even if you have other people writing for you, the stories need to come from you. Walking around helps you to

> *You can't be afraid of the information. Take the difficult step, determine what needs to be measured, measure it, take appropriate steps, and communicate every step of the way.*

constantly gather fresh material to drive home those messages about mission, purpose, and values.

When you're actively engaged in talking to people in all corners of the organization, people see you as a highly connected leader, and they are motivated to go the extra mile for you. And when you're out there listening, you create insurance that no one person or group gets your ear or distorts what's going on. If you rely too much on any one source, you put your organization at risk. Take it into your own hands to be around, available, and accessible, and you'll also inspire other leaders to behave the same way.

Feedback Loop Accelerates Results

A strong feedback loop accelerates results and also fosters cooperation, teamwork, and motivation. Jeff Neufeld says, "It's hard to put a price on the benefit to an organization when there is clarity and communication about goals and measurements." People are inspired when they see that what they are doing is making a difference. They stay connected with the mission and purpose of the organization. It is easy to lose sight of why you are working so hard if you aren't hearing about the results. On the other hand, all of us feel that work isn't so hard when we know that what we're doing really matters.

You accelerate progress and create energy and enthusiasm as people share the milestones and celebrate their successes. They look forward to hearing what's going on. They feel valued and important to the organization and therefore are motivated to contribute. They feel a stronger connection to purpose and more passionate about what they are doing. Even when there are setbacks, people will agonize together and recommit to moving forward. The more they know, the more quickly they can act, and the more energized they are.

> A strong feedback loop accelerates results and fosters cooperation, teamwork, and motivation.

Once you have your feedback loop in place, the next step is to make sure that you can sustain momentum toward your goals. How do you keep momentum going in your organization? This is what we'll discuss in Chapter 7.

Summary

- You must continually track and measure how your company is doing. You need to know the answer to this question: "Do people understand where we are going and why?"
- Business results are the ultimate measure of your success, but they often come too late. You need to set up a system that allows you to be in the loop all the time.
- You can do this by creating a feedback loop—a constant, reliable pipeline and source of information.
- Determine the most important success factors to measure and the simplest, most accurate way to track them.
- Setting expectations and measuring progress create positive feelings. You accelerate progress as people get more and more enthused about the milestones.

7

Create Momentum and
Keep It Going

Motivation is everything. You can do the work of two people,
but you can't be two people. Instead, you have to inspire the
next guy down the line and get him to inspire his people.

—LEE IACOCCA

RANCH KIMBALL IS CEO and president of the world-renowned
Joslin Diabetes Center, a Harvard teaching facility and the world's largest
diabetes research, clinic, and educational center. The Joslin Center was
founded in 1898 by Elliot Joslin, a brilliant physician and researcher who
blazed a path to modern-day research and care. At the turn of the
century, the Joslin Center took a radical approach that became accepted
standard practice—helping patients manage their own diabetes. Back
then, there were none of the tools that exist today to monitor and manage diabetes. However, despite its rich heritage, the Joslin Center was
now at a low point. Kimball took the helm as the center faced significant
financial challenges and, along with them, low morale among the clinical group, the original heart of the operation.

The rest of the organization had come to blame the clinical group
for the Joslin Center's poor financial situation. The center had always
provided a very high level of patient care, but it was costly. Critics saw
it as a drain on resources. Doctors and nurses were feeling resentful,
marginalized, and unappreciated.

Most organizations undergo ups and downs over time as founders leave, missions change, and new people join. Every business or enterprise has to figure out how to adapt to new situations, opportunities, consumer demands, and needs. There are always bumps in the road: economic downturns, competitive pressures, and geopolitical changes. This makes it challenging to sustain momentum and keep an organization moving forward.

How can you help your organization get reinvigorated? How can you generate positive momentum and keep people engaged? A purposeful, motivated workforce is vital to your success, and sustaining enthusiasm, energy, and passion over long periods of time requires great leadership. The challenge of building and maintaining momentum falls to the leader—and let's face it, we all lose steam from time to time. Sometimes corporate politics, unanticipated setbacks, the loss of key personnel or customers, and just balancing your life with your work make it difficult to sustain your own energy. Yet motivating leaders are the spark that lights the flame. It is possible, in fact, and perhaps not so difficult to stay enthusiastic and share your enthusiasm. The secret is to make a conscious effort to look for the positive story and tell it to others.

> *A purposeful, motivated workforce is vital to your success, and sustaining enthusiasm, energy, and passion over long periods of time requires great leadership.*

Connect People to Purpose

Here's how Ranch Kimball started—by learning and understanding the organization and then looking for opportunities to tell the story. Kimball became a student of the Joslin Center's history and heritage. He studied where the organization had been and, in so doing, gained a deep appreciation for the high-touch patient care approach that was part of the center's heritage. He realized that the organization needed to be reminded of its roots and that he could do this by telling the stories that promoted this mission.

When visitors came to his office on the seventh floor, he would seat them at his conference table and then pull down original artifacts from Elliott Joslin's turn-of-the-century practice from his bookshelves. Kimball would proudly demonstrate Joslin's antique scale for measuring the weight of food in grams (a new concept in the early 1900s), a daily log for tracking intake of protein and carbohydrates (a breakthrough idea at that time), and a photograph of patients boiling urine on a stove. It was an entertaining "show and tell" that demonstrated the revolutionary "patient involved" model of care that was born at the Joslin Center. In a short few minutes, Kimball was able to help visitors appreciate how the Joslin Center changed the care of diabetes patients.

Kimball's passion and enthusiasm are obvious and somewhat remarkable because he had no previous experience in health care (he was a policymaker in state government prior to this). He embraced the role of championing the center's philosophy and clearly communicated the mission in an exciting way. Word drifted back to the physicians—they heard about how Kimball was promoting the Joslin Center approach—and they genuinely appreciated the effort he made to spread the word. For the first time in a long time, the patient care group felt valued.

The lesson from this story is that the leader can ignite momentum simply by becoming the custodian of the story, talking about the mission and purpose in a compelling way and communicating with everyone who interacts with the organization and its people. The leader looks for opportunities to communicate and connect people with purpose. When morale is low, as it was at the Joslin Center, ask yourself, "What is our story, and how can we make sure that people hear it and are moved by it?" At the Joslin Center, Kimball was able to change the perception that the clinical group was a drain on resources by reframing their mission as essential to the enterprise.

> *The lesson from this story is that the leader can ignite momentum simply by becoming the custodian of the story, talking about the mission and purpose in a compelling way and communicating with everyone who interacts with the organization and its people.*

Table 7–1 will help you to organize your thinking around the topic of reigniting momentum by examining the stories of your own organization. Use it to analyze how these stories can connect people with purpose and engage them. Consider how you would like people to think and feel about the organization and what actions you want them to take as they connect with that purpose.

This approach—looking at the stories of your organization—will help you to understand it better and connect others with it. It is really very simple—all you need to do is look at what has happened—stories of yesterday and today—the great moments in your company. Sometimes what is wrong with the organization when morale is low is simply that people have lost their connection with what you're doing and why. Stories will help you as a leader to reconnect people and help them to remember why they work there and what really matters. As you do this, you'll find lessons to share. Kimball says that once he understood the story and shared it with others, it was easy to motivate people with a powerful promise. While he acknowledged the truth—that the clinic was losing money—he told them that they would find the money to keep providing great patient care. "That was very motivating for them," he says.

Table 7–1 The Story of Your Organization: An Analytical Tool

What is the story of our organization?	Why does this story matter?	What, if anything, has caused us to lose this connection to purpose?	How can I reconnect people to purpose? What are the stories that will resonate for others?	What is the feeling I want to create, and what are the actions I hope people will take as a result of hearing these stories?

How Else Can You Communicate to Create and Build Momentum?

As you seek to motivate your team and build momentum, you also need to talk about values and culture. Sometimes organizations lose momentum because of a culture of negativity, internal competition, or blame creeps in. As a new leader in an organization, you may find it easier to see these behaviors, but every leader should evaluate the cultural issues of the organization periodically and communicate to encourage positive behavior.

As a new CEO, Kimball noticed almost from the start that this academic institution was different from business or government. In advocating for their projects, researchers had grown accustomed to having to go behind closed doors to get funding. The budget process in the past had not been open, which encouraged researchers simply to look out for their own—no one really had an accurate view of what was best for the entire enterprise. This was not only a budget buster and bad for the balance sheet, but it also created a negative environment where favoritism reigned over fairness, and people had to compete instead of work together.

Kimball communicated right away that the practice of competing behind closed doors and lobbying for projects would end. He stopped taking meetings this way and let people know that he would not be granting special favors. He insisted that the entire organization work out a budget that was real. Members of the team had to make decisions out in the open; there couldn't be closed-door meetings where projects were approved without the knowledge of others.

As you examine the culture of your organization, you may see negative behaviors that have crept in over time. It is important to pay attention to these because no matter how worthy your goals and purpose, a negative cultural issue will completely undermine motivation. Analyze negative behaviors, curb them, and talk about how you want people to behave instead. Even if you haven't been told directly that negative behaviors are dragging people down, you can be

> *Analyze negative behaviors, curb them, and talk about how you want people to behave instead.*

sure it's happening. For example, if one person or group gets special attention or resources, *you* won't hear about it, but *everybody else* will be talking about it, and you'll be wondering why. If you have your radar up for situations that create a perception of unfairness, dishonesty, or inequity, you'll be able to address them quickly and keep the energy focused on achieving important goals.

Take a Long-Term View Toward Building Positive Momentum

As we learned in earlier chapters, when Mike Daly became CEO of Baystate Medical Center, he realized that he wouldn't change the culture overnight. In fact, it took a ten-year commitment to build positive feelings and improve morale. Daly and his team identified new behaviors and values around which the center would operate. Through their patience, perseverance, and long-term view, they were able to unify the three warring hospitals.

Taking a long-term view means that you have to repeat the message in many ways over months, even years. Even if you think that you have said a thousand times what needs to be said, say it again. Constant reinforcement is one of the keys to building and sustaining the positive momentum that will make you successful. When new challenges arose and the staff pointed out, again, how Baystate wasn't living its values, Daly would change the policy and communicate his message again. The result was that year after year, employee attitudes improved. "It became clear that employees really, really liked what the organization was becoming," says Daly.

When you see that moving the organization forward is going to take some time, you need to celebrate each victory and keep track of your progress over time. As we noted Chapter 6, you can keep in touch, walk around, listen to the stories, and make sure that the "wins" are communicated through a feedback loop. If you have a baseline on employee engagement or attitudes, you can track your progress. For example, at the beginning of the merger that created Baystate, the medical and front-office staff reported seeing "work as a chore," a place to "work locally and get a decent paycheck," so it might have been easy to get discouraged about momentum. By tracking it, however, as time went on and people reported looking forward to going to work, helping their patients, and interacting with colleagues, this was news that the leadership team could share. "This is something I take immense pride in," says Daly. "When you take a long-term view, you get results over time, and you fulfill the vision."

With the rapid pace of business today, leaders are judged most frequently not by what they've accomplished over a five-year period but rather by what they've delivered this quarter, even this week. The short-term goals, which are typically financial results, don't tell the whole story of your organization. Organizations and leaders not only must take the longer view, but they also must communicate the longer-view wins, such as upward trends in how employees feel about working there. These are things that take time, but they matter. "I think a ten-year horizon is appropriate," Daly says.

Don't confuse patience with complacency. You don't need to be satisfied with the status quo. A complacent leader creates a complacent organization. People become discouraged if they don't see things change. A complacent leader doesn't expect things to change; a patient leader believes that things can change and will change and looks for slow but steady improvement over time.

Create and Sustain Momentum with a Focus on Driving Values

As I've mentioned, creating and sustaining momentum happens not only because you achieve financial goals but also because your organization documents, talks about, and lives by a set of shared values. When people share values, they work together, act as one organization, and enjoy coming to work. The foundation for building a culture of people who care about the company and are excited to come to work is the value system you create and live by. Your business plan is the roadmap; the values tell people how to operate every day and make decisions in their own best interest as well as that of the company.

At Baystate Medical Center, Mike Daly says that shared values were very important to the center's success. Daly set about to change things by talking about and living the values. He had a vision for a vibrant organization that could become the crown jewel of the region. The most important asset of this organization, and any organization, is its people. Determining and living by a set of values stabilized a rocky, warring, disparate group, and that ultimately created one of the best places to work in the region.

> *When people share values, they work together, act as one organization, and enjoy coming to work.*

Values are not just "nice to have"; they are essential to your success because they provide a basic guideline for how people should work, interact, and make decisions. "To me," says Daly, "this is the way you ensure success." As the values are communicated and take hold, people become more enthused and excited about coming to work. You don't have to tell them what a great place to work the organization is; they already know it. When Baystate was finally recognized as a "top 100" hospital, it was simply proof of what people inside already knew had happened.

Empower People to Act

You cannot build positive momentum by trying to carry the organization on your back. You have to empower people to act. Remember the story of John Fish, who started Suffolk Construction Company? For the first few years in business, he succeeded by being on overdrive and pushing everyone else to their limits. He got to work every morning at 4:30 a.m. and was the last to turn out the lights. However, eventually, his company grew so large and faced issues that were bigger than Fish could fix with drive and determination. He had to empower people in the organization to make choices and to do so according to their shared values.

When you give people the power and authority to make decisions and provide a framework of values, they become your partners in building momentum. If you don't, you doom the organization to fail. Rich Krueger, CEO of DynamicOps, whom you met in Chapter 1, told me a story about a time earlier in his career when he worked for a company whose CEO couldn't let go and let his own leaders run their groups. He directed everything, overrode decisions, and second-guessed every single person. The company started with great promise, but over time, Krueger says, the morale sank because the CEO wouldn't empower his people.

"This guy was really smart," says Krueger. "He was probably smarter than everyone on his team. The problem was [that] he thought he could do other people's jobs better than they could. He also didn't want to accept an answer that wasn't the one he wanted, even if it was the truth." The CEO's unwillingness to empower his team created a significant drag on the business. The company "didn't reach its potential, disappointed investors—eventually it fell apart," says Krueger. "The world was their oyster" early on, but eventually more than half the senior management team left, future funding was in jeopardy, and the sale of the company was looming.

> *When you give people the power and authority to make decisions and provide a framework of values, they become your partners in building momentum.*

If the organization loses momentum, you can blame the economy, market pressures, or bad luck, but the real reason may be that people are not empowered to do their jobs. Examine your own motives. Whatever the challenges in your business, think about whether you can let go and what is the worst that will happen if you do. If you don't have the right people in place, hire them; if you are overmanaging them, take a step back. Talk about the mission and values—these become the framework for their decisions. Then you just need to coach them. Don't be the reason that people lose heart. Encourage them to take risks—to act—and always remind them of the mission, purpose, and values by which they should make those choices. Without empowerment, there is no real commitment, and momentum dies.

Be Inclusive

You won't build momentum unless everyone is part of the plan. Every person in the organization should feel that he or she is important to the mission. As a leader, you have to make a conscious effort to include all parts of the organization and every individual. One simple way to be more inclusive is to just get out there and talk to people. I discussed in Chapter 3 the value of starting a 90-day listening tour and meeting with people to gather collective wisdom. Think about the areas of your organization that are often ignored. Maybe they aren't the "sexiest" or most "fun" group; perhaps you don't understand or feel connected to what they do. Don't let that deter you from talking with them, seeking them out, and including them in your communications.

It's important to make an extra effort to reach out to the people you don't know well or don't understand. They appreciate it and can become your best allies. In the television world, general managers came from the sales world; they were therefore sometimes afraid to venture into the newsroom. We weren't "their people." Yet those general managers who did venture in had tremendous support from the troops.

Including people who often are on the fringes of the organization can make them into your greatest allies. Ranch Kimball at the Joslin Center is delighted to tell you that he has walked every inch of the facility—from the labs to the storage facilities, to patient accounts offices, to "freezer farms" where 30-year-old blood is stored, to the backup generator on the roof. He doesn't just talk with researchers and physicians; he talks with *everybody*.

The connections have to be real, not superficial. Kimball doesn't just shake hands; he makes an effort to *learn*. He describes sitting with a researcher who carefully explained how to read a blood glucose pattern in a printout from a diabetic high school wrestler. He learned how to inject himself with a needle. Over the top? I don't think so. Kimball sees it as inclusion and knows that it builds morale. He wants to know people, and they want to know him.

Can you really get to know people when you run a large organization? The answer is, You can certainly try! You'll get points for getting out there even if you don't remember everyone's name. The Joslin Center has 700 employees, and in the first month Kimball invited every one of them to meet with him—90 percent took him up on it. He continues that practice by making sure that at least once a year every single employee gets an invitation to a small group lunch with the CEO.

A Small Army of People Building Momentum

You need a small army of people out there to help you communicate the mission because you simply can't do it alone. Enlist every leader and influential person in your organization in helping you to energize people and generate positive feelings. This is important because you can't be everywhere. Most employees think first about their own boss when they evaluate how they feel about the company. Every manager, supervisor, and executive needs to be aware of the impact they have on others. Make sure to let them know that you consider it their job to talk about the vision and values and share positive success stories; this job is as important as managing their business. Their contributions to building momentum are essential. Your small army of leaders should have the knowledge, skills, and opportunity to communicate the mission, purpose, and values.

Paula Johnson, executive director of the Connors Center for Women's Health and Gender Biology at Brigham and Women's Hospital, creates this opportunity by enlisting physicians, contributors, and staff as advocates for the mission of the organization. The Connors Center was founded to advance research in women's health and to promote integrated health care for women. This is a new concept—combining breakthrough research on women's health and clinical care that puts the theory to work on patients. "Our work is cutting-edge, and it needs to be easily understood by all the people we might touch in any given day," says Johnson. "The Connors Center must give philanthropists a true appreciation and feel for the work. We have to orchestrate the opportunities for them to get the message."

Johnson regards every board meeting, event, fund-raiser, or update as a significant opportunity to connect people with the mission of the Connors Center. "To keep the momentum moving forward, we have enlisted other people to deliver the message: faculty and nonfaculty, hospital administrators, and people who have already given and believe in our mission," she says. Of course, this means that everyone, absolutely everyone, needs to be on

> *You need a small army of people out there to help you communicate the mission because you simply can't do it alone.*

message, on mission, on purpose. "We actually work with all those people on how the message is communicated. We get together and talk about how we are going to frame each presentation."

The Connors Center started as a concept and has become a cutting-edge research and medical facility with a strong base of significant donors who understand the mission. How did it happen? This army of people is all on the same page. Presentations are prepared by several people, reviewed carefully, and rehearsed with feedback from the group before an event. "We want to be sure that we are delivering the same information and that the way we deliver our information is consistent. Even if someone is a very good speaker, we assume [that] they need to be as sharp as they can be, and that requires input from others." So it's a *team* approach to a *consistent* message to keep building momentum.

Imagine what would happen if you actually had people in your organization go through training to be able to talk about the vision and values. What if they could stop and talk to anyone, anytime, about what they do and why it matters? At the Connors Center, this is what happens. "Every single person who works with us from the physicians to the administrative assistants can answer the question, 'What do you do there?' We want them to be comfortable and confident when they talk about our mission and how the work gets done," says Johnson. "Everyone has to understand in a visceral way what we do and why it matters. It is hard work to make everyone feel confident that they can articulate the mission and values," she says.

> *What is the impact of having an "army" of people delivering a consistent message? "The outcome of this is that we have a larger team of both faculty and staff with a much greater appreciation for the potential power of our work," says Johnson.*

What is the impact of having an "army" of people delivering a consistent message? "The outcome of that is that we have a larger team of both faculty and staff with a much greater appreciation for the potential power of our work," says Johnson. She makes sure that they have the tools to articulate mission and vision, and she says that this makes them feel part of something very important. "They all feel they are working toward improving the health of women. It feeds the *momentum* because they are empowered when they can articulate it," she says.

Whatever the mission of *your* organization, it's easy to bring many people into the mix. The more ambassadors you have out there speaking enthusiastically about what you do and why they love it, the easier it is to sustain momentum and achieve long-term goals.

How to Evaluate Your Organization's Momentum

How do you know that your organization is building positive momentum? Is there a way to measure excitement, enthusiasm, and engagement? Employee surveys are one effective way to evaluate people's attitudes and engagement. You also can start a conversation among your leaders, managers, and supervisors. A robust conversation about the level of engagement, energy, and enthusiasm is a good thing—you'll learn whether there are challenges company-wide or just in one or a few areas of the business.

Bring your leadership team into this exercise. You may want to send them on a "listening tour." Ask them to sit down with influential people in their organizations and figure out what is demotivating or getting in the way. Sometimes, when an issue has existed for a long time, people don't really talk about it anymore—they just accept that it's the way things are. By starting these conversations, your leaders and managers can show people that they are interested in how they can make it a great place to work. As you look at new input with a fresh eye, think about simple ways you could start to turn things around.

Here are some questions to ask your team:

- What issues have been raised by employees that we should be concerned about?
- How are these affecting motivation?
- What is the history of this issue? What has led to the current situation?
- Have we tried to address this before? If so, why didn't it work?
- What would be a better way, and how could we make it happen?

- What resources, people, and time would it take to make a significant improvement?
- What is the outcome we are looking for?

As you engage your managers, supervisors, and leaders in this process, the simple act of asking the right questions can create positive feelings. When you engage your team not only in managing the business but also in being responsible for the kind of workplace they create together, you may find that they have simple, creative ideas that can make a world of difference. As you build momentum, it is also important to create ownership—the feeling that everyone is responsible and accountable. This is what we'll discuss in Chapter 8.

Summary

- Even the greatest organizations undergo natural ups and downs; no one is immune to market pressures and economic downturns that strain morale and halt momentum.
- The challenge is also at the individual level; even the most passionate, energetic person has to sustain drive, enthusiasm, and creativity.
- You have to figure out how to rekindle your own spirit and reconnect to the mission—determine what keeps it fresh for you.
- Create a small army of people to help you connect people with purpose and keep momentum alive. Don't try to do it alone.

The foundation for building a strong culture with people who care about the company and are excited to come to work is the value system you create and live by.

8

Create Accountability and
Drive Results

There are two ways of exerting one's strength; one is pushing
down, the other is pulling up.

—BOOKER T. WASHINGTON

WE HAVE LOOKED AT the building blocks of motivation—your purpose and passion, connecting people with a purpose, linking what with why, and aligning the organization and building momentum. The next logical step in the process is to harness this momentum and create ownership for outcomes. This means setting up accountability and driving results. Your motivated team is now working toward purpose and is excited about doing great things. By creating a culture of accountability, you get results, and people feel greater satisfaction, which, in turn, reenergizes and motivates the organization.

Achieving results is highly motivating. This is why accountability is so important. Communicating who does what, when it needs to be done, and what the outcomes should be is your job as a leader. When you communicate accountability, you set people up for success. This is the kind of leader people want—one who not only motivates people but also communicates expectations and holds people to their commitments.

People in your organization are very busy. The question a leader has to ask is, "Busy doing what?" Are people working on the highest-priority projects—the ones that are closest to your purpose and aligned with your strategy? If you suspect that people are not always working on the highest priorities, it's your job as a leader to communicate (or make sure that your managers and supervisors communicate) to get people focused on the right activities and make sure that they "own" the outcomes.

People in your organization want to do a great job every day. They just need to know what to do. They need to have ownership. By making sure that people know that they "own" projects, you give them a chance to succeed, and then you can recognize and celebrate them when they achieve good outcomes. The biggest challenge for most employees is that they simply have too much on their to-do lists. When they come to work each day, they have to look at the list and decide how to spend their time. They may believe that they are choosing well, but if leaders aren't communicating accountability and ownership, chances are they may not choose well.

You have to communicate priorities, ownership, and accountability so effectively that it is easy for people to choose the best, most productive way to spend their time. A simple example of how this does not happen in organizations is what goes on in meetings. Too many meetings end after a discussion on several topics, without the leader assigning responsibilities and setting expectations, deadlines, and desired outcomes. You may assume that people know what to do only to learn days, weeks, or months later that no one has even started the project or that it has languished or died because no one "owned" it. As a leader, you need to constantly state what may seem obvious by talking about what needs to be done and who is responsible.

> *You have to communicate priorities, ownership, and accountability so effectively that it is easy for people to choose the best, most productive way to spend their time.*

As one participant in our survey said, "If the strategy isn't . . . effectively communicated, there cannot be a common endgame. Without a common endgame, individuals are unable to pull together collectively and, even worse, may be working at cross-purposes."

If you are just beginning to look at accountability in your organization, a good place to start is with project management. There are many sophisticated computer programs and processes for project management, but you can start with a simple Excel spreadsheet such as the one in Table 8–1. Distribute it at a meeting, and complete it on the spot so that everyone knows the project's goal, responsible party, next step, and deadline. Customize the categories as you wish; just be sure that it conveys the most important information. Writing it down and reviewing it weekly ensures that your people will remember what needs to be done and when.

You may have worked in an organization where people were very busy doing things that didn't matter that much. This is not a failure of the employees; it is a failure of leadership. Leaders have not organized what needs to be done and have not communicated the plan. They may assume that people know what they are supposed to do and when. The result is not only frustration for the leader; employees are frustrated, too.

People Like to Be Held Accountable

Here's the big thing about accountability, and it is very important to understand: If your people haven't been held accountable before, they may be afraid of it. They may feel anxiety about meeting expectations. However, this is simply because they have not worked where they've experienced the rewards of working in a culture of accountability. They may never have worked for a leader who clearly communicated expectations

Table 8–1 Project Tracker

Project	Goal	Team/Individual	Next Steps	Deadline

and empowered people to achieve outcomes. They may never have worked for someone who clearly defined success.

If you communicate accountability and define success, people appreciate it and *want* to be held accountable. When they experience how exhilarating it is to achieve results, they are willing to take on even more. Once they do a great job on a high-priority project, they gain confidence and embrace a culture where people are expected to "own" the outcomes.

Think back to a time early in your career. You couldn't wait to prove yourself. You were eager, excited, and committed. You wanted to impress your boss and get a pat on the back. All you needed was the opportunity to prove yourself and to have a chance to work on a high-visibility project that mattered. As a leader, you can create an environment where everyone, not just new employees, feels the same way. You can communicate well and manage outcomes.

> *If you communicate accountability and define success, people appreciate it and want to be held accountable. When they experience how exhilarating it is to achieve results, they are willing to take on even more.*

Ellyn McColgan, of Morgan Stanley, puts it this way: "Ninety-eight percent of people who come to work every day want to do a good job and want to get recognized for doing a good job. Whether you work in the mail room or you're the CEO, everyone wants to do a good job and make the enterprise valuable." What is accountability, if not that!

What people are *afraid* of is that they won't match up to expectations. As you communicate expectations, you also want to boost their confidence. Therefore, when you talk about expectations, it is also important to express your faith in the individual or team. This is often what is missing from a leader's presentation. It's fairly common, in my experience, to see a leader get up and talk about the strategy and forget to let his or her people know that he or she believes they can do it! Communicate your confidence in your people, and they will find a way. Of course, you must make sure that they have the power to make decisions and the resources to accomplish the task, too.

When people express concern that they won't be able to meet a goal, McColgan answers, "Of course you will! You will be recognized for doing a good job." Just telling someone that you believe in him or her is a shot in the arm—the person will throw himself or herself into it and give it his or her best. McColgan tells people when she gives them a tough assignment, "You are good enough, more than good enough. And when you achieve the objectives, you own them and can celebrate them."

Here are a few things to communicate:

- Let people know that you believe in them. If you believe, they believe.
- Discuss the resources they will need. This is important to motivation.
- Tell them that they can make decisions. This speeds results.
- Explain that you want them to stretch. One reward is to learn new skills.
- Congratulate them for milestones. Build momentum toward the next goals.

> *When people express concern that they won't be able to meet a goal, McColgan answers, "Of course you will!"*

Accountability Starts at the Top

Creating accountability isn't just a matter of command and control. In fact, if you don't make yourself accountable to your people, they won't feel accountable to you. One thing a leader is accountable for is making it possible—and easier—for people to get their jobs done. A leader can remove or mitigate obstacles.

John Fish, CEO of Suffolk Construction, whom you met in Chapter 5, says that the first person he holds accountable is himself. Once he has a plan, he tells the team so that if he varies from it, he'll have to explain himself. "You are held accountable to people when you take a detour," he said. "Even though we are privately held, I have a responsibility to those people, too, and feel personally responsible. I don't want to let them down or let my family down." You are accountable to your team, and your team is accountable to you. To instill a positive culture of accountability, make commitments to your team and fulfill them.

Ellyn McColgan learned early in her career through a disastrous business failure why leaders should take this seriously. While employed by Bank of New England from 1987 to 1990, she and the top managers were aware that the bank was starting to fail. Although nothing was public, internal rumors were rampant. McColgan was responsible for the securities operation, which included the people who worked in the "cage," a vault that was below ground. "These were operations people who typically had 25 years of service," says McColgan, "and all they really expected is that they would have a nice place to work and be able to retire."

> You are accountable to your team, and your team is accountable to you.

McColgan was a relatively young manager at the time, so she was taken aback when an older supervisor named Joe approached her. Nearing retirement, he asked if he should move out of the company stock in his 401(k) plan. "He was about to lose everything he had. I knew that by the time we announced the decision, he would be too late getting out of that stock, and it was his whole retirement. So I said, 'Yes, I think you should move the money.' And then he said, 'Ms. McColgan, do you think I will be okay?' and I said, 'I don't know. I hope so.' "

McColgan has since told this story to every management team she's ever led. She wants to drive home the point that as leaders they are responsible for the welfare of the organization. She wants them to see that the decisions they make affect people's lives. "Through the completely incompetent leadership of that bank, thousands of people lost their jobs and retirements and future. I was the one who had to stare them in the face, not the big banking executives who made these bad decisions. So I promised myself I would never run a business that wasn't profitable and growing and where we didn't do what we said we would do."

As Americans, we have grown accustomed to opening up the *Wall Street Journal* and reading stories about a failure of accountability at the top. Executives do not always hold themselves accountable for the welfare of their organizations, and the result is that their employees, customers, and the public suffer. These people are not leaders. Accountability is a tenant of leadership that we all need to take seriously. Democratic societies and free markets cannot sustain themselves unless people hold themselves accountable—the damage in the wake of their failures is too great. It is impossible to succeed or build a motivated workforce if leaders don't hold themselves accountable first. When employees know that the leaders of their organization are serious about being accountable, they take it seriously, too.

> *"I promised myself I would never run a business that wasn't profitable and growing and where we didn't do what we said we would do."*

While it's tragic when a company closes its doors, people lose their jobs and retirement savings, and investors lose money, this worst-case scenario isn't the only thing we should fear. When companies and their leaders are not accountable, mediocrity reigns. Mediocre performance is a far more common problem in business today, and much of it can be traced to a lack of accountability. A company might not go under—however, it simply will limp along if people don't "own" actions and outcomes. If the people at the top aren't accountable for results, then how can others be expected to drive forward and help the company achieve its potential?

McColgan feels fortunate that this incident happened early in her career. She witnessed the consequences when leaders didn't take responsibility for their decisions. She vowed to make it her mission to run a healthy business and to hold herself and her senior leaders accountable. "This is what it means to run a good business. Nobody gets to walk away from that. This is the issue in leadership, isn't it?" she says.

A Culture of Accountability

How do you create a culture of accountability? It starts with taking personal responsibility and then communicating what you will do. It is important not only to make a commitment to yourself but also to *let others know what that commitment is.*

> *It is important not only to make a commitment to yourself but also to let others know what that commitment is.*

When you talk about your own commitment, people respect you and want to emulate you. When you set a high standard for yourself, they do the same. Creating accountability by example is effective because you are not only issuing directives, but you are also making a commitment to your people. People are highly motivated to work for a leader who holds himself or herself accountable.

Once you set the standard by communicating what you will do, you can create a structure that supports a culture of accountability. At Suffolk Construction, CEO John Fish structured each of his business units as a separate profit center. These units and the individual leaders who work in them have responsibility for generating profit. They have clear, written roles and responsibilities: "Every individual has a job description, every individual has a comprehension of the business units they intersect with, and they also know the roles and responsibilities of all the people they work with," Fish says. "We measure success based on how well they perform according to the roles and responsibilities."

Fish considers clear assignments and responsibilities essential; accountability is the Suffolk "brand." Each business unit is held accountable for its own success. "We can measure success and failure of each of those silos, or business units. It is crystal clear; we can see it in our measurements. There is no hiding. You can't dodge a bullet—it is what it is," he says.

By holding business units and individuals accountable, you create clarity and eliminate infighting. Everyone knows that they have to strive to achieve success as it is defined for their organization. McColgan agrees that people need to have their own assignments and expectations. "Everyone, no matter how good your business plan and communication strategy are, needs to be assigned a clear role," she says. "If every person doesn't understand they play a role, you will not achieve the optimal results."

Transparency

Holding people accountable works when people know what they are supposed to do and what *others* are supposed to do, too. This means communicating with everyone in the organization not only about their jobs but also the jobs of the people around them. When you communicate with your entire team about what expectations are of everyone in the group, you have transparency. Transparency is simply communicating more clearly and informing people about what should and must be done throughout the organization.

Sometimes you may find people in an organization complaining that others in their group are not pulling their weight. This may be true; it also may be so because they don't know who is supposed to do what and when. Instead of making people wonder and guess whether their colleagues are "pulling their weight," you pull back the curtain and talk about expectations. You also encourage collaboration and cooperation by making teams, as well as individuals, responsible for outcomes. If you know the person next to you is accountable or that several members of the team are accountable for various aspects of a plan, as a member of that team, you stop worrying about what other people are doing, and you get your own job done. When you get your job done, you get recognized; if others don't do their jobs, there are consequences. If you make it clear that the expectation is that they will work as a team, more often than not they will join forces and solve problems.

When you communicate in a transparent way about roles, responsibilities, and expectations, you send a message that performance counts, not office politics. People know that they are accountable not just to you, but to the whole team. This communication gets them to focus on the job at hand. They don't want to let anyone down. And you eschew favoritism for performance. People learn from you that what counts most is what they get done. It takes time and a conscious effort to communicate everyone's responsibilities to the team, but you will earn respect and trust as team members see that what matters to you is teamwork and performance.

Communicating with transparency accelerates results. At the end of the year, you will look back on conversations with your team and see how they produced positive business outcomes. Tracing back and remembering tough conversations, you'll have proof of how your words mattered.

> *When you communicate in a transparent way about roles, responsibilities, and expectations, you send a message that performance counts, not office politics.*

Communicating with transparency not only creates a positive business atmosphere, but it also leads to faster results and higher profits.

Holding people accountable doesn't mean that every individual, team, or business unit has to produce *the same* results. You set expectations appropriately and explain why. You may have a pilot project or a beta test that is expected to lose money but help your business to move forward. You may have a team that provides service and doesn't make money but builds your brand. As long as everyone's roles are clear and you are communicating expectations, you foster a healthy, motivated culture.

In the construction business, which is more cyclic than many, CEO John Fish says Suffolk Construction expects every team to communicate in real time on progress against goals. He says that this is one reason that in the volatile world of construction, for every one of the 26 years that he's been in business, he's made a profit.

Meetings: Where Accountability Is Communicated

Meetings are the place where accountability is communicated. At the end of each discussion, and at the end of each meeting, you should be talking about who will do what and when. You may assume at the end of a discussion that people know what they are supposed to do, but you shouldn't. Leave time on the agenda to talk about assignments, roles, and deadlines so that you are assured that people understand and don't forget.

Many of us work in industries and companies where there are too many meetings back to back. Many meetings are run poorly; people are overscheduled and stressed, but they arrive late and leave early, and the meeting leader does not manage the meeting well. Pretty soon, people are racing out the door before next steps, assignments, and deadlines are communicated. And guess what happens? The meeting convenes the following week, and the same old discussion starts up again. Nothing has been done. This does not motivate people. It only reinforces the belief that meetings are unproductive and a waste of time.

Whether or not you have finished discussion on a topic, the last ten to fifteen minutes of every meeting should be reserved for stating accountability, deadlines, and next steps. This is when you review decisions, assign individuals to tasks, and set expectations for completion or updates.

My firm often works with organizations and their senior leaders to evaluate their meeting culture and recommend changes that will foster a more productive meeting culture. This often means creating an agreed-on list of meeting guidelines and practices that everyone must live by, and I believe that this is one of the main reasons that we have started to achieve better results.

If you let people leave without communicating next steps and accountability, it doesn't mean that the job won't get done; you're simply leaving it to chance. Some people still may take the ball and run with it, but you have no assurance. They may forget, other priorities may arise, or they may not be clear that it has to be done, so they'll put it off until next time. The only way to guarantee that assignments get made is to put it on your agenda and leave time to talk about it.

> *No matter what you are doing, the last ten to fifteen minutes of a meeting should be reserved for stating accountability, deadlines, and next steps. This is when you review decisions, assign individuals to tasks, and set expectations for completion or updates.*

Meetings are the place where decisions are made. This is why it is so important to build and foster a productive meeting culture that sets up your organization for success. Strong, well-written guidelines and a commitment to those guidelines will make meetings more productive and motivate people. Your organization should review its challenges and problems with meetings by surveying the organization, and out of that, you should discuss a set of meeting guidelines that you will practice and enforce. If your meetings are not efficient and productive, it is extremely difficult to create a culture of accountability, make people feel good about going to meetings, and ultimately drive results.

What goes into your meeting guidelines?

- An agenda for every meeting with a purpose for the meeting, names of participants, date, and time. It should be e-mailed in advance with attachments so that participants can prepare, participate, and make decisions or recommendations.

- A template for the agenda, including a code for each topic, a description of the topic, the person responsible, time allotted for discussion, and desired outcome, such as decision making or brainstorming.
- Behaviors and norms for behavior that everyone agrees will make them more productive and engaging.
- A rock-solid rule to start and end on time.
- Policy on use of cell phones, BlackBerries, and interruptions.
- Plenty of time at the end of each meeting to wrap up, determine next steps, assign tasks and responsibilities, and set deadlines.

Consistency

Consistency is doing things the way everyone has agreed all the time so that you have predictability in your business practices and outcomes. Being consistent in your actions, policies, and practices is very important to accountability. You can't have one rule for some and another for others. If you are not consistent in asking people to do it the way you've agreed, you will not be able to hold them accountable. If people perceive the organization as unfair, even if a manager or supervisor has "reasons" for making exceptions, people will not be motivated. In fact, they will resent it tremendously, and you will kill motivation.

I remember a particularly challenging time in my television career when I experienced this first hand. I worked side by side with a coanchor who was very talented but, for some reason, was not expected to go out and report news stories. Each day, after the news show was over and we went back to our offices, he read the paper, and I was assigned to go out and cover a story. While I had a producer who worked closely with me to help me get these stories on the air, it became obvious that my workload was very different. My producer and I were expected to turn out at least two or three stories a week, a significant addition to anchoring the program.

Setting and communicating consistent expectations is very important to motivation.

I never asked why in part because I enjoyed the reporting, and I didn't really want to sit around. However, we were paid roughly the same salary, and I couldn't help but also feel resentful. I never discussed it with my boss, but I did think it was unfair, and it certainly didn't give me any confidence that my coanchor and I were both being evaluated in the same way.

When People Don't Report to You

It can be a challenge to make sure that you get a job done when some of the people working on a project don't report to you. In many organizations, people have to work together across functions or divisions without the involvement of their bosses. If you have a team, but you do not have the authority to hold them accountable, it can make it very difficult to get people motivated and get the work done. You may find yourself working behind the scenes and pulling strings to build consensus, cajole people, and even beg. But if you look at this job as one of influencing others, it may help you to gain momentum and still get people to "own" the outcomes.

Paula Johnson, of the Connors Center at Brigham and Women's Hospital, works hard to bring people together and influence them. Her center is part of a Harvard University teaching hospital, so many physicians and researchers operate independently. At this stage of their careers, they value autonomy and may need to fight for their own programs and projects. In a teaching hospital setting, many depend on the same resources, and this can discourage cooperation. There is often little or no incentive to get together and work on joint missions.

"A good part of my energy is spent carrying out a strategy that focuses on the cross-departmental work," says Johnson. "In order to make transformational change in women's health, we can accomplish a lot at the Connor's Center. However, the truly transformational part of the work is what occurs across every part of the institution." Johnson is striving to reinvent the "model" for patient care so that it includes the entire hospital; patients have access and doctors cooperate in unconventional ways. "If you think about that strategy, my ability to communicate what is compelling about the model, why it is important to patient care, is critical to getting the work done. If I can't get other physicians and the management on board and get people to cooperate with us, the work doesn't move forward."

The leader who is able to influence others, win buy-in, and get people to share in a commitment is able to achieve great things. "A lot of the initial work in a project like this is communicating why this is important to *each* audience," says Johnson. As we've discussed, in motivating people, one of the challenges is to make it relevant to *them*. "We have to show them how it benefits everyone when we work in an interdisciplinary way. I have to explain the win-win strategy with every person I talk with."

> *"A lot of the initial work in a project like this is communicating why this is important to each audience," says Johnson. As we've discussed, in motivating people, one of the challenges is to make it relevant to them.*

"If I don't make an effort to communicate with all the stakeholders on their terms in a powerful way, there is no interdisciplinary work there; it doesn't exist," she observes. "You can create a structure like the Connors Center and fund it, but without communicating with all the other departments, we will not bring about change because the work has to happen way beyond the confines of a single center here in the hospital."

Flexibility

While creating a culture of accountability, you must be flexible. For example, in a technology business, defining success only as bringing an innovation to market is a mistake. Many innovations will fail. Accountability in an industry such as high tech may mean something else entirely. Keith Blakely, CEO of NanoDynamics, whom you met in Chapter 1, says, "There is a cultural challenge in holding people responsible and accountable for something beyond activity. You can't reward for activity; you reward for results. However, the challenge is that sometimes people can work tremendously hard and intelligently on things that don't work out for reasons that couldn't be known when they started the project but became clear later."

Blakely believes in taking a less unbending approach to accountability. "We try to maintain an informal nature to the company because rigid goal setting and performance evaluations that are inflexible or not appreciative of the challenges that early-stage companies encounter will tend to be very frustrating to employees," he says. If people feel that the boss doesn't understand the challenges they faced that were beyond their control, such as another company building a better "mousetrap," it is actually demotivating.

> *"We try to maintain an informal nature to the company because rigid goal setting and performance evaluations that are inflexible or not appreciative of the challenges that early-stage companies encounter will tend to be very frustrating to employees."*

In any organization, you have to be flexible about outcomes, and you must make sure that you're correctly defining success. Communication again is the key. If you evaluate and communicate as you go, people don't get discouraged. You still hold them accountable; you simply make sure that everyone knows what's changing and why.

If you are a company trying to drive innovation, then people should be accountable and rewarded for coming up with great ideas and pursuing them, and you need to figure out the best way to communicate this. Doing so may mean a different standard as well as different channels for talking about it, but you still can have accountability. "We tend to try and have a culture and environment that encourage much less structured communication, not reporting but interfacing between personnel and departments," says Blakely. Accountability in this type of organization is less about having a boss looking over your shoulder and more about staying in close touch and supporting people.

Message Discipline

As you work to develop a culture of accountability, you need to have discipline in the way you communicate your message. You want to be consistent and clear at all times about where you are going, how you will get there, who "owns" it, and what the expected outcomes are. If you have discipline about the message, it means that everybody hears the same thing many times. You should review all important communications to make sure that they are consistent or make sure that the people who create and deliver the message have a plan and know precisely what you intend to communicate.

Good message discipline means sticking to the three to five messages about what you are trying to get done as a company this year. Repeat those messages so that there is no doubt in anyone's mind about the goals. Update people regularly on the progress you are making to encourage people to stay focused. Focus ensures that the right things get done, and when that happens, your organization is highly productive.

Message Discipline Exercise

What are the top three messages I want to deliver this quarter?

Message:

_____

_____

_____

_____

Message:

_____

_____

_____

_____

Message:

_____

_____

_____

_____

Who needs to hear it?

_____

_____

_____

_____

With consistent messages and a culture of accountability, it is much harder for people to fail. They won't come back as often and say that they didn't know what they were supposed to do, and when they do, you'll know that you need to work a little harder to communicate and make sure that they get the message. A clear, consistent message will keep everybody focused and improve accountability around the things that matter.

Summary

- Everyone is busy; the question is: Busy doing what? Are they really working on the most important priorities that will produce business results?
- Every day people come to work wanting to do a good job and have a choice about how to spend their time. If you have accountability, they will be busy doing what really matters.
- Good people who are empowered to do the work actually *want* to be accountable, especially when they realize how exhilarating it is to be responsible for success.
- What people are *afraid* of is that they won't match up to expectations, so you have to clearly communicate expectations and encourage people by letting them know that you have faith in them.
- Accountability starts at the top. When people see that you are accountable, they feel a stronger commitment to you.

9

Create the Story: The Secret to Winning Hearts and Minds

Stories can conquer fear, you know. They can make
the heart bigger.

—Ben Okri

THERE'S NO BETTER WAY to motivate and inspire people than through a good story. Stories connect people with purpose and passion. And it's easier than you imagine to find stories that make powerful points and to tell them well. Stories are a tool of leadership, and you can use them in all your communications. Good stories are all around you. Look inside your own organization and you'll find that people are overcoming obstacles and accomplishing great things. These are the seeds of stories that will help you to communicate your mission and values with purpose and with passion.

Stories are a great way to inspire people as well as to highlight behaviors and values that you want to drive through the organization. Tell a story about a success on your team, and feature a value or behavior that made the team successful. Voilà, you communicate your expectations in a powerful way. People really appreciate being recognized in a story. They talk about it with colleagues, friends, and family, and they see you as a leader who is in touch and cares about them.

151

For the rest of the organization, these types of stories are motivating and memorable. People see their colleagues being recognized for good work and start thinking about how they might receive the same type of recognition. Not only that—stories are memorable. When people remember a story, they remember the point. This helps you to drive home your message. If you tell stories well and often, people look forward to your stories and expect to hear the "lessons." Stories demonstrate that as a leader, you're in touch—that you know what's happening in your organization, care about the people who make things happen every day, and value their contributions.

You may think that a good storyteller is born, but storytellers are actually made. Storytelling isn't a gift; it's a skill that anyone can learn. Learning to write and tell good stories should be the goal of every leader. A story creates powerful visual imagery that makes your message stick. People remember what they see in their mind's eye. And telling stories makes you a more interesting, compelling, and charismatic leader. People learn something about you, seeing you as a person, not just a title. And stories take you away from the humdrum, sleepy style of speaking with PowerPoint graphs and concepts to genuinely connecting with your audi-

> *Stories demonstrate that as a leader, you're in touch—that you know what's happening in your organization, care about the people who make things happen every day, and value their contributions.*

ences. You can motivate and inspire people only when you connect with them. You have to grab them so that they put down their BlackBerries and start listening. Thus, if you have not yet started incorporating stories into your communications, this is a good time to start.

Anytime you communicate with your organization, you can make a more powerful impact with a story or two. Let's say that you're leading a company meeting, kicking off an off-site conference, rallying your sales team, or talking with important customers or business partners. Tell a story and engage people from the start at both the logical and the emotional levels. You'll stand out and make a big impression as a motivating leader and engaging person. By starting with a story, you will get your meeting off on the right foot and set the stage with a theme or big idea. Stories demonstrate confidence, knowledge, and understanding.

The Power of the Story to Drive Change in Your Organization

Dr. Archelle Georgiou, the former chief medical officer at United Health Group, is an influential leader and a good storyteller. She uses stories to communicate powerful messages and make her talks memorable. During her time at United Health, she became a thought leader in her industry and was able to drive significant changes in her company's business practices in large part because of her ability to communicate through storytelling.

Here's her story: Dr. Georgiou reviewed some standard practices and noticed that United Health required primary care physicians in its system to call the insurance company to get permission for a procedure whenever their patients needed a specialist. She says a whopping 99 percent of the time when the physician called, the answer was "Yes," but that practice was costing United Health $108 million a year.

> *A lot of people think that a good storyteller is born, but storytellers are made. Storytelling isn't a gift; it's a skill that anyone can learn.*

Georgiou determined that not only was this practice costly for the company, but it also was eroding relationships with doctors and patients. It was a waste of the company's resources and a big hassle for clients. "I wanted to redeploy the people making the calls so that they checked on how patients were doing when they got home, making sure that they got a prescription filled and set up their next doctor's appointment," she says. But it wasn't going to be easy to get approval. Georgiou had to open people's minds and hearts to change. At the next company leadership meeting, she chose the theme "Reach for the Stars."

The featured speaker was an astrophysicist from Paris, a renowned scientist who discovered the existence of water molecules in space. This scientist explained that she had felt so certain that she would find water (even though most scientists doubted its existence) that she invested in building a telescope her team could use to locate these water molecules. She was so passionate in her belief that she created an instrument to find it. "The message," says Georgiou, "was that when you are forging new ground in health care, you have to create your own path, too."

What did this story have to do with United Health? "They were so mesmerized by the story that they became open to hearing how in health care they could create new tools and didn't have to be on the same planet or operate like every other company," says the former chief medical officer. This was a huge turning point. The story got people thinking that anything is possible. They were primed. Georgiou got up to speak. "We centered on one fact, we were spending $108 million a year to say yes." Georgiou proposed that they spend that money to help patients and improve health care.

Story Impact

The impact of the story was remarkable. In the year following the decision (yes, they agreed) to institute Georgiou's proposed new process, United Health saw the biggest membership growth ever: The company added *one million members.* Employers who had left United Health and gone with other insurance providers came back, says Georgiou, because they believed that this was the right way.

> *"They were so mesmerized by this story that they became open to hearing how in health care they could create new tools and didn't have to be on the same planet or operate like every other company," says Georgiou.*

Importantly, the decision that resulted from that meeting positioned United Health as a thought leader. "We were creating a sea change in the industry. That has probably had the longest-lasting impact. Everyone remembers that United was the first to take that step, and many other insurance companies followed suit," says Georgiou. Stories make the message "sticky."

Did the message stick? "That happened seven years ago," she recalls, "and people who attended that meeting still remember the number. They remember the 1 percent denial rate and the 108 million to say yes."

Not only are stories memorable, but they also are effective because they respect the wisdom of the audience. Georgiou would say that she would not have been as successful had she simply stood up with charts and graphs and cited the numbers. The powerful story *opened their minds and hearts*. The story respected the audience's ability to connect the dots. The audience enjoyed hearing the scientist's experience and relating it to their own.

> *The powerful story opened their minds and hearts.*

Where to Look for Stories

How do you find stories for your presentation? There are so many places to look! You can start with your own experiences through your career and also look at the stories of colleagues, mentors, clients, and friends. If you are not accustomed to telling stories in your presentations, don't worry, it's easier than you imagine. Coming up I will give you a simple list of questions that will trigger your memory about things that have happened in your life. These questions will uncover things you haven't thought about in years that have shaped you and made you the leader you are — by recalling these events and looking at the insights and lessons, you will develop great material for inspiring stories.

A story doesn't have to be an "over the top" experience. Sometimes the best stories are born from simple, everyday occurrences. What makes a story great is whether it delivers a point or lesson with punch and whether it is relevant to the audience. The best motivational stories have a theme that is usually about achieving goals, overcoming challenges, persevering, and discovering what is possible with drive, effort, and adherence to important principles. Stories such as these are what audiences long to hear — and trust me, when you open your eyes, you'll find stories everywhere. Once you get into the habit of looking for them, you'll be tripping over them.

Exercise: Original Stories

When we teach storytelling skills to executives and leaders in our coaching programs and boot camps, we begin by asking them to close their eyes and listen. We present "categories" of stories. You can use this list yourself and do the exercise with your eyes closed if you ask a partner to work with you. I have found that by closing your eyes and listening, you're able to recall stories more easily because you see them in your "mind's eye." So the idea here is to close your eyes, ask your partner to read these categories out loud, and then think, in silence, for a minute or two. During that time, allow your mind to wander. Pay attention to whatever pops up, and follow the thread. We always discover that people remember things they haven't thought of in years. Write down whatever comes up. Don't worry yet about whether it's a story. It's a seed that you need to nurture and grow.

Story Categories
Personal challenges, difficult decisions, choices, hurdles, obstacles in your life or the lives of people you have known

_____

_____

_____

_____

Startling events, major changes, new experiences that shaped you or people you know

_____

_____

_____

Embarrassments, awkward situations, dumb ideas, lost opportunities, failed attempts

_____

_____

_____

_____

Inspiring people, mentors, individuals you admire, remarkable achievements, memorable events that you witnessed or experienced

_____

_____

_____

_____

Travel stories, interesting people you meet, places you've been, things you've discovered along the way

_____

_____

_____

_____

Inside your organization, interesting projects, developments, achievements, successes, or failures that made an impact on you and others

_____

_____

_____

_____

You Use "Personal" Stories in Business?

Steve Rendle, president of The North Face, part of VF Outdoor, wanted to plan a great meeting with his sales team. He was searching for a way to convey the passion he felt for the company and its products. The plan for the meeting was to lay out the business strategy. He started brainstorming to create a visual image and story that would capture the goals.

Then it came to him. He thought about the first time he went on a climb; he was 17 when his mentor gathered a group of kids his age together to teach them the sport. Rendle described with great animation what it was like to set up the base camp, make the climb, reach the summit, and look out over that vast Washington State mountain range. This was the powerful image that he was searching for—reaching summits.

Summits were the perfect way to communicate how the divisions of his business would approach the big goals they had set. The visual would resonate, and the story would demonstrate his personal connection to the mission.

The analogy was ideal because it naturally provided powerful visuals. He had an artist create sketch renderings of several mountain summits, each representing a pillar of the business plan. He found a photo of himself as a 17-year-old kid making his first climb. You can imagine what a great reaction he got with that. The audience loved it!

His personal story was a very powerful device—people understood so much more about him and why he felt passionate about the company and the product. Talk about connecting purpose and passion—he emblazoned his personal imprint and made a lasting impression on his team. This event enabled him to sit down on a stool in front of an audience and speak from the heart. One guy told us, "Everybody in this company would take a bullet for Steve."

Why did Rendle go to so much trouble to develop the story and the visuals? He says that when he became president of The North Face, he realized that just "issuing directives" was not how he wanted to lead. It didn't work. He wanted *to motivate people* to accomplish great things. "In today's world, we're all so busy. But you can't just send e-mails; it simply doesn't work." What is the impact of telling a story that motivates and connects people to your mission? In an industry that at that time was barely growing, The North Face was rapidly expanding at five times the average company.

"It was eye opening when I finally realized how effective it is to stop and really find powerful ways to articulate your strategy," says Rendle. He believes that it humanized the concepts. "The impact that has, versus barking orders and expecting things to be done, is very significant," he observes. While Rendle says that he realizes that not everyone has a natural gift for telling stories, you are better off as a leader if you learn.

> Why did Rendle go to so much trouble to develop the story and the visuals? He says that when he became president of The North Face, he realized that just "issuing directives" was not how he wanted to lead.

When you tell a story from your own experience, people connect with you as a person, not just as the boss. You give them an opportunity to know you and understand how you think. The story not only connects you to them—it engages them at both the intellectual and the emotional levels. You can't do that with PowerPoint bullets and busy graphics that no one can read. If you give thought to the heart and head message you want people to hear—to the intellectual and emotional connection you want them to make—you'll be amazed at how stories come to you. Remember, you want your audience to both think and feel something when you walk off the stage or out of the meeting. Logic clarifies; feeling motivates.

Story Worksheet

It is easy to write a great story by following a step-by-step formula for story development. This worksheet provides you with four story "elements" that you should be thinking about as you write your story. The first step is to just put the whole story on paper. Then break it down into these story elements. This process will help you to focus in on the most important moments, characters, and elements of the story to streamline it and make it "tell well."

Story Elements	Your Story
Element 1: Set the scene: Who, what, when, where (enough vivid detail to take the audience there without overwhelming them with detail).	
Element 2: Expand the "moment": Relate the conversation between your "characters" or show the action (don't just *tell* what happened; relate the actual conversation back and forth or act out what happened—this is much more interesting).	

Element 3: Make your point: Conclude the story and draw from it a lesson that emerges from that story.

Element 4: Expand that story lesson to a universal theme that applies to each audience (the same story may have a different point for different audiences).

I encourage you to try this and see how much easier it is to write a good story with a powerful point by using a tool and a process. Fill out the "Story Worksheet," and consider what to put in, as well as what to leave out. Don't try to incorporate too much—a good story is really just a little "slice of life." Think of it as a snapshot, or picture, with a feeling that when told well will stick with your audience. What makes it a good story is that it has significance beyond the event itself—in other words, the story has something to teach your audience. The lesson should not be "preached" but rather "learned" through your characters, dialogue, and insights. And remember, a story should make only one clear, powerful point.

If you find that your story has more than one point, that's okay; just don't dump it on your audience all at once. You may want to deliver a point, continue your talk, and then return to the story later in the presentation to make another point. You also may find that you can use a story to make one point with a particular audience and another point with someone else. By finding many ways to use the same story, you'll find that the material you are creating can become part of your narrative as a leader. You can tell the same story again and again with different audiences and travel on it for years.

Storytelling: Not a Natural-Born Skill

If you've read my first book, *Speak Like a CEO*, you know one of the fundamental principles is that there is no such thing as a natural-born speaker. Good speakers are made, not born. Speaking is a skill, like learning how to tie your shoe or solve an algebra problem. To become an inspiring speaker, you need to approach storytelling as a skill to learn and master.

A common misconception among new speakers is that storytelling in particular is a natural gift. They see a speaker get up and tell a good story and assume that they just have a knack. Speakers work hard to come up with great story ideas; they craft their stories and practice them so that they "tell" well. While it would be an advantage to grow up in a family that tells stories, you can learn this skill anytime in life. The best way to start is by observing inspiring speakers. You also can take courses and hire a communications coach.

> *Good speakers are made, not born. Speaking is a skill, like learning how to tie your shoe or solve an algebra problem.*

Steve Rendle says that becoming a more inspiring speaker requires a new mind-set. "It's something you become committed to," he says. Now Rendle notices when people on his team or vendors pitching their services tell stories, and he appreciates the effort they are making to communicate their message. "I was sitting in on a consulting group's presentation. The topic was dry, but the speaker was able to relate his points through stories about customer experiences. This presentation was four hours long, but it went by quickly." It struck Rendle that "this is the way you present—to tie your points to a story that allows the audience to experience and understand."

Story Development

The best way to develop stories is to work with a coach or partner. Tell your story, and have your partner listen closely and reflect back to you what he or she hears. Encourage the coach or partner to just listen at first, asking only clarifying questions. Tape-record the session so that you capture everything. Have this person ask questions from the list below. Don't stop too soon. Keep going, exploring more details, and ask your coach or partner to listen for significant moments. Resist the temptation to jump to a conclusion too quickly about the lesson from the story. This is one of the biggest mistakes speakers make—they decide that they want to make a point and then try to stuff a story into that point. Allow the story to tell you what it is telling you. The following sidebar lists some questions that your coach or partner can ask to draw your story out.

The reason that it is effective to work with a coach or partner is because he or she undoubtedly will hear things differently. He or she can reflect back ideas or insights that haven't yet occurred to you. Remember, ask your partner not to interrupt at first except with clarifying questions. Then, as you go along, have your partner reflect back what he or she is hearing. The point may not be obvious at first. It will be *inside* the story. Don't *force* a point that you want to make; let it emerge. This will help you to avoid that common mistake of delivering a story with a conclusion that doesn't make sense for your audience.

These prompting questions will help you and your coach or partner to search for the point (and there may be more than one point for different audiences, which is fine). One more thing—keep in mind who might be in the audience as you tell the story. This will help you and your partner to identify a point that is relevant to them.

> *Don't force a point that you want to make; let it emerge.*

Prompting Questions for Story Writing

- Set the scene: who, what, when, and where.
- What happened first?
- Describe the key characters.
- What happened?
- And what happened after that?
- And after that?
- What else?
- Why was that significant?
- Who said what to whom? Use exact words or as close as you can come.
- Why was it significant?

- What was the painful, difficult, or challenging part of this?
- What was the significant moment?
- Why do you recall it now? Why did it matter?
- What did you learn?
- What was the take-away?
- Why is that important or significant to this audience?
- How would the audience members apply that and make it relevant to them?

Repetition—The Mantra

Aside from stories, another excellent way to drive home a message is through repetition of a phrase, theme, or idea. People need to hear an idea more than once, and usually many times, in order to remember it and act on it. Repetition is a great tool in inspirational speaking because people get excited when they "get" a concept. If you repeat it several times, they will walk out the door with a memorable idea in their heads.

A good example of the use of a mantra is how my friend Gloria Larson, president of Bentley College, anchored an important concept during her inaugural address. Quoting E. M. Forster's words, "Only connect," she returned to this mantra as she talked about her plans to move Bentley from a college to a university. Connection was an appropriate theme for Larson's presidency because her entire career had been about connecting. One of the reasons the college hired her was because she had already seen great success as a cabinet-level officer in Massachusetts government, as a successful attorney in a large law firm, and as president of the Boston Chamber of Commerce. Because she straddled and mastered so many worlds and was respected in all of them, the mantra about connection made sense. She spoke eloquently about connecting students, faculty, the city, the state, and global partners.

The mantra really hit home; people got the message. Larson received an enthusiastic, heartfelt standing ovation and dozens and dozens of wildly enthusiastic e-mails after her speech. Less than one year later, Bentley became a university. Larson's mantra was making a big impression on all the stakeholders and setting a course for the university for years to come.

So a mantra, or repetitive word, phrase, or idea, can drive your message home and make a real impact. Once established, the mantra also can be used in many presentations and communications. You can carry it from presentation to presentation, meeting to meeting, and modify it for each topic and audience. The mantra is an effective device for helping people to remember and act. The more you repeat it, the more likely it is that people will remember it, repeat it, and organize their activities around it.

Another example of the use of a mantra comes from Archelle Georgiou. After she made her initial presentation to the leadership of United Health, she delivered a scaled-down version to numerous groups of managers and teams who had not attended the meeting. She and her team told the story again and again, with the mantra "99 percent of the time the answer is 'Yes,' and its costing $108 million."

So never be afraid of repetition. It works! "I can talk about something 160 times in a week, over and over again," says Georgiou. She had a mantra and three key messages—very simple. She went back to them again and again. Eliminate the hassle, make it easy for people to get care, and restore respect to the patient-physician relationship. "If you create a mantra, it keeps the vision and the mission very visible in a simple way in front of people."

Creating an Audience Experience

Approach the development of a presentation with the idea that you want to include stories and mantras that deliver an audience experience. Your goal is for your audience to walk out the door saying, "Wow!" This doesn't mean that you need to be the world's most polished, practiced speaker. It means developing strong, memorable material that, when well told, connects your audience to mission and purpose on both the logical and the emotional levels.

You will be amazed at how the simplest stories, mantras, and devices create a memorable audience experience. For example, I once attended a lecture on planning for retirement—an important topic that can be dull in the hands of an unimaginative speaker. However, this speaker was creative and made it an experience by opening up her presentation with a Slinky in her hands. If you're a baby boomer, you probably remember that Slinkys are wiry spiral toys that will "slink" down a stairway on their own wound-up coil power. They're classic toys, which means that those of us over age 40 would connect with the example—on both an intellectual and an emotional level. The speaker's point was about approaching retirement planning with flexibility, and it worked like a charm. She then gave the toy to someone in the audience who answered a question correctly.

As a leader, you should always look for ways to incorporate devices such as this in your communications. Create a memorable moment that you can share with people. Look for the device that will make it stick. Whether you're giving a formal presentation to your organization, speaking at a conference, or just sitting down for an informal meeting with your direct reports, these devices work. Take the time to think creatively, and brainstorm ways to make a lasting impression.

Why is this important? Because one of the greatest challenges a leader faces is making the message stick. If you set out to create an experience instead of just "telling," you'll create sticky messages. One CEO client of mine wanted to get people to think "outside the box," but since this is now a stale phrase, I encouraged him to think of a way to visualize it or make it fun. Thus, as he stood on stage holding a box, he asked the audience to remind him of some of the "old" ideas they'd already tried. After he pretended to "catch" them in thin air and pretended to "put" them into the box, he then gave the audience a smile and hurled the box to the side of the stage. The point was that you can't think outside the box until you define what the box is.

What works when you want to create a device that is memorable? You have to do it with gusto and conviction! When you appear genuinely enthusiastic, passionate, and excited on stage, your emotion is contagious, and the moment is authentic. You won't get away with it if you don't believe in it and act it out. In this case, the box visual was memorable, and the CEO's genuine enthusiasm was convincing. The audience returned to their teams and talked about it with everyone! The impact reverberated throughout the organization. Now the message had "legs." Even people who didn't attend the meeting were talking about it.

You may wonder how leaders come up with these types of creative stories, mantras, and devices. One tip is to start early and let the ideas come to you. All the leaders I know who take this creative approach to communication start early and follow a process. For example, Archelle Georgiou starts thinking about what she wants to convey weeks, even months in advance. This gives her the time to consider different ways to motivate and inspire people and connect with them at their level.

Here is a step-by-step description of the creative process:

Step 1: Decide What You Want People to Know or Believe

"Early on, when I know what I'm going to talk about, I try to get very clear about what I want people to walk away with or learn," Georgiou says. "I'm very practical about that from a business perspective." While reflecting on the end game, you should solicit a lot of input. You can't expect to come up with all the ideas. "What I do is I begin to talk with people in a very spontaneous way about the three things that I would like people in my audience to learn," says Georgiou.

> *"Early on, when I know what I'm going to talk about, I try to get very clear about what I want people to walk away with or learn," says Georgiou.*

"I catch people after a meeting and run it by them because I want it to be as spontaneous as possible. I see right away whether they understand what I'm saying, and that helps me refine it. Do I have too many messages? Is it too esoteric, too broad, or not succinct?"

Talk to many people and gather ideas. Georgiou describes a time she was asked to talk to high school students about portable health care. It wasn't her usual corporate audience of leaders, so she went to a credible source—her own daughters. "Mom," said one of them, "portable health care sounds just like carrying around all your music on an iPod." "Believe me,"

Georgiou says, "When I used this analogy, that Battle Creek Michigan high school audience was awake and listening. If you can drive home a message with them, you can speak to a corporate audience."

Step 2: Start Early—Long before You "Have To"

When you start early, you have a far better opportunity to make the most of the time you have with your team. Let's face it; it is a tremendous effort and expense to bring your organization together for a major meeting. Recently, I worked with a CEO and senior leadership team who typically had started just a few days before the company's annual meeting to put together their slides. They never rehearsed, and the results were dismal. They realized they needed to put in more time.

Georgiou looks at preparing a major corporate meeting presentation the way you might approach building a dream house. You spend a lot of time talking about it, drawing, planning, thinking, revising, editing, and finalizing the plans. Then you build. "The same approach works very well with a presentation," she says. "The more time you have, the better house you will build, and the fewer headaches, change orders, and costly mistakes you will incur."

"Two years ago I was giving a talk on coordinating health care to 2,000 nurses, and I had a year to prepare. I started then, not because I am inefficient, but because I believe creativity occurs in spurts." The more time your ideas have to simmer, the better. The human mind can only create so quickly.

Step 3: Find Inspiration in Articles, Books, Movies, Quotes, News Items, Photos, and Other Sources

With the luxury of time, you can keep your eyes open to inspiration. It may be a single quote, a photograph, a movie, an article, or an experience that becomes a good story. This is what Bentley College President Gloria Larson did. The "Only Connect" sentiment came from a book she loved. It was the perfect inspiration for weaving together all the ways that the Bentley president wanted to make connections, as well as Bentley's philosophy of connecting a business education to a broader liberal arts education.

To find inspiration, you need to read books, magazines, and newspapers that you might not necessarily pick up—widen your search.

> *To find inspiration, you need to read books, magazines, and newspapers that you might not necessarily pick up—widen your search. Don't just look to the* Wall Street Journal. *Pick up a magazine in the airport or at the dentist's office and read something "foreign."*

Don't just look to the *Wall Street Journal.* Pick up a magazine in the airport or at the dentist's office and read something "foreign." Watch popular television shows (even if you don't see them regularly), and listen to radio just so that you are plugged into what is going on. Watch a movie or go to a show, and cultivate a genuine sense of curiosity.

The simplest device can inspire you. For example, you've probably heard the famous Faith Whattlesey quote, "Ginger Rogers did everything that Fred Astaire did, except backwards and in high heels." I liked this quote for a presentation I was giving to women leaders in the food and restaurant industry. The point I wanted to make was that women executives still face challenges that men don't face—and that it is important for them to become very, very good communicators. I found a movie clip of Astaire and Rogers gliding across a stage singing and dancing and used it to open and close the presentation. The movie clip anchored the quote in their minds and created an upbeat feeling as well. Many people in the audience remarked about it after the speech. So it was memorable, and perhaps equally important, as the speaker, it inspired me and made me feel better about the presentation.

Step 4: Throw It into a File

Archelle Georgiou says that it's important to get organized and make your approach to communicating as a leader more fun. "I take as much time as I can take, cutting out articles, quotes, and phrases that are inspiring." For the talk for nurses on health care, she found a *New York Times Sunday Magazine* article about Aristotle and his approach to rhetoric, pathos, ethos, and logos. "I thought with my Greek background it would be a wonderful framework," she says.

Ideas don't usually come to you while you're sitting in front of a blank computer screen. Read, watch, and listen for inspiration, and then, when you find it, throw it into a file. You never know when you're going to come across something that hits you as good material, and if you have a place to put it, you'll be able to refer back to it when you need it.

If it resonates for you, in all likelihood you'll be able to sell it to your audience. If you feel the power of the idea, you will speak in an inspiring way. Gloria Larson found a quote that resonated for her, and it allowed her to deliver an inaugural address that made real, emotional impact. It's amazing how one device can transform your presentations and allow you to communicate with purpose and passion.

> *Ideas don't usually come to you while you're sitting in front of a blank computer screen. Read, watch, and listen for inspiration, and then, when you find it, throw it into a file.*

Step 5: Create and Organize Your Visuals

I have a cartoon in my electronic files. It shows a group of comical-looking businesspeople sitting around a table, staring approvingly at the boss, who points to a pie chart. "Don't turn the page!" one of the team says. "That's the most fascinating pie chart I've ever seen!" declares another. The caption reads, *"George suffered from classic signs of attention surplus disorder."*

I use this cartoon to make a humorous point about how dull most visuals are. Most presenters spend hours and hours on tiny little graphics and bullet points that their audiences can't even read, much less comprehend. While it may be the norm in business, there is no point in using visuals that don't have impact. You're better off with no visuals at all. You stand out as a leader and communicate your ideas clearly and powerfully when you have great visuals that make an impact.

One mistake that many leaders make is to start preparing their presentations by creating their PowerPoints first. They spend hours and hours on this, with the misguided idea that at the end they will figure out what they're going to say about the slides. If this sounds like your approach, don't worry—it's what most people do. But when you think about it, it makes far more sense by starting with what you want to say and then building your visuals around that. You may, of course, include some bullet points, but you don't want to read your presentation from the slides. Bullet points are boring for your audience and do nothing to enhance your communication or your stature as a leader. You cannot afford to be boring, and you cannot motivate when you are reading slides.

One way to create visuals that have more impact is to start with blank sheets of paper. Think about pictures, photos, and creative ways to elegantly and simply make your point. Archelle Georgiou says, "I lay out 20 to 30 blank pieces of paper on the floor. Each piece of paper represents a slide. Each paper gets one picture or sentence. The sequences of sentences must make sense and tell a story. It has to end in a conclusion," she explains. Each slide you prepare should be simple, easy to grasp, and memorable. By applying this rigorous standard, you can ensure that when you walk away, people will be talking about your presentation.

As CEO or a senior leader, you may have people who can help you to create your presentation visuals, but don't just turn it over to someone without spending time talking about the outline and key concepts for your presentation. If you make the mistake of asking someone to go off and create a presentation for you, without outlining and defining concepts, stories, and elements, what you will get back is a slide deck out of someone else's head that you will find impossible to deliver with conviction. Work together, prepare your talk first, and then bring in people who can help you visualize the concepts. Work with them to be sure that they understand the themes, ideas, and concepts you want to convey.

Step 6: Make Sure to Put You in Your Story

People want to know you as a leader. They are inspired by leaders who connect with them. This is why you have to put *you* into your presentation. By this, I don't mean making yourself the center of the story. What I mean is making sure that the concepts and stories *come from you and reflect your purpose, passion, and values.*

When working with a speechwriter, it is important to spend time with him or her so that he or she can gather your original stories, ask questions, and understand your viewpoint. As a CEO or senior leader, you get the product you deserve. Get involved in the speech development, and you greatly reduce the risk that the talk will fail. If people in your audience don't believe that it's you speaking—that the words on the page are your words—they simply won't connect. A nice talk written for you is transparently obvious, and your audience won't find it credible. Make time to work closely with your speechwriter, and allow him or her to capture your words in your way.

Other Ways to Use Stories

Use the stories in all your communications so that your message is repeated. Have a speech posted on the intranet (not just your slides, but a full text, including the stories). Videotape every important speech, and stream the video on your Web site. Write the story into your blog if you have one. In your public relations efforts, you can incorporate the story in your interviews with reporters. As I have pointed out before, repetition is a great tool in motivation.

Once you have learned how to develop stories and material for your meetings or presentations, it's time to consider how to enhance your leadership presence. People are inspired by a leader who commands the room with confidence and energy. It is a skill to speak with passion and conviction. In Chapter 10 we'll look at strategies that motivating leaders use to convey energy, enthusiasm, and intensity.

Summary

- Stories connect people with purpose and passion. And it's easier than you imagine to include stories in your presentations.
- Good stories are all around you. Every single day people are doing interesting things that could become a story for your next presentation.
- A lot of people think that a good storyteller is born, but storytellers are made. Storytelling isn't a gift; it's a skill that anyone can learn.

■ When you tell a story from your own experience, people really connect with you as a person, not just as the boss. They understand a little more about how you think.

Focus on creating an "experience" for your audience. Take them on a journey—it will transform your presentation.

10

On Stage: Speaking with Passion and Conviction

Nothing great was ever achieved without enthusiasm.

—Ralph Waldo Emerson

I HAD THE EXTRAORDINARY opportunity to participate in a "music para-digm" workshop by conductor Roger Nierenberg, who, after a distin-guished career at the helm of two American orchestras, became a well-known speaker on the topic of "orchestrating leadership." It was a memorable, inspiring presentation. Members of the audience, all CEOs and presidents of companies, were invited to sit in the orchestra pit next to professional musicians and to watch and listen from the musician's point of view.

As the orchestra played short passages from Mendelssohn's Fifth Symphony, Nierenberg drew parallels between conducting an orchestra and leading an organization. At one point he comically walked away from the stage and instructed the orchestra to play without him. The group did a pretty good job. "Scary, huh?" he said. Yet, when he came back to the podium, took up the baton again, and then resumed direct-ing with *intention* and *intensity*, he extracted from that same group a peak performance. His energy and intensity produced a far richer sound than had occurred without him, a much more cohesive piece that included perfect interplay between the musical sections. This performance moved almost every audience member to tears. A few actually were outright sobbing.

At one point I had the chance to move up to the front. Sitting no more than five feet from the conductor was incredibly intense. From this vantage point, I felt energy radiating from every part of his body and emanating from his baton. Sweeping his arms upward, he urged his musicians to play up into the crescendos; lowering the baton and conveying tiny snippets of movement, he urged them to play more tenderly. I had not seen nor felt this intensity from afar.

Up close, I could see how passionate he had to be to bring out the best from the individual musicians and therefore produce a powerful, cohesive musical performance. It struck me that a leader who wants to communicate and inspire has to communicate with the same energy and passion. You must communicate all the way to the back of the room in order to connect with each individual in your organization and orchestrate a powerful performance from your team. It takes intense effort to do this—to communicate in a way that connects and moves people. If you are able to raise your level of intensity, people will "read" and resonate with this emotion coming from you, and they will be inspired to perform at the highest level.

> *His energy and intensity produced a far richer sound than had occurred without him, a much more cohesive piece that included perfect interplay between the musical sections. This performance moved almost every audience member to tears.*

In our survey, people often talked about how vital it is for leaders to reach out, connect, and communicate with passion. "If a leader isn't passionate about the strategy he or she wants others to follow, then the results will be marginal and difficult to measure. Good communication skills and passion create something intangible that drives an organization forward," said one respondent.

At the same conference, I had the opportunity to hear a keynote speech by Sung-Joo Kim, chairperson and CEO of Sungjoo Group/MCM, a purveyor of designer handbags and luggage. She spoke eloquently about how important passion is to running her successful company. She mentioned that while people assumed that she must run a global organization like a military operation, that wasn't her style. "The definition of power," she told us, "is earning their heart."

For every leader who hopes to motivate and inspire others, the goal must be to not only speak with passion and intensity but also through your stories to earn their hearts. Kim connected with her audience through a compelling story about her upbringing in a wealthy family in Korea. Although she grew up the daughter of a billionaire Korean businessman, her privilege provided her no real advantages because she really wanted a career. In Korea, women of her generation were discouraged from going to college or even speaking up at the dinner table. She was punished often for countering her brother's opinions. Remarkably, she convinced her father to allow her to attend Amherst College in the United States. After earning several degrees and launching her fashion career at Bloomingdale's, she then founded Sungjoo Group, the parent company for brands including Gucci, Yves Saint Laurent, Sonia Rykiel, and a recent acquisition, MCM. She built a very successful business without an ounce of support from her father and brothers. In fact, they essentially disowned her.

Yet Kim is obviously an upbeat, compassionate businesswoman who is able to convey this emotion on stage. She talked about how she developed her philosophy of business—rather than "serve to succeed," she seeks to "succeed to serve." She talked about giving back, helping to raise the standards of living in her native Korea. Telling her unusual story with a "heart" message made a real impression on the audience of women leaders. While I had not previously known the brand, I was so impressed that I started noticing its signature handbags in high-end department stores.

What I took away from her talk was a reminder of how important it is to share your story in a passionate way that is authentic with your audience. While Kim was not a fiery speaker—in fact, she was rather reserved—her quiet energy came shining through because the story had heart. When you take a risk, tell a personal story and deliver it with authentic emotion, you make an impact. You don't have to be theatrical to convey passion and energy to your audience.

Passion Comes from Within

The first rule about passion is that it comes from within. The second rule is that it is expressed differently in each of us. There is no one way to communicate passion, except for this: You have to *feel* it. This is why it is so important to get in touch with your purpose and mission. You can communicate passion and enthusiasm only if you feel it inside.

Whatever your personality, introverted or extroverted, quiet or outgoing, you can tap into your authentic feelings and convey emotions with an appropriate level of intensity that resonates for your audience. Don't confuse passion with drama. It is not necessary—in fact, it is inadvisable—to be overly dramatic. For most people, that would not be authentic. Passion isn't about shouting, flailing your arms, or pacing the stage. It's about getting in touch with your feelings and revealing those to your audience.

> *The first rule about passion is that it comes from within. The second rule is that it is expressed differently in each of us. There is no one way to communicate passion, except for this: You have to feel it.*

It's important to find your own comfortable way to express your passion. It should be authentic to you. You may need to dig deep to find or rediscover what you feel passionate about. Once you're in touch with it, hold onto it, and learn to tap into it when you need it.

One way to evaluate how effective you are in conveying passion is to record a presentation in front of a live audience and review the videotape with a coach or trusted advisor. If you have ever watched your presentation on videotape, you know that the video doesn't lie. You may have been surprised or disappointed that your energy seemed low, your voice didn't carry, or you didn't make good eye contact. You may have thought that you were really connecting through body language, voice, and strong material. The reason most people don't connect is because they need to bring more intensity to the performance in order to convey it to an audience. So you need to tap into those genuine feelings and convey more intensity. The rule is to feel it and then to express it.

Business speaking is not the same as a theatrical performance, but there is more than a dash of performance art to it. We can all learn from the great "method" actors because they don't pretend; instead, they draw on their personal experiences to locate the emotion they need for their performance. In telling a business story, for example, you will be more effective if you transport yourself back to the moment and feel the feel-

> *Business speaking is not the same as a theatrical performance, but there is more than a dash of performance art to it.*

ings you felt then. Getting in touch with these feelings and being able to call on them at any time is the secret to conveying genuine passion on stage. You don't need to "act" so much as just convey the actual emotion you feel.

David Woods, an outstanding and passionate speaker and executive director of the nonprofit organization Life and Health Insurance Foundation for Education (LIFE), puts it this way: "There is an element of show biz to it. You have to be able to display sincerity and passion. You have to be a bit of an actor. But I don't talk about things I don't believe in; I only talk about what I care about. By caring about it, I don't have to reach too deep. I'm an emotional person; if I know my messages very well, then I can let myself go, to get emotional and passionate." Woods says that he is not ashamed and embarrassed because he knows that he can make an impact.

Authenticity is essential. People know when it's not real. When you speak with *authentic* passion and conviction, when it comes from inside you, people connect with you. If you were disappointed that the talk felt flat and uninspiring, chances are that your audience felt the same way. You are far more effective as a leader if you convey a range of emotion. Leaders who speak well do the same thing actors do—they get "up" for a performance.

Is Passion Appropriate for Business?

If the word *passion* makes you uncomfortable, I can understand that. But passion really isn't a scary thing. One definition of passion is "a strong emotion, a great enthusiasm for something." As leaders, I think that we all want to convey enthusiasm. We want everyone in the organization to feel enthusiastic about their work and their contributions. Speaking with passion, therefore, is simply about conveying the emotions that you feel and hope to invoke in others.

Is passion appropriate for business? I think that it's *missing* from business. Your work is an expression of who you are in the world.

> *Is passion appropriate for business? I think that it's what's missing from business. Our work is an expression of who we are in the world.*

Yet, if you get up and give a robotic presentation, you are not projecting the real you. Too many leaders miss the opportunity to connect with their audiences by sharing their excitement, joy, enthusiasm, and conviction. We often paper it all over with a "businesslike" demeanor and fancy, meaningless jargon, flat language, and an avalanche of complex, unreadable slides.

Ellen Parker, of Project Bread, knows the importance of getting in touch with your passion. When she analyzed hunger programs and saw how she could change things, she became genuinely excited, and her excitement ignited a desire to communicate her ideas. She became committed to going out and talking even to skeptics about what was possible. "If I weren't passionate about making change, none of this would be happening. I'm passionate about process, and I hope [that] others connect with that passion when I can tell a different story about hunger."

Another executive who has spent a career in financial services told me that he feels passionate about helping people save for a secure retirement. He came by this passion because of personal experience. It wasn't that he grew up poor—in fact, his was a middle-class family; his parents sent him to college, but as a result of sacrificing for him, they were not able to save much for retirement. Fortunately, he became financially successful and thus was able to help out with their bills, but he shuddered to think how it would have turned out had he not had the resources. So helping clients secure their future became a personal crusade for him. The passion was real. It is easy for him to speak with passion because all he has to do is recall the sacrifices his parents made.

Your Words, Your Way

Have you ever been in a situation where you absolutely had to deliver a presentation that was not your own? If so, then you know how difficult it is to give a talk that came out of someone else's head. They wrote the words and created the slides, and you had to do your best to guess what they meant or interpret the material as your own. You may have struggled to find examples or to provide context because you frankly didn't follow their thinking. This is the opposite of the preceding examples, where leaders talk from the heart. Audiences have a high degree of radar for presenters who are delivering someone else's material. They know when you're not delivering your own words in your own way.

This is why, when speaking from a script, you need to be sure that *you* are *in* that script. We discussed this in Chapter 9. Whether you write it or someone else writes it, your presentation needs to have your ideas, stories, phrasing, and language. Even a practiced professional speaker would struggle to deliver a talk that someone else wrote without his or her significant input. It's just very difficult to get up and speak energetically using someone else's words. It's especially challenging—in fact, nearly impossible—to do a great job if you have only practiced the speech once or twice. In that case, you're still trying to figure out what's on the next page! Speaking with passion and connecting authentically with your audience is only possible when the words are your own, or at least you make them your own, by mastering the script.

In suggesting that the presentation has to be yours, I don't mean to say that you have to write every word. If you are running a large company, this may not be practical. However, you do have to be a full participant in the process. Andrew Liveris, CEO of Dow Chemical, an exceptional speaker, doesn't write his own speeches anymore, but he works very closely with his speechwriters and spends significant time with his communications advisor. They know him so well that they can

> *Audiences have highly tuned radar. They sense when you're not delivering your words in your own way. Even when speaking from a script, you need to be sure that you are in that script.*

pretty much write a speech the way he would say it; they can "hear" his voice when they write. Thus, while he may not be sitting at the typewriter, his ideas, phrases, and even cadence are easily accessible to the writers, as if he had written the speech himself. Liveris spends a lot of time with his writers. He also practices speeches many times so that he internalizes the message.

Liveris discovered how important it is to use your words your way when he was a young leader of one of Dow's business units. He was preparing to give a talk to the company's Asian Diversity Network. "At that time, I wasn't used to having a speechwriter," says Liveris. "However, our communications group gave me a detailed outline and talking points they thought this audience would appreciate."

Liveris sat in his hotel room the night before, pouring over the talk. "I was reading the script and saying, this isn't me. So I looked inside myself." The topic was "How Asians Can Adapt to Western Culture." It turns out that Liveris had spent years on assignment in Asia, so he felt that he had better insights than the communications group about how this mostly Asian audience felt. "So I scrapped the talk, wrote down five things I wanted to say, walked onto the podium the next morning with 600 in the room, and spoke from my heart," he says.

What happened next was amazing. He had an overwhelming feeling of empathy and connection with his audience. He could see that they felt the same way; he was really connecting. "As I looked around the room, people seemed immobilized. Clearly, I was saying something that resonated. I was saying what *I* believed. The standing ovation was mind-numbing. People had tears in their eyes and came up to thank me."

This was the moment when Liveris realized that if he spoke about what *he* believed in and articulated it his way, he would be able to connect with any audience. "That is something that I saw myself doing again," he said. "Now I try to find ways to connect with individuals in the audience, to say what I believe, and to say it in a way that is clear and not ambiguous."

Gather Audience Intelligence

To be a leader who speaks and inspires, you have to know your audience. If you don't know your audience well, you need to gather some intelligence about them. Even if you are speaking to a team in your own organization, you need to pick up the phone and find out what's going on. If you are completely unfamiliar with the group, you or the writer should call and talk with the meeting planner—a simple step but one that many speakers simply never take. Set up a 15-minute call, ask a short list of questions—and you won't believe how much you can learn. The meeting planner is always grateful to any speaker who takes time to do this.

With a few questions you can usually find out exactly what is on the mind of the audience, what their challenges are, and what they'd like to know from you. Your speech to the same audience could be different in July than it would have been in January—because their lives, industries, and challenges change. A speech on the same topic will be different for an industry group in a different part of the country or the world. You can have a lot more fun if you're completely in tune with your audience.

For example, I imagine that when Sung-Joo Kim speaks to a fashion audience, she's going to tell "insider" fashion industry stories that engage and inspire audience members. However, when she speaks to an audience of women CEOs, such as the one I attended, she will tell stories about what it's like to be a woman CEO of a global company. We will be inspired by those experiences, the lessons she has learned, and the wisdom she has gained.

To create a motivating, inspiring talk for each audience, here are questions you can ask the meeting planner:

- What is the goal of this meeting or event?
- Who will be in the audience?
- What is their interest in this topic?
- What are their challenges in this area?
- What are their needs as individuals and as a group?
- Why would they be interested in hearing from me?
- What would you recommend I keep in mind as I prepare my talk?
- What is the benefit to them?
- What will be happening before and after I speak?
- What will be the mood at the event?
- Is there anything I should be sure to do? Or not do?
- What have other successful speakers done that really worked?
- What else do I need to know to make this a great talk?

Once you and your speechwriter understand the audience, you will find it far easier to brainstorm creative ideas and come up with great stories and devices that make your presentation memorable. You'll feel far more confident as you go into the presentation about your prospects for connecting with that audience and make an impact. When you walk on stage, you'll feel better prepared and have appropriate remarks and material. This means that you'll be able to focus on how to communicate, project, and radiate energy and confidence. There is nothing worse than walking into a room and thinking, "Gee, I hope this talk works." There are enough variables in speaking; eliminate the mystery and give yourself a better chance to connect by being prepared.

> *Find out what is on the mind of the audience, what their problems and challenges are, and what motivates them.*

You don't have to write a brand-new speech for each group; just tailor it with relevant examples and stories. Whether you are speaking nationally or internationally, include examples that you know your audience will appreciate. Make it a practice to understand cultural issues and be sensitive to how your message will come across. It always changes: There is even a difference between speaking to a predominantly male audience and a predominantly female audience. Pause to consider how your stories and advice will come across. You want to include stories, examples, quotes, or videos for women that are about women.

Imagine how much easier it will be to connect with your audience and speak with passion if you have done this background work and feel confident that you've got a speech that was created for them. This is such a simple rule, but it makes a big difference to your audience. So many leaders miss out on opportunities to do this; you can travel the country or the world, but the trip is only worthwhile if you really connect with your audience. If you're going to make the effort to get on an airplane and take time out of your schedule to speak, do it well, and do all you can to connect.

Tune in While on Stage

When Andrew Liveris gave his speech to the Asian Diversity Network, he stumbled onto another important insight—that is, how important it is to watch the reactions of the audience. When he looked out into the audience, he could see that audience members were moved to tears; he could feel the emotion in the room. This energized his performance and helped him to push forward and make an even stronger connection at the end. The longer he spoke, the more engaged he was with the audience.

When you pay attention to your audience and really tune in, you will be amazed at how it fuels your performance and helps you to give a more inspiring talk. You need to know what you want to say, of course, so that when you stand on stage, you're able to look out there and see people. It is part of the joy of the experience on stage to watch them, read their faces, and gauge their reactions. The best, most inspiring speakers and leaders take joy in connecting with the audience throughout a speech.

No matter what your personality type, you can connect with your audience by just tuning in. Ken Leibler, former president and CEO of Liberty Financial Companies, is an analytical person who discovered the power of tuning into how people are feeling. Under Leibler, Liberty grew from a relatively small asset management firm with two subsidiaries and $15 billion under management into one with eight subsidiaries and $65

> *Imagine how connected you will feel to your audience if you are relating a story about them.*

billion under management. He went on to become CEO of several other companies, including the Boston Stock Exchange.

"For people to feel committed to a strategy, you have to touch them emotionally," he observes. "You have to get beyond pie charts and logic, and you have to try to engage people in doing something that has meaning to them," he advises. "People really want meaning in their work. They want to go home and tell people [that] they are making a contribution to something bigger than themselves, and not just making a larger profit." He concludes, "To be effective, you have to think about how to engage people beyond the financial and analytical and make it relevant to their work."

Work the Room and Connect

A good way to connect with people is to walk around before and after your talk. The short conversations help you to pick up information and vibes you can bring to the stage. This helps you to adapt your message and suit the mood of the audience. It is always difficult to stand at the front of a room full of strangers. However, if you take the time to "work the room," shake hands, say hello, make "friends," and pick up these signals, the faces are familiar and you adapt your material so that you can connect as a friend. Plus, audience members will be far more favorably inclined and actually will smile back if they've already met you.

It's amazing how quickly you can pick up on the mood of the audience in a few short conversations prior to your talk. Not long ago I was getting ready to give a presentation to a client company. These were people on track to become senior leaders, and they were also in jobs that brought them close to their customers. They were in touch with their marketplace, aware of their customers' challenges, and had a real sense of how things were going. Prior to the meeting, standing in a circle of about five, I asked a few of these leaders who were from Asia, Europe, and the United States, "How's the company doing?" and heard a consistently positive message from all of them. This helped me to assess quickly how well my talking points would resonate, whether I would have to adapt the message, and also to know whether I would need to take a different tone when I walked onto the stage.

Many speakers stand on "ceremony" and wait in the wings prior to their speeches or sit at the reserved front table until the moment they get up to speak. There is no rule that you need to stay hidden prior to your talk; in fact, it creates emotional distance between you and the audience. It also makes it more difficult when you finally do walk on stage and look out at this sea of people. You may feel shocked or surprised, and it can throw you off your game. It's far better to circulate so that audience members become familiar faces before you begin. Hang out in the lobby, shake hands at the tables, or greet people in the back of the room before the program begins so that you get to know them, and they get to know you.

"To speak with passion and really connect, I have found that it's really good to get there in advance of the talk and mingle with the crowd to get a sense of the mood," says David Woods, executive director of LIFE, the insurance industry organization. "You want to understand the overall feeling of the crowd." Mingling does require some energy and planning on your part. And there will be times when it just isn't possible. "But it is well worth the effort," says Woods. "It sets everything off on the right foot and tells people [that] you want to be there."

Love Your Audience

Woods also says that it may sound corny, but to show emotion, you need to *love your audience.* "To trust the audience is to love the audience." Early on, when he first started giving a lot of speeches, he wrote in block letters on the top of each manuscript the word LOVE. "It would remind me that I have to love that audience; I have to care about them. If I feel

> *. . . [I]t may sound corny, but to show emotion, you need to love your audience.*

that way about them, I am not afraid to show emotion or passion, and I can let it all hang out," he explains.

Woods admits that this advice is more than some people are prepared to act on. When people see him speak and ask him, "How do you do that?" he shares the technique. Some of these friends say, "Great idea!" and others say, "Thanks, but no thanks." However, the "good ones" come back and thank him later, he says! "They tell me [that] they were a little afraid to try it—but it worked."

Woods' idea of writing a message on the top of your manuscript is a great device. Whatever words you want to remember that will help you connect on an emotional level with your audience will work. This technique can help you to immerse yourself in the moment with an intention. It will be the last thing you see before you start your talk.

Of course, there are other ways to get revved up for a presentation performance. Some speakers listen to upbeat music, sing along, even dance. Some take a walk outside and breathe fresh air to get their blood moving. Some get energy by chatting with people right before they hit the stage. Experiment and find out what works for you because this is a very personal thing. The point is to do what it takes to get up for the performance and feel energized as you walk on stage.

The Importance of Practice

Knowing your message is all part of connecting with your audience at an emotional level. In order to be effective in motivating and inspiring people, you simply must practice your talk. You need to be so familiar with your messages that when you get up to speak, you are able to focus entirely on connecting with people and moving them to think and feel. Practice is the secret to a great performance every single time. It allows you to be with your audience completely while you are standing at the front of the room. You worry a lot less about what's on the next slide or in the next paragraph of your script and focus again on projecting energy and confidence.

Practice also helps you to act like yourself when you get up there. Believe it or not, you have to rehearse this; it doesn't happen naturally. Many people go into an awkward "presentation mode" when they step to the front of a room. They turn formal, move stiffly, and come across as serious or robotic. While you want to appear professional, that doesn't mean stiff. You want to look comfortable, at ease, and confident. Through practice, you learn how to exude that comfort and fluid movement. Whether you plan to speak from notes, script, slides, or index cards, it has to be easy and flow naturally. No matter what your format, your body language, voice, and facial expression should convey comfort. The image you should hold in your mind is that you are having a conversation with your audience. You want audience members to see you as comfortable in your own skin.

Practicing and learning the material well frees you to do what you want to do physically on stage. You can stand up, sit on a stool, walk around, lean on the podium, or even walk out into the audience. The way you use the space on stage can enhance your communication tremendously. The physical part of speaking is important, especially in motivating people. As you move freely around the room commanding the space, people will enjoy watching and listen more closely.

> *Knowing your material also frees you to do what you want to do physically on stage. You can stand up, sit on a stool, walk around, lean on the podium, or even walk out into the audience.*

Prepare for Surprises

Even with the best preparation, there will be surprises. In fact, what is surprising is when everything goes exactly as planned. Speaking is a live event; anything can and will go wrong from time to time, so you have to be able to "roll with the punches."

I remember a time when I was speaking at the close of a sales meeting for a client in Atlanta. The team was tired after two days of training. Ten minutes before I went on stage, the room started buzzing—and not because I was the speaker! A rare sleet-snow storm was about to descend on Atlanta.

These seasoned travelers immediately opened up their cell phones and BlackBerries. They wanted to get out of town on the next flight! Even I was calling my office! When I finally walked onto the stage, it was obvious that no one was interested in the program. I acknowledged the situation all of us were facing with a few jokes and significantly shortened my talk. I took no offense when people started trickling out of the room in the middle of the program. I would have done the same thing. I probably should have ended even sooner.

The point is that anything can go wrong, so you have to adjust. Every presentation won't be a home run, although you always should give it your best effort. Don't worry about the things that you can't control, just the things you can.

No matter what happens, focus on speaking with energy no matter what snafus befall the meeting. Never let the situation throw you. Go up and deliver your presentation the best way you can, and your energy will carry you through. Andrew Liveris, of Dow Chemical, says, "What I focus on in speaking is . . . how to convey [the message] with the right energy. It is connectivity; trying to get a sense of the mood and environment. [You] . . . adapt to your audience and the setting so [that] you have maximum impact."

Find opportunities to get up and talk, formally or informally, whenever you can so that you can develop a higher level of intensity and passion in your speaking style. Effective leaders look for ways to get in front of people and practice these skills because they know that the better they get, the more effective they are—and the more fun it is. Whether you have 200 or 2,000 people in a room, don't miss the opportunity to develop these skills. They are important to your success and the success of every leader in your organization. In Chapter 11 we'll look at how you can involve your entire team of leaders in making communication job number 1.

Summary

- You must communicate with passion and intensity so that everyone "reads" you like the conductor of an orchestra and is able therefore to perform at their peak.
- When you express this passion, you can't help but inspire others. The first rule about passion is that it comes from within.
- Don't confuse passion with drama. You do not need to be over the top—just in touch with the fire that burns within, because people know it when they see it.
- Transport yourself back to the moment and be in touch with the feelings you felt when the story happened. You don't need to "act," just convey the actual emotion you feel.
- Your work is an expression of who you are in the world. Don't miss your target with a "businesslike" demeanor and fancy, meaningless jargon, flat language, and an avalanche of complex, unreadable slides.

Knowing your message is all part of connecting with your audience at an emotional level. Practice builds confidence and helps you to be yourself on stage.

11

Everyday Motivation: Make Communication Your Job Number 1

Today is your day! Your mountain is waiting.

So . . . get on your way.

—THEODOR SEUSS GEISEL (DR. SEUSS)

A FEW YEARS AGO, Jeff Taylor, founder of Monster.com and Eons, started collecting the name badges he wore with the title "speaker" on them. He was on the road giving so many presentations that the collection quickly grew to fill several shoe boxes. He considered photographing them for the cover of a book to make a point about his role as "master sales person." He says, "I think that's my job. Speaking is my natural spot as a leader, and I probably crafted that role, even though I was a pretty shy kid in high school."

Like Jeff Taylor, you have to make communication your top priority. As a leader, you must influence people to affect change and drive the company strategy forward. This means that you have to think about communication as a daily, even hourly activity. This may be a big change in how you see your role and schedule your time. If you have come up through a series of operational roles where your success was based on your technical skill and project management, you may be unaccustomed to taking time for these activities. Most of us are rewarded in the early part of our careers for "doing," so it is not natural for us to spend so much time communicating and motivating others.

In a strategic leadership role, you need to spend the majority of your time communicating with other people. This is why it's so important to develop the skills we've discussed in previous chapters. You and every single leader in the organization have to shift your thinking to embrace the idea that communication is job number 1.

The way to make things happen in your organization is to embrace communication and take charge of when and how you deliver the message. If you accept and adopt this role, you have an enormous opportunity to inspire people and move your company forward. The time you invest in your speeches, presentations, and meetings takes on considerable importance because it is your highest priority. Where in the past you may have seen making a presentation as a necessary evil, now you will see it as perhaps the most important thing you do. When your mind-set shifts, it is far easier to schedule these activities and honor the time on your calendar. As you reorient your thinking about how you can best make a difference, communications with employees, clients, customers, analysts, board members, the media, and the public move to the top.

Your communication role evolves as you move to higher levels of the organization and as your company grows. Jeff Taylor describes how his role progressed: "In the beginning, it was about directing the innovation and product development; later, I became more of a traditional CEO, taking on an outside role." Later, Taylor says, as ". . . Chief Monster, my job evolved further to 'pound the brand table at critical junctures.' It was . . . a Pied Piper role. I had the brand in my title, and what I communicated had to be more vision-oriented."

As chairman, Taylor relished the role of telling his company's story.

> *Your communication role evolves as you move to higher levels of the organization and as your company grows.*

"The more you 'get' leadership, the more you will be drawn to communicating outside the company. Storytelling is the best way to get your message across. I find through storytelling [that] you also learn something because you have to retell it."

Every Leader's Job

Every leader in an organization has responsibility for communicating, motivating, and aligning the organization. In today's business world, good communication skills are a "must have." If leaders are not effective communicators, it will be much more difficult to reach every employee and every customer. Great organizations know how important it is to promote leaders who are good communicators.

Bill Lane, Jack Welch's speechwriter at General Electric (GE) for 20 years, wrote in his memoir, *Jacked Up*, "Every single one of the . . . [people] who were in the original field of 23 potential GE CEOs is a good-to-great 'presenter.' Some have some weaknesses, usually related to PowerPoint, but none could ever be described as 'deadly.' You simply cannot get a job at this level if you can't stand up and teach, and persuade, excite, . . . and lead."

As a CEO or senior leader, think of executive communication as a team activity. Develop a group of leaders whom you know have the skill and desire to make communications a priority. They should work as hard as you do on communication and be as focused as you are on motivating and inspiring people to get great results. As you consider who you want to have on your team, who you want to promote and put into the succession plan, this should be one of the top considerations. You cannot afford to bring on people or move them up if they do not have this skill. They need to have not only the technical, business, and analytical skills but also the ability and strong desire to communicate and inspire others. Their professional development plans and your leadership development programs should focus intensely on leadership communication skills, going far beyond basic presentation training.

> *In today's business world, good communication skills are a "must have."*

You may have noticed that new leaders often don't see communication as their strength, so they avoid it. When they are not good presenters or communicators, they tend to fall back to old skills that involve doing rather than leading. They go in and micromanage their teams and get involved in minutiae that don't advance their team or organization.

This is so primarily because it feels comfortable to default to the things they like to do.

Usually these leaders have no idea how much this will hold them back in their careers. Sometimes their bosses don't realize how much it is holding back progress toward business goals, too. As a leader, you have to help these people "face the music" and get comfortable learning a new skill. Even if they resist, make it clear that you expect them to develop the skill, attend training, or work with a communications coach. Young leaders also will follow your example. I have more than once heard from a new executive that his or her goal is to speak as well as the CEO of the company. When you set the example, leaders in your organization will want to be good, too.

So make it clear how important it is to develop communication skills, and push your high-potential leaders to get out there to do it. If they feel a little uncomfortable at first, that's okay. It will help them to raise the level of their game. Jeff Taylor says, "I have this expression that 'If you are nervous, you are in danger of learning something. And if you're not nervous, you didn't do a big enough presentation!' I lean into the adrenaline rush as opposed to leaning back."

I remember a first-time CEO who had two people on his team who were terrible presenters. They had a major meeting coming up, but the two were not working on their presentations and resisted his suggestion to get coaching. They told him that they would work on it, and then they would cancel their coaching appointments. Yet the CEO was reluctant to push them. It wasn't until after the meeting, where they gave poor presentations, that he realized that he should have insisted. The lesson is: Don't wait until it is too late—if it is an important meeting, if you are investing significant resources, if important people will be there, you need to set people up for success by getting them the help they need.

> *Don't wait until it is too late—if it is an important meeting, if you are investing significant resources, if important people will be there, you need to set people up for success by getting them the help they need.*

In the case of this CEO, he was reluctant in part because he didn't realize that he couldn't do it all himself. As we discussed the importance of the CEO getting his entire team to focus on communications, I took out a napkin, and I sketched out the organization chart. There was the CEO at the top, and below him a bottleneck of people who were not communicating with their teams. It was virtually impossible for him to drive the message and strategy forward without their participation. He noted that there was no one on his team who was helping him with this enormous task. He was a lone ranger, trying to communicate and motivate the entire organization (see Figure 11–1). I encouraged him to imagine what it would look like if every leader were engaged in communicating the vision and strategy. "I get it," he said, "I have to push for this to happen."

Bottlenecks

If you look at the figure and think that it looks like your organization, it is time to think about how you can make communication *everyday job number 1* for every leader on your team. If people are not pulling their weight or have become lackadaisical about giving good presentations and

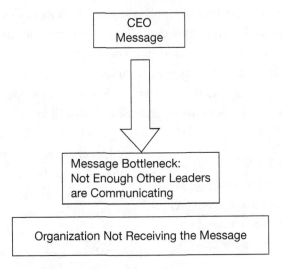

Figure 11–1 Communication Bottleneck

communicating effectively with their teams, you can change things and *must* because you cannot reach everyone yourself.

If there is a vacuum of information and people aren't getting the message, they certainly won't be motivated and inspired. In fact, you'll have a vacuum. This is when people will start making stuff up. If they don't know what's going on, they will invent it.

Greg Case, CEO of Aon Corporation, says, "It's essential that our [entire leadership] team communicate all the time. It's not the Greg Case show. I'm not good enough." Case insists that his team come together around a game plan for communications and then lock arms to get it done. "We're aligned around the game plan, we model behaviors we ask others to do, and we trust each other. I expect our senior team to absolutely drive the plan and help people understand."

Set the Expectation

Vikki Pryor, of SBLI USA Mutual Life Insurance Company, sets an expectation by including people at every level in her company as speakers at meetings. On the roster, she places senior leaders, managers, and even people in front-line positions. "I tell people [that] the quarterback is not the most important person on the team. A front-line person can communicate. Of course they can!" Pryor says that the message is that everyone should contribute and that you have to believe in the intelligence and capability of every human being.

Greg Case suggests that you assemble a team of leaders who feel as passionate as you do about the organization. This will make the job of communicating effectively easier. With every leader on your team communicating well with their people, you will get faster results. He says that if leaders aren't communicating well, they are not managing well, and that creates chaos. "We expect our leaders to create calm, not chaos," he explains. "When you think about all the things that happen every day, leaders can either amplify the chaos or dampen it. Leaders that amplify aren't effective."

> "I tell people [that] the quarterback is not the most important person on the team. A front-line person can communicate. Of course they can!"

If you set expectations that leaders in the organization will make communication *everyday job number 1*, you may be surprised at how positively they respond. They may never have really thought about how important it is. I have worked with leaders who previously were regarded as terrible speakers and watched them make dramatic improvements. It usually happens when they learn from the boss how important it is to their careers. Their progress accelerates once they give a good talk and get a positive reaction; they are often *elated*. Even the most skeptical, resistant leader or manager can become an enthusiastic communicator. Deep down, many thought that they could never do this. Once they see it can be done and what an impact they can make, they don't have to be pushed. They look for reasons to speak.

This is why it is important to create lots and lots of opportunities for members of your team to speak in formal and informal settings. If you have a heavy load of meetings and presentations, tap them to take on some of them. Start with a low-stakes presentation, and let them work their way up. Don't relinquish your speaking role when it counts or you have an audience expecting you, but look for ways to spread the wealth of speaking opportunities out and cover more ground. This is more exposure for your company, better professional development for your leaders, and ultimately, greater impact on your marketplace.

How do you decide as CEO when you should speak and when others in the company should stand in? The public relations firm for one of my top clients came up with a very effective "triage" system to determine this. In a hospital emergency room, triage means that certain criteria determine which patients go where. My consulting group team thought that this was such a good idea that we adopted a similar triage system for our firm. We now look at every request that comes in and cascade speaking opportunities so that more people have a chance to get in front of audiences.

When You Encounter Resistance

When you encounter resistance, make it absolutely clear that you consider this part of every leader's job. You aren't doing a person in your organization a favor by giving him or her a pass. If the person can't improve, you may need to move him or her out of the leadership role.

I worked with one CEO who had a guy named George on his team—technically brilliant and dedicated to the organization but a poor communicator. George was always telling his boss that he was "planning" to have a meeting with his team, but somehow it never happened. He avoided calling meetings, and when he did, he canceled them for ridiculous reasons. When the meetings came around, he would sit at a table and read notes. He would ask other team members to speak so that he didn't have to suffer long. The CEO believed in this individual and depended on him for technical advice.

> *Make it absolutely clear that you consider this part of every leader's job. If you don't deal with resistance, you only delay the inevitable.*

However, eventually, painful as it was, it became clear that George simply was not effective in the role. The CEO decided to move him into an individual contributor role. It was the right thing to do. George actually was happier there, and the CEO was able to find a leader who had the technical skill and also was effective in communicating with the team. The move immediately improved productivity and morale.

Another leader, Steve Rendle, president of The North Face, makes it a point to look at the communication skills of each leader on his team as part of the complete package. If his team is not skilled in this area, he says, "The risk is [that] it's not shared, it's not as powerful, and it can become like a dictatorship." It comes back to being an influencer versus a dictator. "You want to have a team that is communicating and completely aligned."

While you may have more experience, you can still ask your team to aim high. Expect them to learn to speak with the same passion and enthusiasm as you do. Rendle says that one of his criteria for leaders is not just how well they communicate but also how well they communicate the passion. "A question I ask [when hiring and promoting a leader] is whether they have the same passion for the issues that drive your strategies. If not, you're not going to win." Rendle looks for leaders and employees who are deeply invested in the concept of helping The North Face customers enjoy the outdoors and preserve the environment. "It's essential to a positive corporate environment. People feed off that energy and know what to do."

How Much Training Do People Need?

At dinner one night, I sat next to a senior vice president of a bank who made sure that he told me that he had "already had training" in presentation skills. He added, "Everyone should do this . . . at least once." He explained that 20 years earlier, he had been through what he felt was an effective one-day presentation skills course. It was his first year on the job. This executive now was in his forties, and he had never invested in any further training in this area. What was interesting was that the CEO of his company had recommended that he get into a coaching program with us. The senior vice president didn't understand why. He thought that he was a pretty good presenter. It was obvious that we would face an uphill battle convincing him that he needed to invest in himself.

> "A question I ask [when hiring and promoting a leader] is whether they have the same passion for the issues that drive your strategies. If not, you're not going to win."

It is not uncommon for executives to assume that one round of presentation training is enough. They don't realize how many different types of communication skills they need to develop as a leader. They regard presentation as a "soft skill" and usually have checked the box with a single training and a little experience that allowed them to stand up and speak without embarrassing themselves. Yet motivating leaders know that to speak well is to influence, and they spend years seeking advice, practicing, and improving their skills. The smart ones know what kind of investment it takes to be the speaker and leader they want to be.

One way to encourage leaders in your organization to improve is to offer an array of training that continues to advance their skills at every stage of their career. You wouldn't want to send senior-level leaders through a basic course they've already taken or lump them in with more junior people who are still getting exposed to new skills. Offer them more and more challenging courses that focus on all aspects of communication and leadership. In this way, as each offering comes along, they will see it as a worthwhile investment of their time.

Leaders who have recently had presentation training might benefit from a course in storytelling for business, in leading effective meetings, or in communicating vision and values. Keep it fresh, offer individual and group sessions, and make sure that the trainers make it interesting, exciting, and relevant to them. If you offer a succession of courses as well as individual coaching, you will encourage continuous development and engage people at every level in improving their communication skills.

Looking at the continuum in Figure 11–2, it's easy to see how effective you can be in moving people through a series of workshops and coaching opportunities. They begin with basics; move on to tactical skills such as listening, influence, persuasion, and negotiation; and then, when being considered for senior roles, they move on to communicating vision, strategy, and values and the art of inspiring and motivating others.

Promote Skills, Not Dependency

As you encourage people to get better and better at this, they still may be intimidated, especially if you, as the CEO or senior member of the team, are a very good communicator. If they don't believe that they'll

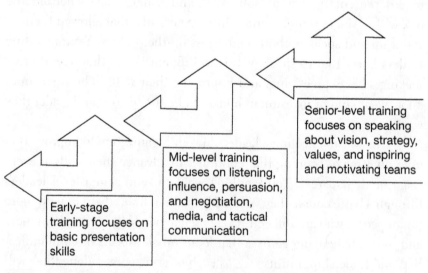

Figure 11–2 Model for accelerating communication skills.

ever compare to you, they may make excuses or avoid trying at all. This is when you need to encourage them to develop skills, not dependency. What I mean by this is that they need to know how to do things for themselves and take responsibility for the success of their presentations and what it really takes to be good. It is not enough for them to direct their teams to prepare a set of PowerPoint slides; they must master the skills to make their presentations great.

> *It is not uncommon for executives to assume that once is enough. They've checked the box. Yet leaders who speak well work at it for years and know what kind of investment it takes.*

The way to promote skills, not dependency, is to keep offering new and different experiences that help leaders and emerging leaders to build on the skills they have.

- Locate new types of workshops, coaches, and programs that you haven't offered.
- Create a mentoring system and suggest that individuals pair up to help each other.
- Set up opportunities for teams to rehearse and critique presentations together.
- Hire a coach and make it a "reward" for good leaders to get coaches.
- Videotape meetings and have review presentations with a mentor.
- Talk about leadership and communication during all performance reviews.
- Make communications part of each leader's development plan.
- Ask leaders to tell you what support they need to get better.

By making it *everyday job number 1* and offering new and different opportunities for people to develop their skills, you will see them improve more rapidly and develop greater confidence.

Choose People Who Raise Their Hands

How can you identify the leaders who will step up into this communications role? Vikki Pryor says that she has learned to choose people who put up their hands. "I was a person who always volunteered. Sometimes I had a teacher or a boss who still wouldn't accept it; they went with the person they 'thought' should be in that role." She saw it happen to other people in school and on the job. "I decided that if people were stepping up, they ought to get picked. Of course, they have to get the job done and done well. But why would I pass up the person who is wildly raising their hand and not give them a chance?"

Some people are self-starters. They realize from the beginning how important it is to present their ideas effectively and gain visibility through speaking. After a very good presentation, I asked the executive vice president of human resources and sales in a large company how she had become so good at it. "It was so simple!" she exclaimed. "Looking back, I realize that I enjoyed making presentations. I blew the socks off my bosses early on. It was like this light was suddenly shining down on me. Everyone noticed." After that, she put up her hand and offered to present as often as she could. She got better and better. "I wasn't any smarter than anybody else. I just gave myself the chance to stand out," she said.

So choose those who raise their hands, praise the self-starters, and give them a chance to shine. Offer everyone the chance to get training, and pay special attention to the high-potential people who are both technically skilled and interested in improving their communications as well. The good ones will rise to the top, those who are okay will still be okay, and those who are not interested will fall behind.

Help Your Team Communicate by Sharing How You Think

As you work with your leadership team to help them become part of the communications plan, you need to not only encourage them to develop skill but also share the way you think. You should never assume that your team understands; go out of your way to talk with team members, and give them deep background. In this way, they will be fully capable of standing in for you and speaking for you.

Keith Blakely, CEO of NanoDynamics, says that he also knows that he won't have the team behind him if he doesn't spend time with them sharing his thoughts. "What I know [that] I need to do is make sure that I give my executive staff both enough information and enough time to come to believe what it is [that] we are attempting to do, why, and how so [that] they can become great sales people, too. Most human beings have a great capability for sensing nonsense, and it doesn't matter what your IQ is. If my leadership team doesn't have inherent confidence that what we are doing is real and solid, they won't be able to convince others either."

> "What I know [that] I need to do is make sure that I give my executive staff both enough information and enough time to come to believe what it is [that] we are attempting to do, why, and how so [that] they can become great sales people, too."

Blakely spends time in groups and individual meetings letting people get as comfortable or as cynical as they need to. "Until they have that degree of confidence in the plan, they won't be able to motivate others around it. Leaders have to be confident in their own ability to deliver the message to peers and superiors," he says. "This is what makes an executive team function well, communicate, and motivate others."

Stay Visible, Stay Involved

Once you have a team of people helping you to communicate, you can give them many opportunities while still staying visible and involved. You take on the role of chief motivator and provide an example to other leaders. Ken Leibler, who has been CEO of several companies, including Liberty Financial Companies, the American Stock Exchange, and the Boston Stock Exchange, says, "To drive strategy forward, *you* have to be sure [that] everyone is communicating all the way down the organization."

Liberty Financial acquired several other companies until it had $65 billion under management. "Since each [company] had [its] own culture, and many had been in business for 30, 40, or 50 years," he recalls, "it was critical that they understand our strategy. But it wasn't easy. You couldn't just tell the person who had been in charge for years to do it our way."

Leibler visited every office. "Usually the CEO can be effective with his [or her] own reports, and then some of those reports will actually translate the message down into the organization. But others won't do it so well." Leibler found it frustrating when he assumed that people were getting the message, and it turned out that they didn't. "It didn't always happen. But I would encounter an employee who had no idea what we were doing; whether there was a meeting or a memo, it didn't get all the way down there."

Leibler created forums so that he could speak directly to people about the strategy. "At some point the CEO should be touching everyone in the company. You can't take the chance [that] they won't hear it." Taking the lead was vital to bringing the company together. "This is the job of the CEO; you have to take the time to personally communicate the message, as well as to ensure that other leaders are engaged."

Other Ways to Make It Job Number 1

Speaking and presenting aren't the only way to drive the message home. For example, you can use e-mail and written communication to reinforce your messages. Written communication is a tool for building in repetition, and when used properly, it can be an excellent tool for motivating, inspiring, and moving your strategy forward. Most people use e-mail to conduct the business of the organization, but the way you use it also sends an important message. Of course, managing e-mail is difficult, and every leader handles it differently. Bill Swanson, chairman and CEO of Raytheon, whom you met in Chapter 2, tries to answer all his e-mail within 24 hours. He does this for a very specific strategic reason: He wants to be sure that in a company that is making important decisions, often on defense systems, every person in the organization feels that he or she has access to the top.

"They should have all the resources of the company available to them, and I am a resource," says Swanson. "If I can understand what is going on, I can often help." He adds, "If someone knows of a problem and doesn't do anything, it can't be fixed. So I want them to believe [that] they can get in touch and communicate with me if they have a concern."

Strategic use of e-mail and the phone provides ways to drive a message home. As you look for ways to motivate and inspire, don't forget how effective a well-written e-mail or timely phone call can be.

Use Electronic Communications to Your Advantage in Motivating People

It is easier today than ever before to be in touch with employees, clients, prospects, the media, and the public because of electronic communications. While managing the volume of e-mail you receive can be a headache, it is still a very effective way to connect, motivate, and inspire. A note with a personal touch, even a phrase, can make someone's day. And you can do it from anywhere. With the effectiveness of electronic communications today, you can be "there" or "present" for people.

E-mail gives people access to you. This access is a relatively new phenomenon in business. Just a few decades ago, before e-mail, if you called the CEO's office, you reached a secretary who took a message. Not only was there no way to reach someone electronically—voice mail hadn't been invented—but sometimes you got a busy signal, or the phone just kept ringing. Without this access, employees had a different, more distant relationship with their leaders. "Years ago, when I was coming up through the company, you wouldn't have contacted the CEO directly; there was a hierarchy," says Swanson. "It wasn't acceptable. Today, however, young people are different; they don't see that hierarchy. They are very comfortable sending me an e-mail, and they want to work for a company where they feel connected."

Understanding how to speak with all generations of people in your organization is also important to motivation. You are far more effective when you connect with people the way they like to communicate. Swanson says, "I am a boomer. They are 'nexters'; they are the 'thumb' generation." He can almost always tell by the tone and formality (or informality) of the message which generation of employee is e-mailing him. He answers everyone. "I find it very frustrating to send someone an e-mail and not hear back for two or three days. I realize [that] not everyone is wired the same way I am, but to me, if you don't answer an e-mail, it says [that] it wasn't important. So I just take the time to do it," he says.

The New Demands on Leaders

Does this style of communication create new demands on leaders? Of course! If you have worked in business for decades, you may feel a little uncomfortable with all this access. However, there is no turning back. Technology is here to stay. So you have to manage your time and find your own way to make it work. Recognize the power of the tool, and then decide when and how you will use it. Learn the art of brevity. Brevity doesn't mean being abrupt; you can be personable and still be efficient. "I've learned to be very brief and to the point, but people get an answer," says Swanson. "From time to time it does create a bit of a challenge. But I answer because I also think it sets a standard of accessibility that is part of our company philosophy."

> "I've learned to be very brief and to the point, but people get an answer."

A major advantage of electronic communication today is that it allows you to spread "good news" quickly, which is a tremendous asset in motivating people. When Jones Lang LaSalle won "Supplier of the Year" at General Motors, Peter Roberts says he immediately went into action. "That was huge!" he exclaimed. Within minutes, he sent an e-mail to the account manager and asked her to forward the note to the entire team, and then he copied *her* manager on the note: "I told her super job, thank you on behalf of the firm for setting the example and allowing me to set an example of what being 'the best' really means."

Roberts also believes in jumping in appropriately even if he is not the person who ultimately will handle an issue. He responds to a call or e-mail and immediately gets someone to take care of it. Two examples:

- An employee on disability who failed to sign up for a benefit e-mailed him directly to say that he had a problem. "At an organization as large as ours, it isn't feasible for me to fix the problem, but I personally intervened with our legal and benefits department and said, 'I don't have the facts, but if there is a problem, we need to get to the bottom of it.'"
- The chief operating officer sent out a personal note to the top 20 percent of his managers who received exceptional ratings on manager effectiveness, and Roberts sent him a note, praising him for walking the talk. "It just happened this morning, and I wanted to get to him right away." Roberts says that *immediate* praise is one of the most powerful ways to align the organization around values. This is why it's an "everyday job."

The Impact of Making Communication Job Number 1

What difference does this level of commitment to great communication make to your organization? You can measure the positive impact it has in many ways. Peter Roberts says, "Our organization has been through massive amounts of change [during] the last four years. I came into the role in 2003, and we had two tough years righting the ship. But once we set the strategic direction, we evolved the message and stayed true to its core, bending over backward on communications." Because of that effort, through a major reorganization, changes in compensation, and four acquisitions, Roberts maintained a motivated and engaged workforce, and his firm was named a "top workplace."

"The external metric is we've been tracking our performance against our competitors, and in the past two years we've seen a dramatic differential in organic revenue growth," Roberts says. "Separate from acquisitions, we have an organic growth rate in revenues about three or four times that of our competitors." What is the reason for this success? "We have translated our mission for the organization so [that] people understand. They know we don't want to be the biggest, or the cheapest, but the best. That's a unifying goal, underscoring our strategic direction."

As you develop your own approach to making communication job number 1, you will find that there are many ways to make it work on your terms. But you do need a team of leaders working side by side with you, and they need to know how to use the tools of communication to drive a strategy forward and connect people with purpose. While the tools of communication have in some ways made it challenging to manage our time, they also have given us unprecedented opportunities to make an impact and accelerate results. If you get a team of people focusing on communicating well, you can rapidly move your organization forward.

Summary

- You are in a unique position to make a world of difference by speaking in a powerful, purposeful way about your company.
- In a strategic leadership role, it is important to start thinking of communication as everyday job number 1. Create opportunities for all leaders in the organization to speak often so that they develop skills.
- Stay visible; be involved. Today's employees expect leaders to be more accessible than ever before. Learn to manage e-mail and phone calls while remaining responsive.
- Learning to speak well takes time. Don't just check the box after you have gone through one presentation training. Some people are self-starters, but most need encouragement.

Communicate more than the plan. Ignite the passion in others, and help them to connect with the mission.

12

Making Time for Motivating People

Talent is cheaper than table salt. What separates the talented
individual from the successful one is a lot of hard work.

—Stephen King

MAKING TIME TO DO the things that ultimately will motivate people and move them toward a common purpose can be a challenge. Whether you work in a small or a large company, the demands on you are great, and just getting things done when they need to be done can be a full-time job. Yet, to have a truly extraordinary company that gets exceptional results, it is important to motivate people. This means that you have to deliberately, mindfully, and consistently choose moments to communicate and motivate others. You have to develop the discipline to incorporate communicating and motivating people into your daily business life.

Is there a secret to finding time to do this? Yes there is, and it's very simple. First, accept that you will never "find time." The secret is to adjust your thinking about the use of your time. And then you employ a three-part strategy: set intentions, schedule intentions, and discipline to stick to the plan.

> *The secret is to adjust your thinking about the use of your time. And then you employ a three-part strategy: set intentions, schedule intentions, and disciple to stick to your plan.*

207

As I mentioned earlier, you don't find the time—you *make* the time. You do this by first admitting that whatever you focus on will get done. This means that you have to change thinking as well as habits. But, if you adopt the concept that you have to make time, you will have all the time you need. After years of coaching executives, I've found that this change in mind-set is the most difficult aspect of making the transition to leadership. It is hard work to change your thinking and realize that you do have a great deal of control.

When I start working with a client, they frequently tell me at the end of the first coaching session, "I'll *probably* get to that by the end of the week" or "I don't know when I will do this, *maybe over the weekend.*" This is a clear indication to me that we have some work to do around the way they think. The way you think determines the way you act. You have to be deliberate in the way you think about your time. While there are always times in business when we face a crisis, a deadline, or a crunch, most of the time we have to be operating under the principle that we make choices about our time.

However, leaders who do learn to think differently and exert control over large portions of their time and who spend significant time communicating and motivating others are more likely to get to the top, to drive their organizations forward, and to achieve high levels of success. They somehow learn to set the intention, schedule the intention, and follow through, which produces real results.

Let's look at this strategy—setting intentions, scheduling intentions, and disciplining yourself to follow through—and examine how it can help you to *make the time* to communicate with everyone, connect them with purpose, and move them toward worthy goals.

Setting Intentions

Setting intentions means determining what must be done and deciding that you will do it. By setting intentions, you make choices about what is important and what is not. You tell yourself that this is what I will do and this is what I will not do.

For some people it is extremely difficult to let go of the notion that you can do everything. Let's face it, there are so many things that you could choose to do each day. If you don't accept that you will be able to do some things and not others, you will never get ahead in the game. Success starts with an intention about what your priorities are and how you will spend your time. Every action you take begins with an intention, and the intention should be connected to your highest priorities. Intention is the first step.

If you want to be a leader who communicates purpose with passion and moves an organization forward, you need to get very clear about what you want to accomplish. Think of the process of setting intentions as creating a "reset" button in your head. No matter what comes up during the day or week, if you have intention, you can hit the "reset" button and decide whether to do something or not do it.

The clarity of your purpose is essential. Clarity makes it easy to create intention. For example, you might set the intention to have a great meeting with your customers or sales team; your goal is to deliver a motivating presentation that defines your strategy and builds excitement about the direction of the organization. By setting that intention, you will begin scheduling and doing things that move you toward that goal. You will carve out the necessary time to make it a phenomenal presentation.

Or imagine that you want to build the morale of a group in your organization that is feeling forgotten or unappreciated. Setting the intention will lead you to put time on the calendar with them. It also will help you to choose between activities, even spur of the moment activities. You might be inspired to take a detour over to their site and pop your head into a few offices; if you're suddenly free, you might set up a lunch with a key person. The clear intention will remind you to do these things, as well as to send out notes of thanks or congratulations, pick up the phone, or send a gift. Intentions are one of the most powerful forces in the universe. What you intend to do and schedule, you do.

Scheduling Intentions

Once you have created the intention, the second step is to make your calendar reflect those intentions. Your calendar should be a statement of your priorities. While there are some things you must do, you *do* have a choice, every day, about how you spend your time. As you look at your calendar today, you may not believe it, but on closer examination, you'll discover that it is true. A closer analysis of your scheduled activities usually reveals that a significant percentage of them are discretionary. This is especially true if you are a senior executive. And as a leader, how you spend your discretionary time determines your success.

As you review your calendar with your intentions in mind, you may find that you need to make some very different choices not only about *what* you do but also about how *much* time you spend on each activity. Reviewing your calendar regularly and evaluating your appointments based on your intentions is very important. In *Speak Like a CEO*, I talked about how to delegate, delete, or delay. If you delegate what you can, delete what doesn't really need to be done, and delay the rest, you'll find more time for what matters, and you'll be able to balance activities as well.

If you find that the activities on your calendar don't adequately reflect your intentions, you need to delegate, delete, or delay those things and schedule more time for communicating and motivating activities.

> *Once you have created the intention, the second step is to put it on the calendar. Your calendar should be a statement of your priorities.*

Clear the clutter first, and then think about whether each appointment you add is a high-priority activity. Whatever is important goes on your calendar. Whatever is not does not. The calendar is your ally if you so choose. It can affirm your purpose, move you more rapidly toward your goals, and help you to achieve great things. The calendar can and should be a liberating tool that tells you and the world how you're going to lead your organization with purpose.

No one is saying that this is easy. Scheduling your intentions can be challenging because everyone wants some of your time. Yet relatively small changes in managing your calendar can make a big difference. Schedule only high-priority activities, resist the urge to fill up your calendar, and review it regularly to be sure that it reflects your intentions. You will begin to feel relieved and consequently feel more energized, motivated, and even exhilarated about your work. There is nothing like looking ahead to your day, knowing that you're going to be doing things that really matter. You actually can schedule yourself to work with purpose and passion.

Discipline to Stick to the Plan

The third step is to discipline yourself to stick to the plan. Once you set intentions and put them on your calendar, there still will be pressures to attend meetings that are not a high priority, jump in and handle emergencies, or accommodate other people's priorities. While it is important to be flexible, you also need to make sure that you have built-in time for the inevitable events such as these.

Discipline around your priorities often can be the one thing that separates you from other leaders and helps you to stand out in the crowd. Many talented young executives have the skill and knowledge to lead, but those who have the *discipline* to set intentions and keep them on the calendar get things done. Setting intentions and scheduling them makes you far more effective. It's important not only to exercise this discipline yourself but also to encourage leaders around you to do the same. And make sure that the people who support you understand this strategy—every time they put something on your calendar, it should be with the full knowledge of your priorities and intentions.

> *Discipline around your priorities often can be the one thing that separates you from other leaders and helps you to stand out in the crowd. Many talented young executives have the skill and knowledge to lead, but those who have the discipline to set intentions and keep them on the calendar get things done.*

Practice the art of saying no. If you're already doing this, I congratulate you. You would be surprised at how many people in very big jobs have not yet figured this out. I've worked with senior executives who are killing themselves working way too many hours. While the demands are great, another issue is that they haven't just learned to let go and say no. *No* is a word that frees you to do the things that will help you to succeed and move your organization forward. Whether you're worried about disappointing people, not looking like a superhero, or just letting go of things that you've always done but don't need to do anymore, think about the reasons that it is hard to say no, and then think about what would happen if you could instead say yes to your highest priorities.

Time Flies

If you're old enough, maybe you've had this experience: You get in bed at night and feel as if you were just there. The day has flown by. It isn't that you didn't accomplish anything; quite the opposite. You just can't believe the day is already over. The older you get, the faster time flies. You become acutely aware of how important it is to make every minute count.

As you spend more of your time working with purpose, setting your intentions, and scheduling the connection with people, you will feel a greater sense of satisfaction in your career. Because time flies, why not devote the time you have to doing the things that really matter, that fulfill purpose? The fact that we each only have so much time can be a debilitating or an empowering concept. You can get depressed about it or look at it as a gift. If you do the things that move you toward important goals, you feel exhilarated at the end of the day. When you are working with purpose and scheduling activities that fulfill you, you feel motivated and energized before the day even begins.

If you are scheduling your intentions and working with purpose, you also will find it easier to step back when necessary to take time for family, friends, or yourself. This strategy makes you not only busy but very productive. If you feel that you have achieved many of the important things on your list, when a crisis comes up or your family and friends need you, you can be there for them. You can go away from time to time and return, ready to engage again in purposeful work. It is easier mentally and emotionally to take time out for unanticipated events when you are generally happy, working with purpose, and feeling a sense of accomplishment.

The Language of Commitment

"I Hope" Means "I Probably Won't"

As a client of my firm was walking out the door, his coach reminded him to complete the outline for a big sales team presentation and e-mail it back by that Friday. The client said, "Gee, I don't know when I'm going to do it, but I will try to get it to you." As he got on the elevator, the coach and I looked at each other and knew he was in trouble. The coach undoubtedly would be calling and e-mailing him to remind him, and he probably would miss the deadline. This is another example of the behavior that I've mentioned previously. You set this behavior in motion with words. When you hedge your words, you are only hoping.

Hope is not a strategy for getting things done. As we've discussed, you have to set intentions, schedule them, and have the discipline to follow through. Your language has to reflect action, not hope. What you say to yourself and others matters. Your words will determine, ultimately, how you behave and choose to spend your time. If you use such words as *hope, would like to, try, plan,* and *wish,* you are not making a commitment. You are not setting an intention. You are instead setting yourself up to fail. Instead of saying, "I'll try," say, "I will" or "I won't." Try is not a trigger for an intention. Intentional language sets intentions and tells your brain what you will do.

Not only will your language tell you what to do, but it also will tell you when to do it. You are less likely to postpone activities that keep you moving toward purpose. Frequently, executives will spend their entire day on scheduled activities, leaving the very important activities of thinking, writing, preparing, and practicing until the late evening hours. They get home after a long, hard day with several interruptions and meetings or calls that ran long, have dinner, and at 9 p.m. get in bed to review that PowerPoint presentation. They start to get sleepy, so they look through it quickly and vow to go over it more thoroughly during the first 20 or 30 minutes at the office tomorrow. They get to work a little late and get an unexpected call or visitor. The presentation is at 10 a.m. They crash through it once more at 9:45 and then go in hoping for the best. It doesn't go as well as they'd wished. This is time management on a wing and a prayer and a fairly certain recipe for frustration and quite possibly disaster.

My advice is to use intentional language that commits you to activities and tells you when you will do them. Here is how you might use language to make a commitment to others and to yourself: "This is a high priority, so I am clearing my calendar Thursday starting at 2:00 p.m. I will e-mail you the outline Thursday afternoon. If there is an emergency, I also have time Friday morning, so no matter what, you will have it by Friday at noon." Now there is someone who knows how to use the power of language to make things happen!

What are some of the things you can do to carve out more time for working with purpose and passion?

- Brainstorming about vision, values, and purpose alone and with the team
- Writing (presentations, stories, and material to convey the message with passion)
- Informal meetings with employees, customers, stakeholders, etc.
- Brown bag lunches and "walk-around time" to listen
- Off-site visits to clients and customers to make a personal connection
- Phone calls and e-mails to thank, congratulate, and acknowledge people
- Formal presentations to employees, customers, stakeholders, etc.
- Speeches to conferences and events
- Private coaching to improve communication skills
- Leadership communications training in a group setting
- Practice time to improve skills

Here are some tips on how to make it happen:

Schedule Chunks of Time

Put chunks of time on your calendar for these activities, and schedule more time than you think you will need. You don't have to do it all at once; in fact, that would be a mistake. However, it does require a stretch of time to brainstorm, write, and practice.

If you schedule, for example, a two-hour chunk of time to brainstorm a creative approach to your presentation or write a story, you will get it done. What gets scheduled gets done. If an emergency comes up and you need to take a phone call at the beginning or end of the brainstorming or writing session, you'll still have had enough time to accomplish your goal. If you schedule only 30 minutes, and something comes up, it just won't get done.

If you are not accustomed to "chunking" your time this way, start by scheduling a couple of these sessions a week. I have worked with many executives who tell me flat out that they simply do not have time to work on presentations. What I usually do is to go through their calendar and evaluate the meetings and activities on their schedules. The question I encourage them to ask themselves is, "Do I really *have* to do that? Can someone else do it? Does it need to be done at all?" Since usually someone else can attend some of the meetings or they can skip them, we capture those one- to two-hour blocks of time and redeploy them to writing, preparation, and practice. What these executives often opt to do is give others in the organization the opportunity to attend the meetings and give them a briefing. This gives that direct report or individual an opportunity to learn, be involved, participate in a meeting, get exposure to the organization, and develop leadership skills.

Table 12–1 is an example of how you might write out your intention, determine the activity, and get it scheduled. This is something you could write on a note pad in five minutes.

Table 12–1 Schedule Your Intentions

Intention	Activities	Schedule
Deliver an outstanding presentation on the new business plan at our annual employee meeting	Meet with the communications team to review the plan and discuss the top three messages	October 1
	Work with a speech-writer or write my presentation and develop stories and material	October 5
	Review the presentation with other leaders to get their input and revise	October 12

Create Blank Time

As I mentioned earlier, the way to ensure that you will get everything done is to allow blank time to exist on your calendar. Get comfortable having blocks of unscheduled time because every important activity takes more time than you expect. Blank time ensures that when something important comes along, you can still fit it in and achieve your goals. Blank time protects you when a project takes longer than you expected. Calendar management requires discipline as well as flexibility—discipline to get the high priorities done and flexibility to meet the unanticipated demands of your business. Blank time helps you with both discipline and flexibility.

You may have some blank time in your head, but if it isn't on the calendar, that time will not be protected by you or others. Be sure that you have some blank time every week, and get your assistant or others who schedule things for you to take it as seriously as any other appointment.

You may have some blank time in your head, but if it isn't on the calendar, that time will not be protected by you or others. Be sure that you have some blank time every week, and get your assistant or others who schedule things for you to take it as seriously as any other appointment. Communicate very clearly with everyone that they need to check with you before they infringe on the blank time. Make sure that you and that person are on the same page about who and what can usurp that time.

Many people like to have a full calendar—they falsely believe that a schedule chocked with activity equates to productivity. You may hear a new executive brag about the number of meetings on his or her schedule. Each scheduled activity should be evaluated against your purpose and the priority activities that make it happen. You can add activities that are important, but once you are committed to lower-level activities, it can be hard to get out of them. Still, if your calendar is too full, review what's ahead at the beginning of each week and again at the end of each day, and change it if it doesn't reflect your highest priorities.

What to Do About Too Many Meetings

Most people I know complain that they are going to too many meetings. Often, they work in companies where meetings are long, disorganized, and unproductive. I rarely meet someone who works in a large or medium-sized company who doesn't tell me that there are too many meetings. Of course, there are meetings that you must attend. However, you may discover on closer examination that you don't have to go to them all. As in the preceding example, you can send someone else, give them an opportunity, and have them exercise their communication skills by briefing you later.

If you're running the meetings, you can create a more productive, efficient meeting environment. You can do more in less time if you adopt good meeting practices. This will give you more time for doing the work and make you feel more energized. Imagine how it will energize and motivate your team if they are not spending all their time in meetings. It is possible to take control of meetings and eliminate the "drag" that so many people feel after they've spent the day sitting in conference rooms. Not only will they be more productive, but they also will be more excited about coming to work each day knowing that they have more time to do their work!

Good meeting practices are essential to making meetings productive and getting people in and out of meetings. Decisions get made, people get assignments, and off they go. It is so important to motivation to respect your people's time and allow them to work with purpose. If your business is not conducting efficient, productive meetings, you need to review what's wrong, institute best practices, and insist that everyone follow them. As we discussed earlier during our conversation about accountability, good meeting practices include making decisions, handing out assignments, setting deadlines, and creating accountability. If you do this, people will walk out the door knowing exactly what they need to do, planning their week, and feeling more enthusiastic.

> *Imagine how it will energize and motivate your team if they are not spending all their time in meetings.*

I will never forget what I learned while working for Massachusetts Governor Jane Swift. While she was in office only a short time, I admired how she ran our meetings. I always arrived early at the State House, as did the rest of the governor's communications team. At the precise appointed time, Governor Swift would walk in the door, sit down, and start the meeting.

There were always brief greetings, and the tone was very friendly and pleasant, but we were all about *business*. We knew that we had limited time and that we needed to get the job done. Many organizations do have leaders with this kind of discipline and skill, and they institute excellent meeting practices in their organizations. But most of the time I hear from people about how terrible and unproductive their meetings are. The experience with Governor Swift showed me that even the busiest executives can bring discipline to the meeting culture. I always felt energized when I left those meetings because they were so productive.

If you aren't getting enough done in your meetings, then you need to take a hard look at meeting practices in your organization. Do you start on time? Do you get right to work? Are people prepared? Do people leave with clear accountability and an action plan? If your meetings feel instead like the movie *Groundhog Day*, that is, always the same old topic, the same old issues, the same old things left unresolved, then do something about it! Poor productivity and a lack of accountability in your meetings should not be tolerated. You will be amazed at how much more motivated people are when they go into a meeting knowing that the leader is running things well and that they'll be out on time and will be clear on what needs to be done.

Back Time to Priority Projects

Another secret to getting things done is to *back time*—work backwards from a goal to figure out what you need to schedule and when. *Back timing* is a TV term that producers use to determine what stories will go into the news block, how long they can run, and what the writers need to do to shorten or lengthen content. For you, it means preparing for an event, meeting, or presentation. You look way out in advance and figure out what it is going to take to prepare for it. Imagine how relieved you will feel and how much more effective you will be if you have scheduled all your preparation in advance and have had the opportunity to really prepare.

People in your organization may be accustomed to working last minute, even on important events. It isn't uncommon to see a senior leadership team start putting together their presentations a couple of days before a major event such as a sales conference or annual meeting. However, when we lay out what really needs to be done to do it well, they see how such a strategy is a recipe for failure.

Back timing priority projects is just good project management. Consider everything that needs to be done, and space out the activities so that the process can unfold as it should. There is nothing that builds your confidence or makes you feel more energized about an event than knowing that you have set aside blocks of time well in advance to think, strategize, collaborate, develop a talk, write the presentation, prepare the stories, practice, and deliver a dynamic, motivational presentation.

> *Imagine how relieved you will feel and how much more effective you will be if you have scheduled all your preparation in advance and had the opportunity to really prepare.*

The following table is a visual I use to begin a conversation with my clients about what they need to do. Sometimes, when I show this on a PowerPoint slide during a workshop, I just put it up on the screen and

Monday	Tuesday	Wednesday	Thursday	Friday
	Brainstorm		Prepare first draft	Review first draft
Second brainstorm		Out-loud editing, collaboration	Writing time	
	Out-loud editing, collaboration	Second draft prepared	Practice and edit	Practice and edit
	Write or receive final draft	Practice	Dress rehearsal	Speech or presentation

stand there, letting it sink in. Then I say, "If you don't have time to do this, you probably shouldn't accept the engagement." I always get nods of recognition from the audience. After a day of working on ideas or stories, they realize that it all takes time. And they want to schedule things because they realize it will set them up for success.

Hit the "Pause" Button

Ideas need time to gel. You need to do the work and then go away for awhile. Create some space between these activities. During that space of a day or two, or longer, you may not be thinking about a topic all the time, but your brain will be working it over subconsciously. You can play it over again in your mind and reformulate, rework, and reconsider.

Many people find it productive to go to bed and think about a problem they would like to solve. They go to sleep and wake up, and sometimes they get a great idea first thing in the morning. This is a testament to how our brains work. We need time to figure things out. It's an example of how to use the "pause" button to get your brain started working on an idea.

If you start too late on any project, you won't have time to hit the "pause" button. So plan, schedule back time, and take advantage of time. A good friend of mine in marketing and advertising says, "The 'pause' button is the best tool you have for thinking. If you don't have time to pause, you don't have time to allow the idea to cook. If the idea doesn't cook, it's half-baked, and everyone knows it."

Right Time, Right Activity

Another way to get things done more efficiently and get better results is to do the right thing at the right time of day. Mornings, afternoons, and evenings are usually good for different types of activities. Know your own body rhythm, respect your internal clock, and pay attention to how your energy level ebbs and flows during the day. If you are high energy early in the morning, that's when you should schedule difficult activities, whether for you these are brainstorming, writing, or practicing. Use the same principle in scheduling activities for your team. Remember that most people need a warm-up activity in the morning, lose energy after lunch, and lose steam by 4:00 or 5:00 p.m. Schedule intervals of productive time and breaks so that you get the most from people.

I always ask my clients to schedule their coaching sessions when they feel most energetic and to respect their own body rhythms when scheduling appointments. In my experience, most people are far more productive and able to learn in the morning, but there are those who differ and hit their stride later in the day. Engaging in the right activity at the right time is a good time management strategy because you'll be more productive with the time you have.

Use Technology to Your Advantage

Technology gives us the opportunity to get things done and to communicate efficiently. Prior to mobile phones and e-mail, we were not as productive. Our parents and grandparents couldn't have imagined this 24/7 work lifestyle. They did not typically take calls at home. If the phone rang, it was an emergency. If you were out of the office, your administrative assistant took a message. There was no call waiting, so if you were on the phone, people heard a busy signal (a sound that people under the age of 30 have probably never even heard).

So life has changed, and portable 24/7 communication is never going away. How can you use this to your advantage? The answer is that you can take care of routine matters anytime, anywhere, providing you with the freedom to schedule blocks of time for the major activities that will help you to work and communicate with purpose.

Rather than just feeling burdened by 24/7 communication, you can use it to get things off your plate. Take care of e-mail in the airport, and then spend your time on the plane thinking, writing, and preparing. Use technology to batch your work and free up chunks of time for important or difficult tasks. Manage your work day by managing how you use technology, and you will feel more energized, motivated, and purposeful.

I know a senior vice president of communications and public affairs who is very grateful for the fact that the BlackBerry was invented. Why? When she goes home on the weekends, a two-hour drive from her corporate headquarters, she does not want to have to drive back to the office.

She carries her BlackBerry with her and knows that she will be connected and available whatever comes up. She loves being home and feels more energetic and balanced because she doesn't have to spend as much time at the office as she once did.

Don't allow 24/7 communication to steal your time to think, reflect, write, and prepare. When you are doing important work, turn off the e-mail and create mental space and an environment where you can focus. Don't let constant intrusions make you unproductive. You will feel a greater sense of accomplishment and far more motivated if you give yourself the "gift" of these blocks of brainstorming time.

Example: How to Use Brainstorming Time

Let's say that you're planning the annual employee off-site meeting. You want it to be an inspiring, motivating event that leaves everyone feeling energized. You've hired a meeting planner, perhaps even a production company to stage the event. They will be building the stage, using a theme, and introducing music, lighting, and activities to make it a memorable experience. Of course, as you know, these are the bells and whistles. You need brainstorming time to develop the substance. You need a concept and ideas to communicate an important, inspiring message.

As the leader, you need to set up meetings to brainstorm how you will make this meeting great. Start early, and bring everyone together. Don't leave it to others; get involved and stay engaged, especially at the beginning. If this is your meeting, you are responsible. You have to "own" it.

Many times I've seen leaders make the mistake of turning over the planning of a meeting to their direct reports, only to come in near the end and realize that it wasn't what they had intended. At that point, it is difficult to fix. Important communications and big meetings should involve you beginning to end. A meeting such as this is opportunity to motivate and inspire others and focus them on purpose. No matter how busy you are, make it a priority. Give it your imprint.

In a brainstorming meeting, you might attempt the following:

- Identify the topic and mission.
- Ask each person to give a short "take" on the topic.
- Develop a theme and talking points.
- Determine which presenters are responsible for which messages.
- Record/transcribe the session.
- Write *out loud* in the session by capturing what people say.
- Have someone type up notes of the meeting.
- Read revisions together and out loud to make sure that the messages are clear and powerful.
- Keep everything in a shared electronic folder.
- Assign responsibilities for each aspect of the meeting.
- Write it up and distribute it to the right people.
- Spend time with your team reviewing and making sure that the messages and themes are powerful and clear.

As you set your intentions, schedule your intentions, and allocate your time for important, motivational leadership activities, remember to encourage your own team to do the same. Encourage team members to learn the skills of time management and setting priorities so that they too can focus on the "big things." All your leadership team must come together to motivate, inspire, and move the organization forward. In Chapter 13 we'll look at where, when, and how to do this.

Summary

- Leaders who motivate and inspire others and communicate with purpose make the time for these activities.
- What works is to set your intentions, schedule your intentions, and have the discipline to see them through.
- Time flies, and you can either see this as a depressing fact or use it to motivate yourself to do the things that really matter.

- When you deliberately manage your time better and work with purpose, you will feel more energized, enthusiastic, and motivated.

Use strategies such as hitting the "pause" button, creating chunks of time, back timing, and brainstorming to use time efficiently and work with more purpose.

13

Your Strategy: When, Where, and How to Motivate People

Vision without action is a daydream. Action without vision is a nightmare.

—Japanese Proverb

Steve Rendle, president of The North Face, usually does a "walk-through" with his team when they open a new store. During one of these walk-throughs at the company's state-of-the-art retail space in San Francisco, he was talking with a few people about "The North Face experience." What he meant by this was the feeling that outdoor enthusiasts who are their customers should have from the moment they walk in the door. The way clothing and equipment are displayed, the impact of in-store visuals, how associates interact with customers, everything is choreographed to create the aura of an authentic outdoor experience. According to Rendle, "We want our customers to feel like they are standing next to a premier athlete and that they could actually jump into an athletic activity while they are there."

Rendle knows that every time he talks with associates at The North Face, he needs to share his thoughts about the authentic customer experience. Whether employees have just joined the company or have been there for years, the message bears repeating. Rendle sees the CEO's role as keeper of the brand. "Everything we do has to be the best; it has to be authentic to our core DNA," he says. "We are reinforcing the authentic

225

nature of our brand and choosing our customers through that lens, reinforcing with the assortments we put in front of our customers."

What is the impact of Rendle's consistent message? During a period when competitors in the sports retail industry grew, on average, in low single digits, The North Face was growing by more than 25 percent a year. The company has attained exceptional brand power and, as a result, has become one of the most successful divisions of VF Corporation. Rendle doesn't wait for an employee meeting to drive home his message about rigorous adherence to their brand identity. He talks about it all the time. He wants to be sure that every single employee has a clear vision of what The North Face is and should be.

When, Where, and How

There are so many small opportunities to reinforce your mission and purpose every day. Actively reaching out and communicating the vision and mission is fundamental to your role as leader. Whenever you have the chance, don't squander it—seize it! There are times when you may find people making small talk or doing things that provide you with an opportunity to reinforce the message. Every chance you get, you need to take the opportunity to connect people to purpose.

While in charge of Fidelity Investments with 15,000 employees, Ellyn McColgan did not relinquish communications. The communications team reported directly to her, and she took an active role in all aspects right down to the content of the quarterly company newsletter. She was frequently the featured guest speaker at her direct reports' town hall events and corporate-wide functions as well. Her imprint was everywhere. Her words lived in the organization, and her remarks were videotaped and made available on the company's intranet. It was unusual to leave a Fidelity meeting without hearing at least one comment about what McColgan says. Her involvement and impact are not that common in large corporations, but it is very effective.

It is always best when leaders are actively involved. Matt Davis, corporate director of executive communications, government affairs, and community relations for the Dow Chemical Company, says that his team works to involve executives in all aspects of planning and delivering the message. "I've had leaders like Andrew Liveris [Dow's CEO] who are very involved, and some who initially didn't believe they even *needed* a communications plan," he says. "They were virtually absent from the process. However, I've never had a case where I've gone ahead and written a plan and started to execute and not ended up with a leader who eventually comes around to participating and understanding the value."

When you are actively involved, you ensure that the message is delivered and delivered well. The larger your organization, the further away you are from the people who need to execute the activities of the enterprise. Being involved directly in communications is really the only way to make sure that your message is delivered. The answer to that question: Where, when, and how? Everywhere, all the time, however you can.

In this chapter we'll look at strategies to make this happen so that you have the opportunity to touch people often and drive home your message. The more you focus on communicating and aligning people, the fewer challenges you will face because people will know what to do and what not to do. No matter how large or small your company, you cannot communicate enough. To do this, you need to make communication a priority and create a communication plan.

> *It is always best when leaders are actively involved in all aspects of planning and communications.*

Your Communications Plan

A communications plan is essential to the success of your business plan. The business plan won't be executed unless it lives in the hearts and minds of your team. Communication is everything. Your communications plan will tell you what everyone should be doing, where, and why. It should describe not only how you will *deliver* the message but also how you will measure and track success. Matt Davis of Dow says, "It doesn't have to be airtight or to the 'nth' degree, but you have to know what you are trying to accomplish."

Where do you begin in developing a communications plan? "Any plan has to start and end with the strategy of whatever leader you are supporting," Davis says. He connects his communications plan to the corporate strategy. As it cascades down, members of his communications team work directly with the business leaders, either regionally or by corporate function. Communications professionals are assigned to every top leader because the professional must go deep into the business and understand it completely in order to be a valuable strategic advisor. "Your communications plan links to the divisions' plans and to the accomplishment objectives of the business strategy," he explains.

A communications plan is essential to the success of the business plan—communication drives it forward.

Many executives still view communications as a soft science, but this has to change. One of my colleagues in the firm came up with this concept: "Communication should be hardwired to the business strategy." Everything in the plan should link directly to producing business results. This is why you must have your communications team present for business meetings. You also should consider having them travel with you and meet clients, prospects, analysts, and other business leaders. The more they know and understand, the more they can help you. Your communications team should be given the opportunity to develop deep knowledge about the business and your priorities. This means that you need to hire great talent in the communications department, people capable of fully participating in the business strategy process end to end.

If you are a communications professional and you are working with an executive who is not very involved in communications, Davis advises you to write a plan. Go forward, prepare a document that is aligned with the business strategy, and start executing. He has taken this approach in the past and has found leaders to be receptive. "Eventually, they start seeing results and think, 'Maybe there is something to that,'" he says.

Davis recalls a time when executives at Dow attended one of my firm's visibility boot camps. A few were quite skeptical, that is, until they started to see results. Going forward, because they had improved their skills and had such a positive experience, they became far more willing to work with their communications teams. They began to change the way they worked with these professionals, meeting with them more frequently, brainstorming with them about their talks, and investing more time in preparation and practice. Davis says that it is important for someone to take responsibility for driving the plan forward. "You move forward, and eventually people become total converts," he says.

If you are a leader who has a communications professional or team, by all means invite team members to be involved in the business conversation and to partner with you on the communications strategy. If you are a communications professional, don't be shy about initiating a strategy meeting where you map out the communications plan against the business goals. Talk about the leader's purpose, mission, and values. Make sure that the two of you are on the same page, working toward the same goals, before you walk out the door.

An important element of any communications plan is to name the audiences you want to influence. To motivate and align the organization, you need to analyze the audiences and figure out the best way to reach them. This extends to deciding how to use technology. Davis says, "You need to fully understand [your audience] before you decide on a newsletter or a blog or a broadcast. And it is best if you have a leader who sees the need and has a hand in deciding what you want to do, what the budget is, and what you want to do first, second, and third."

The communications plan also should be in harmony with the *personal* strategy of the leader. The communications professional working with the executive must understand the leader as a person. The communications team must know the leader's communication preferences and career goals as well as the business vision. "If your communications strategy isn't part and parcel of what the leader is trying to personally accomplish," says Davis, "it won't be a good plan. This takes more time and is more complicated, but you really have to get into the mind of your boss."

Working Your Communications Plan

Once you have a plan in place, make it part of your agenda to discuss implementation on a regular basis. As with any plan, you have to make sure that it's moving forward and come up with new ideas to keep it fresh.

Prior to joining Morgan Stanley, during 17 years at Fidelity Investments, Ellyn McColgan never left this to chance. Not only did she encourage the development of a communications plan, but she also made sure that she talked about it with her team frequently so that team members could sustain the drive and momentum. "We had a template. We scheduled many meetings, and I expected my direct reports to have regular meetings with their teams. We also communicated in other ways. The messages came from me. I saw this as my role."

Working the communications plan includes making sure that everyone understands the business plan and getting regular progress updates from your team. McColgan says, "The messages were always aligned to the whole business plan. We focused constantly on the five things we were trying to get done as a company. We would report on the progress." She explains that her division leaders also had their own schedules for communicating the message, as did the managers under them. "So, by the time you got to the margin clerk in New York," she says, "that person understood how the margin business fit into one of our top goals."

McColgan stresses that you need to have a plan and stick to it. Let your team members know how important their role is in connecting people with the strategy. Give them the resources they need to do their jobs effectively. "If you want to communicate, you have to apply resources. You have to apply people to the task of communicating. In some organizations, that is what is cut," says McColgan, "but it doesn't work if you don't have a strong communications team and infrastructure."

Tapping a Great Resource: Your Communication Advisors

Your communications plan is only as good as the team that executes it. It's important to hire and develop an outstanding communications team and to develop a strong, trusted relationship with team members. They are your partners in driving your business strategy forward. You should include the top person on your strategic leadership team and make sure that everyone involved in communications is apprised of the business strategy and ongoing issues.

Building a close relationship with the people who help you to communicate pays great dividends. Empowering your communications team by bringing team members into your inner circle will help you to drive your strategy forward. I once attended an event where Tony Snow, the late White House press secretary and Fox News correspondent, gave a talk to communications advisors; he spoke eloquently about his close relationship with George W. Bush. Snow said that when Bush offered him the job, he had only one condition—that he would be included in *all* important meetings, without exception. Snow knew that unless he was "in the know" on even the most sensitive information, he would not be effective with the tough White House press corps. He had to have a boss who trusted him with classified information and who believed in his ability to answer questions truthfully without jeopardizing national security.

Bush agreed to this extraordinary level of access, and Snow said that the president was true to his word, including him in meetings and even phone calls with heads of state around the world and with Congress, the cabinet, various administration officials, and all other political leaders. Without this access, Snow felt that he could not have performed as superbly as he did. He earned the trust of both the White House and the press for his wit, candor, integrity, and fairness.

When Snow passed away in 2008, he was lauded by the press, the public, and the president. His exceptional ability to balance the interests of the administration and the news media set a very high standard. In the corporate world, his example highlights just how valuable the communications role can be to a leader who wants to communicate effectively and build a great company.

It takes time for a trusted relationship to develop. Dow's Matt Davis says that in his experience, it takes about a year. "You start out doing nuts and bolts; then, over time, you develop a strong sense of the person you work for, and you both develop a high level of mutual trust." Mutual trust develops when both parties treat it as a partnership. There must be mutual respect. The leader must be open to working closely with the professional;

the professional must rise to the challenge by learning the business and by providing real value in his or her advice and counsel.

In my work over the years with communications advisors, I have noted that some are far more effective than others in developing trusted relationships. In order for the communications advisor to become a member of the strategic inner circle, that person must think and act strategically. It's also important to provide the leaders you support with access to expert advice, coaching, and support.

Here are some of the approaches I recommend in building a trusted advisor relationship:

Advice for Communications Professionals

- Advise the leader as a trusted partner.
- Be an expert at what you do.
- Attend all important business meetings.
- Educate yourself on all aspects of the business strategy.
- Tie your communications plan directly to the business strategy.
- Schedule routine meetings with the executives, and bring a tape recorder.
- Capture "their words, their way."
- Look for opportunities for the executive to be highly visible.
- Work closely with the administrative assistant on scheduling.
- Put sessions for creative writing and practice on the calendar in advance.
- Travel with the executive, and take advantage of "found time."
- Develop and improve your own writing and speaking skills.
- Be fearless in providing clear, candid, timely, and constructive feedback.
- Take the lead to recommend coaching and other resources to the leader.
- Protect the leader's and the company's interests at all times.

Advice for a Leader Working with a Communications Professional

- Treat the communications professional as a trusted partner.
- Hire advisors who are strategic, creative, and able to articulate your vision.
- Put time on the calendar every week to meet with your advisor.
- Invite the professional to attend important business meetings.
- Take it on yourself to guide the professional on your business strategy.
- Be sure that the professional's activities are completely aligned with your strategy.
- Evaluate communications activities on a regular basis.
- Write presentations with the professional so that he or she can capture "your words, your way."
- Be open to the professional's suggestions for events, presentations, and media.
- Allow the professional access to your administrative assistant for scheduling.
- Put your preparations for events on the calendar in advance.
- Travel with the professional and occasionally use this "found time" to get things done.
- Develop and improve your own writing and speaking skills.
- Be open to candid, timely, and constructive feedback.
- Accept suggestions for coaching and other resources.
- Make it clear that the professional is to protect your interests and those of the company.

The Big Event: Major Announcements

When your company has a major event, annual meeting, or big announcement, that is a great time to bring people together around purpose. Always connect the message in the event to the larger mission. If it's important, invest in doing it well so that the event is memorable and motivates and inspires your audience. I have worked with many companies that decide that in order to do this, they need outside help. What might this include? Coaches to help the leaders speak well, as well as speechwriters, production teams, and others. You want to deliver a powerful message and to create the right atmosphere with visuals, sound, and lighting. Put creative energy into the planning and execution, insisting that the leaders who will present start to work well in advance of the event, making sure that you have a dress rehearsal, and insisting that people perform at their best.

You'll recall some of the advice from earlier chapters on speaking with passion, incorporating stories, and connecting with audiences. Every leader who presents at a major event should build his or her skills and practice so that he or she can deliver when there is a big announcement. The organization needs to give the presenters time and to invest resources to help them succeed. An example of how *not* to prepare for a big meeting or announcement is to allow the dress rehearsal to be a parade of your leadership team coming in at the last minute, going through the motions, or standing at the microphone saying, "First, I'll say this, then this, and then conclude," and walk off the stage without actually rehearsing. If it's a big announcement, insist that people rehearse. You only get one opportunity to do this right. Plan ahead, prepare, and you'll have a great event.

Once you've had the event, you've launched, but that is just the beginning. You need to have a complete communications plan in place to drive home the message. Make sure that you have written a plan that provides for the message to be repeated in many ways. Get it out through your intranet, newsletter, team meetings, Web casts, brown bag lunches, e-mails, and more. If people don't hear the message again right away, they will discount its importance or forget it, no matter how big the initial splash.

Having a great event without follow-up is like hitting a baseball out of the park and forgetting to run the bases. The score won't count if you don't run all the bases! For every event, prepare a strategic plan to keep driving the message forward. Motivating and aligning your organization is not something that happens in a day—it happens one day at a time.

Figure 13–1 shows how a one-time event, even a successful one, will not have a lasting impact without the follow-through. The event is little more than a blip on the radar screen if people don't hear and see

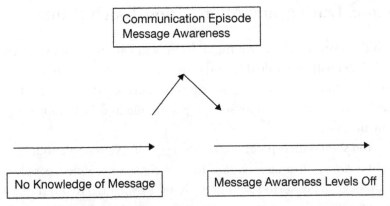

Figure 13–1 Communication: One-time event

the message again. Sometimes a single event without follow-up will even be counterproductive. If people hear it only once, they may assume that you've dropped the ball, and they can grow cynical.

Think of a project, strategy, or brand rollout as a Hollywood movie. You have a potential hit in the making! Weeks or months before the release, TV commercials hit the airwaves, and preview trailers hit the theater. The stars hit the road for rounds of interviews on *Good Morning America* and the *Today Show*. Print ads follow in the big newspapers and listings in the local newspapers. Then you go live with the Web site, blog, and other viral marketing strategies. This is all before it opens. Afterward, you pour on the steam again. It goes to DVD. This is how you get big box office return.

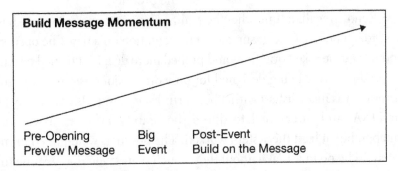

Figure 13–2 Communication: Build on a single event

Before, During, and After: Vision Touch Points

Each time you speak after a main event, you can create another touch point. Meet with individual teams, bring people into your office, send out a weekly e-mail, write a blog, or post your remarks on the intranet. Find ways to create touch points so that people see and hear your message many times.

You should incorporate your message into every single routine staff meeting. Every meeting gives you another chance to connect people with the message. The North Face's Steve Rendle explains, "In our staff meetings we always tie our conversations about projects back to our vision statement. As I work with people one on one, we go through a project planning process where it is documented and written down."

Touch-point conversations, about the business vision and strategy should happen in every part of your business, not just in marketing and sales—from finance to information technology to manufacturing, production, and the supply chain. Rendle uses the apparel design and development process to create three touch points each season. "We don't approve a seasonal design group until we hit a third touch point. Then we sign off on it. It is a laborious process, four days in duration, where each product presents the product line."

> *Each time you speak, you can create a touch-point conversation. Whether it's a formal speech, meeting, conversation, e-mail, handwritten note, blog entry, or whatever, you have many opportunities to connect people with purpose.*

Rendle recalls a time when he realized how important it was to have these touch points. One group gave a presentation on a new line of sports products. As he asked questions and probed more deeply, it turned out that the products were being designed for only one major customer, and that customer was inconsistent with The North Face brand. "It was clearly not our DNA, and threatened to dilute the brand," he says. "I was very unhappy, but at least the system worked. The products were pulled immediately." The point is that without these touch points, you may assume that people know, but they will veer off course. The touch-point conversations will help you to avoid costly mistakes and focus people on what matters.

Your entire team should be communicating the vision using touch-point conversations, too. Make sure that team members regularly talk about it and take ownership for driving the message down through their own organizations. "I would say that each one of us is a steward of the brand," says Rendle. "We are all vested in protecting our authenticity, and we are all very careful about how our brand is represented and portrayed."

Some leaders on your team may have an easier time with this if they've been with you for awhile; those who join you along the way need more reinforcement. With all your team leaders, check in on how well they are communicating by sitting in on their meetings from time to time and listening. "It always surprises me when we go off strategy," says Rendle, "but that only reinforces why you have to constantly check in with your organization and reinforce it with the influencers of the organization to make sure [that] it is upheld."

The Power of Enthusiastic Repetition

We discussed in an earlier chapter how important repetition is to motivating and aligning people. As you consider where, when, and how to create these touch points, remember that repetition is absolutely essential. For every leader it is challenging to keep repeating yourself. You get tired of saying the same thing over and over again. Not only do you need to repeat it and repeat it, but you also need to deliver the message with the same enthusiasm every time. Energy and passion give your message power and make it stick. As one participant in our survey said, "It's not just about leaders saying the right things, or saying it often, it's about putting energy into it." Added another, "That is what energizes a team toward a common goal."

Vikki Pryor, CEO of SBLI USA Mutual Life Insurance Company, said that she found it a challenge to get comfortable telling the same story and sharing the same message "over and over and over and over." But she realized how effective enthusiastic repetition was. She learned to embrace repetition as a powerful tool in her communications. Now she reminds her own team of leaders that they need to do this too because their own teams need to hear the message many times. "An associate meeting can seem repetitive, and afterward the associate might come up and say, 'Great meeting!' which means that even though we've said it 18 times, they are just hearing it for the first time."

One strategy for keeping the message fresh when you have to repeat it often is to modify and adapt your stories and examples for various audiences. Keep looking for new material to open your meeting or make a point. This makes it more interesting for you *and* for them. Pryor adds, "You have to be willing to change what you're saying based on the circumstances." This means taking time to analyze each audience and craft the message in a way that will resonate for audience members. "You have to spend time thinking about that," she says.

There is a psychological component to successful repetition. You have to "get up" for the performance. Matt Davis, of Dow Chemical, recalls how when he was young and acting in a stage show, the play's director, who had worked on Broadway, explained things to the cast. "She gathered us together and told us [that] she realized that this was the twentieth time we'd run through everything, but it would be the first time the audience had seen it. 'They need to believe it is the first time you are saying a line, or singing your song, or crying in a scene,' she explained."

Davis feels that leaders have to approach things the same way. "You may get tired of going around the world [or around your office] repeating a message, but whether you're traveling to Augusta, Atlanta, or Argentina, you have to remember [that] it is the first time for that audience." Look back at earlier chapters on speaking with passion, look for ways to make your message fresh, and make it a goal to deliver your message with energy and passion every time.

Adapting your message for various audiences keeps it fresh for you and relevant for them.

You know it's all working when your words boomerang back. Steve Rendle says, "You measure whether people are repeating the message on the key points. If they can repeat them, if they are articulating the message in their own way, and if they are accomplishing their most important tasks, then you've gotten your point across."

David Woods, executive director of the Life and Health Insurance Foundation for Education (LIFE), agrees, advising not to stop until you "hear the echo." He says, "If people don't get it the first time, they may not get it until the tenth or the 154th time, but if you keep saying it, it'll stick. That's when people dig in and start driving toward the goal."

Use Every Communication Tool Available

To reach everyone, you need to use every tool available. Adults learn in different ways; some are visual, and others are auditory or kinetic, meaning that they connect with a feeling. In addition, people have vastly different preferences when it comes to phone versus e-mail or print versus online. Fortunately, with so many tools available, you can reach people like never before. Today, you can communicate anytime, anywhere, across time zones and languages.

Think of the tools available to you as similar to the way that media now have multiple outlets. The media companies know that people prefer to get their "news" today in different ways—newspaper, online, TV, radio, podcasts, billboards, and elevator monitors. Your employees have different preferences, too. Some love the intranet; others like the company newsletter. Some can't wait to check the blog; others don't even know how to log in. Some check their e-mail constantly; others find it a nuisance. This is why you have to use them all. People listen and process in different ways.

Example: Phase 1 Communications Rollout

Audience	Communication Tool	Timing
Employees	Town hall meeting	May 1
	E-mail blast	May 2
	Blog	May 3
	Newsletter article	May 15
	Intranet interview with CEO	May 28
Public	Media interviews	April 1–May 15
	Three major speeches	May 15, June 10, Sept 8
	Web site announcement	May 1
	Press release	May 1

The larger and more complex the organization, the harder and longer you have to beat the drum. "Hundreds of years ago," says Matt Davis, "villages posted people on the mountaintops to look for floods or avalanches, and if something was coming, they would beat the drum. But their arms got tired, and that's when people in the village assumed, 'Oh, we've averted danger.'" Davis tells leaders with whom he works that they *will* get sick of delivering a message and that at about that same time, people will hear it and get it right. His CEO, Andrew Liveris, is a good example of a leader who keeps beating the proverbial drum even when it feels like too much. "He doesn't have a problem hitting the same message hundreds of times around the world because he appreciates that it'll be the first time that a particular audience has heard it."

Get comfortable with most forms of communication, including broadcast, video, and media. You may be more at ease speaking in an informal setting, but with so many styles of learning and opportunities to get in front of people, you need to master other arenas. Surround yourself with internal resources and with coaches who can help you to polish your communications through various channels. You don't have to be perfect; you need to be authentic so that people can connect.

Everything that goes out of your office reflects on you. You should strive for every type of communication to highlight you in the best light. Wherever you go, no matter who the audience, no matter whether you're speaking to 1 or 1,000, make it great. Your written communications and phone conferences should have the same professional look and feel as everything else you do. Go out of your way to make it the best it can be, and make sure that the people who work with you adhere to the same high standard.

> You may be more at ease speaking in an informal setting, but with so many styles of learning and preferences available, you need to master most of them.

When you are out talking to people, you can take the material you develop and use it in other forums. Keith Blakely, of NanoDynamics, whom you met in Chapter 1, holds small group luncheons to bring people together from different parts of the organization. "They can ask questions about what's going on. It's very informal. These are not well-produced presentations; it's more like—let's get together over wings and pizza and tell me what you don't know about what we are doing or why we are doing it." Not only does Blakely learn what's going on, but he also takes what he learns and puts it into internal memos, blog postings, or his outline for the next company meeting.

The Personal Touch

A personal touch in any form of communication makes the most positive, lasting impact. An "old fashioned" handwritten note or (heaven forbid!) a phone call instead of an e-mail will make a powerful impression. Matt Davis, of Dow Chemical, says, "We find [that] Andrew [the CEO] makes the biggest impact when he writes a note or picks up the phone. It's such a personal touch, and so unexpected."

Davis does it too. "When an employee who doesn't report directly to me received a significant promotion and her boss let me know, I immediately picked up the phone to say congratulations. It's unusual for her to hear from me, and you could hear it in her voice. She was just delighted that I had called," Davis says. The point of all this is to connect people with you and make them feel like they

> *A personal touch makes the most impact.*

are important to you. This is so important to motivating your organization. "These things stick with people," says Davis. "They'll say, 'My leader cares, and I will follow him or her up whatever hill they take me on.'"

You can infuse the personal touch into the most high-tech forms of communication. Keith Blakely, of NanoDynamics, has an employee blog "that is more folksy than technical." Blakely says that he doesn't speak in science lingo or write formally. "People from accounting to shipping read it, and I need to talk to the nonscientists." What makes it work well is that it is written casually in his voice, his style. "What has contributed to my success as a CEO of early-stage companies is that ability to communicate complex technical issues and ideas in layman's terms," he reports.

When Blakely posts his blog to the intranet, he uses creativity to entice employees to click and read it. "I offer a prize for the first person with a rational comment on my blog post: a golf shirt with a logo. It's a tongue-in-cheek way to say, 'I don't want to be a voice in the wilderness out here!'" Folksy personal touches connect you and make you seem like a "real person." They also encourage people to access the information that's out there. "We want people to pay attention to the intranet so [that] they have the information. Everybody gets so busy over the course of a day, or week, or month, you have to make sure that they are plugging in."

Investing in Communications Resources

As a consultant working directly with a CEO or senior team, I am often surprised at how little they are investing in resources to help them communicate when communication drives business results. Communicating has to be a top priority. You need to invest in the people, processes, and tools that will allow you to communicate effectively with all your important audiences. The first step is to analyze how things are working now and what resources you will need to do the job well. Take a close look at what people and resources you will need to carry out the communications plan.

Not only is it frustrating for you, but it is also frustrating for your communications team when they don't have the resources to do their jobs and help you make an impact. Not long ago I received a call from the vice president of marketing and communications for a Fortune 1000 company. She explained that she was one of only two people in the entire global enterprise responsible for marketing, advertising, media, speaking engagements, and internal communications. I know this sounds impossible, but it is true. She was buried, finding it frustrating to make any impact at all. Yet, when she approached her boss about additional resources, he told her that it just wasn't a priority.

"You need resources," says Ellyn McColgan. "You have to apply people to the communications process who know how to write, speak, and communicate. At Fidelity Investments, we had those people. However, I've noticed in many organizations, the communications team is one of the first things that gets cut, and that's a mistake," she says. "We made a conscious effort to build an infrastructure to communicate the message."

Open Channels

As you consider where, when, and how, keep in mind that your communication channels should be wide open. This means a high level of frequency, access, and openness in the communication process. Rich Krueger, the new CEO of DynamicOps, says that wide-open channels of communication and transparency are vital to a fast-moving new company. "We are transparent with everyone in the company about where we stand in landing new customers and developing the product. We even tell them how much cash we have on hand. I show them the balance sheet and answer questions." This open channel of communication is essential to building trust.

Krueger says that people are savvy, and they often can sense bad news when you try to keep a lid on it. "They are all college-educated; even the young guys are smart, so you can't pull the wool over their eyes." When you don't share bad news, people become suspicious. "It becomes us versus them," he observes. "You can share bad news if you have people committed to success. I think no information is worse, because people make their own assumptions, and then you lose them," says Krueger.

Open lines of communication will build trust and help employees to make better decisions. For example, Krueger says, "The engineering manager, sales manager, marketing manager, and CTO are making several decisions on a daily basis. The engineer doing the codes needs to make a decision based on today's information. The sales guy in front of a customer has to make a call then

> *People are smart, and they often can sense the bad news even if you try to keep a lid on it.*

and there. I can't be with everyone; it's impossible. So they have to have the information."

Krueger says that open channels of communication include giving the management team thorough briefings on all aspects of the business and not isolating them in silos. Everyone should know what is going on in all parts of the business at a high level so that they can contribute to the business strategy and also speak intelligently to their own teams about what's going on. Krueger says that the more people know, the more quickly they can act and react. He believes that open channels empower the functional managers. "That way you aren't telling people what to do; you're *informing* them so [that] they *know* what to say and what to do."

Whether you're part of a startup venture company or you work for a mature global firm, wide-open channels of communication will overcome geography, time zones, and other barriers. As more companies go global, they must take a hard look at how to open up channels of communication to be sure that people have the information they need. This also means having the attitude that every question is a good question and letting people know that you have nothing to hide. When you get into a room with people, encourage them to engage with you. "I would answer any question you ask me," says Ellyn McColgan.

Use technology to open up channels of communication. What we have available to us today is just the start. Exciting new technology is going to continue to make it easier to stay in touch, and while not every new communication tool is effective, it is worth your while to stay on the cutting edge and try some innovations. Rich Krueger has found through technology that "even part-time people can be in the loop. They are sharing programs, and they have complete access to what's going on all the time." Krueger says that it's "freeing for people not to be jumping in cars and going to meetings. They can check on things and learn on the portal. They can be busy doing what they need to do and still stay in the loop."

Communicate the Way People Can Hear You

People tune in to what is going on in your company through different channels, so you have to communicate in a way that allows them to hear you. Vikki Pryor of SBLI USA says to pay attention to individual preferences in communication. "One of the key things you have to understand as a leader is that everyone is intelligent, but differently able." Pryor learned the importance of communicating with people the way they can hear you while working for the chief operations officer of another company. She wasn't able to connect. "He was frustrated every time we met. My performance was good, but we weren't connecting," she recalls.

Pryor sought the advice of a mentor. He reminded her that this chief operations officer had been trained as a surgeon, and a surgeon is trained never to go into the operating room without a plan. He recommended that Pryor go in organized with a binder and tabs. "It sounds straightforward, but normally, at this level, this isn't what's expected of a leader, so I hadn't thought of it. The first few times I did this, he looked at the document. After that, he didn't, because I had built up his trust." Pryor says that she learned that by understanding other people's style and preferences, you can build the relationships you want.

Respecting other people's preferences and styles also means speaking in plain, simple language that's easy for anyone to understand. Lose the jargon, and don't make it overcomplicated. Steve Rendle, president of The North Face, says that it's important to stay with a simple message. "I've learned not to overwhelm

> *Lose the jargon, and don't make it overcomplicated.*

people with too many points. Condense, condense, condense, and then constantly reinforce."

You and every single leader should work hard to simplify the message. It is a lot of work to make it simple. But you will find that the effort you put in pays off—with employees, customers, and prospects. Those who communicate make the sale. Speak in terms everyone understands. It's easy to fall back on meaningless jargon, unfriendly acronyms, and fluffy language.

Avoid the trap of falling into "business speak," and just use plain language. Talk to people; don't try to impress them. As you're preparing a presentation, go back and look at the language you're using and see if you can find a simpler, more "ear friendly" way to say it. This is important not just because it makes you seem more accessible and friendly, but also because people interpret the same business buzz words differently. So it's best to root out jargon from your presentation and make it a policy in your organization.

At least one senior executive I know published a list of "banned words" that people were not to use in her presence, including such words as *implement, initiative,* and *scalability.* These are pretty common words in business today, but she saw people hiding behind words that were hard to hear and could be construed in different ways. The entire organization joked about it, but it worked. There was a lot more "plain speak" in the company's business meetings.

Speaking to Different Cultures

As your company grows and does business regionally, nationally, or globally, you need to become more and more savvy about communicating across cultures. There are always subtleties to language, tone, and manner even among people who speak the same language. Understanding these nuances is essential to communicating effectively with people in various parts of the country and the world. Peter Roberts, CEO of Jones Lang Lasalle, says, "In a global organization, we have a lot of different cultures [just among employees]. When you are communicating, the message does not have to change, but it has to be a culture fit."

In considering culture, remember that you bring your own assumptions to a conversation, and it is important to understand what those assumptions and filters are. You will advance your business tremendously if you seek out expert assistance and training in cultural communication. When you and your team hit the road, you should feel confident that you know what to do when you get there. And when you get on the phone or communicate electronically, you also should have a full appreciation of how to do it well. There are many experts available on cultural and etiquette issues. Seek out these experts to help you succeed wherever you go.

The use of humor and emotion often trip up executives, both traveling abroad and in different parts of the United States. "Knowing when to throw in a joke [or not!], or how to tone down the passion and be more resolute, when to use stories or focus on data, or when to poke fun at yourself, these are all the sorts of things that you need to understand," says Roberts. He feels that one of the best pieces of advice he ever received after becoming CEO was from a mentor who suggested that he "dial up" the cultural filter and tailor his delivery and style.

The point of this is to reach out for expert help when you need it. "Don't presume [that] you have all the answers. I have put on my radar screen the need to get advice and help," Roberts says. He is a big believer in having "darn good experts at communication," and then, when you're confronted with a new situation or dynamic, you have someone at the ready to help make you look good.

Summary

- There are many ways to communicate your mission and purpose every day. Take an active role in developing the strategy and speaking often—your words carry weight.
- A communications plan is essential to the success of the business plan because communication will drive it forward. It also should measure and track success.
- Communications is not a soft science. Hardwire your communications plan to your business plan and link it directly to producing business results.
- Develop a strong trusted relationship with communications advisors. They are your partners, so you should include them in all important meetings and decisions.
- Get comfortable with all forms of communication, including broadcast, video, and media. Surround yourself with people who can help you to succeed at all of these.

14

Motivating Your Team: The Coach Gets You Ready

To find out what one is fitted to do, and to secure an
opportunity to do it, is the key to happiness.

—John Dewey

A YEAR OR TWO from now, where do you see yourself and your team, organization, or company? What about five or even ten years from now? Whatever your vision of the future, you need a group of talented people committed to the vision, motivated, and working with purpose and passion. Realizing the vision depends in large part on how you communicate it and inspire people to join you. So it's time to get ready—to look at exactly what steps you can take to connect people with purpose and achieve your goals.

I've talked at length about communication tools and strategies that work. As we near the end of this book, I'd like to act as your virtual coach through the final pages by helping you think through some simple ways to make the concepts real and bring ideas into your daily activities.

After years of coaching executives, I know what a challenge it is to rise above the daily grind. You have all you can do just to manage an organization and keep everybody happy and productive. Yet you probably sense that with the right approach and a modest amount of effort, you can really motivate people and inspire them to do great things. You can look for opportunities every day to add something to the mix that motivates people.

Let me assure you that this isn't about piling on a lot of new projects. Motivating people isn't so much a checklist as it is a mind-set. It's a way of thinking about how you want to lead and what you really want to say. The way to get into that mind-set is to think of motivational communication every day as *job number 1 and make it enjoyable to find a different way to connect.* In coaching leaders, I've noted that those who connect are simply more mindful of what they say to people and the impact it has on them. Motivational communication isn't just about giving an inspiring presentation, although that's a great skill to have. It's what you bring to every interaction that connects people with purpose.

What are some of the small ways you can incorporate productive, positive, meaningful interactions into everyday business activities?

- Get out of your office, make the rounds, and linger while you talk; don't be in a hurry.
- Attend a meeting you don't usually attend, and just listen with interest.
- Observe a part of your business you don't usually get to see.
- Send out a company-wide e-mail to praise a team for an achievement.
- Publish great feedback from your personal e-mail to the newsletter.
- Blog about something you heard from an employee that you found interesting.

> *Motivating people isn't so much a checklist as it is a mind-set. It's a way of thinking about how you want to lead.*

- Plan some fun ways to exchange ideas at your next weekly meeting.
- Organize a brown bag lunch with an unusual, stimulating business topic.
- Invite people who don't usually travel with you to visit a customer.
- Include three great success stories in your next presentation.

- Ask people to share good news with each other at the start of a meeting.
- Make up some new awards and give them out to employees at the next meeting.

If you and I could get together for a coaching session, I would of course want to learn more about you and your business. Since we're not face to face, I will simply share what I know has worked for other leaders and ask you to evaluate how these ideas would work for you.

I also will recommend that you choose a trusted friend, colleague, or partner to help you incorporate the ideas of this book into your leadership style. You wouldn't be where you are today if you didn't have this ability, but it's also very helpful to have people around you who can help you to achieve your goals more quickly and give you honest feedback. Choose someone who understands and supports you and also understands your organization. Give this book to that colleague, friend, or trusted advisor. After he or she has read it, talk together about ways that person might help you to achieve your goals.

In the following few pages I want to share some of the advice that has helped other leaders get started and do the things they need to do to build their skills and become the leaders they want to be.

Do the Little Things

Do the little things like those on the preceding list, and they will lead to big changes. Spend time with people and connect. You'll make an impact that reverberates around the organization. Remember what happened when Bill Swanson visited the Raytheon plant—productivity shot up and stayed high. People long to connect with their leaders. Those are the little things that matter.

Think about how people in your organization might feel if you invite them to a brown bag lunch, as Ranch Kimball did. They would talk about what they're doing and go back and tell everyone that they had lunch with the boss. They would feel like part of the inner circle, "in the know." They've heard it straight from you.

> *Whenever you spend time with people and have a chance to connect, you make an impact that reverberates around the organization.*

Or think about how you will make someone's day if you pick up the phone, as Matt Davis did, and congratulate him or her on an achievement. A five-minute call to tell the person that you appreciate what he or she has done is something the person will talk about with eight or ten other people.

These little acts add up and make you an influential, inspiring leader. Steve Rendle, president of The North Face, keeps a plaque with the word *Influence* on his desk. He reminds himself that every day it's his job to help people understand The North Face mission and strategy and help them to make it live in their work. "I recognize that this is the primary role of this position in the company," he says.

Do the little things, and watch how the motivation meter rises. It takes so little time, and the positive impact on your business is incalculable.

Just Start

Whenever I want to get something done, and it seems like a big project, I tell myself, "Just start." An example of this might be your decision to start a listening tour around the organization. How will you find time? Step one: Sit down at your desk with a full hour to schedule these meetings. Take the first small step, and you'll soon discover that you feel motivated and energized just having it planned. Small investments of time and resources toward a goal in the early stages will pay off. You'll recall from Chapter 12 that the secret to success is a threefold strategy of intention: Set the intention, schedule it, and have the discipline to follow through, and you'll move the needle forward and make progress.

Whenever I'm working with busy executives, I advise them to focus on three or a maximum of five areas where they would like to improve their skills. I find that most people can focus best on three at a time. More than this and your efforts get diluted, you get discouraged, you don't make progress, and you lose steam. Evaluate what's most important, work on that first, make a plan, and do it.

If you don't put it on the calendar, time will quickly slip away. I remember one client firm that was caught up on a company-wide reorganization. The leader of the group needed his people to get up to speed in presenting their ideas to the chairman, so we scheduled individual coaching programs for each of them. My policy is to schedule all coaching appointments for the year in advance to protect the dates and make coaching a priority, but the executive team insisted that it could not under the circumstances make that commitment. Team members said they preferred to come in "when they needed to." As the months went by, I never saw them. It wasn't on their schedule, so they forgot about it. I called and e-mailed with frequent reminders and tried everything I could, but all claimed they were too busy. Soon, eight months had passed, and of course, it wasn't any easier—they were busier than ever.

"Just starting" can be tough when you don't feel assured about the outcome of a project. David Woods, executive director of LIFE and an inspiring motivational speaker, says, "I didn't start out as a very effective speaker. I remember the first talk I ever gave in my first job. I got up in front of the audience, and it was small, maybe 30 or 40 people. I was horrible." He recalls, "I was stumbling and mumbling and wouldn't look at the audience. I was terrified. My boss said, 'For Pete's sake, you know what you're talking about! Just look at them and tell them!' Next time I did better."

As he progressed, he could hear other tough feedback. "I gave a speech in Knoxville, Tennessee," he recalls. "It was beautifully written, every word carefully selected and properly positioned, and I was really into this. I got only tepid applause, and afterward, my host said, 'That was the most beautifully written speech that no one listened to.'" Woods began practicing and internalizing the messages.

> "I didn't start out as a very effective speaker. I remember the first talk I ever gave in my first job. . . . I was horrible."

A step at a time, Woods became a powerful, confident speaker. It wouldn't have happened if he hadn't taken the first step. By just starting, and being okay with the discomfort, he improved. So just start, schedule it, and move forward. Then all you have to do is put one foot in front of the other.

Face Challenges Head On

Motivating people isn't just about positive talk. Sometimes you need to correct behaviors that are impeding work and undermining morale. It's easy to put off difficult conversations and hope that things will just work out, but as most people know, when you delay, it only gets worse.

Let's imagine a scenario where you can motivate by facing a difficult conversation head on: You have a sales rep who you always have liked. It's come to your attention that he has lost focus. You notice that he comes to work every day, gets a cup of coffee, checks the sports scores online, and then heads off to talk on the phone with a few favorite customers. He's not making the difficult calls—he's making the easy ones. You've seen a significant reduction in his productivity. He knows *how* to sell. He knows *what* to sell. But his sales activities are not leading to results. You don't look forward to the conversation, but you realize that postponing it only hurts him and the team. So you face it head on. You ask him what's going on. You tell him how important he is to the enterprise. You build him up by talking about his skills and reminding him of his successes. Then you set very specific targets for calls, meetings, and deals closed. You talk about why it matters. You get him to envision success. You get agreement on next steps. He goes out and sells. (Or he doesn't, and then you get the right person into the job, as we discussed in Chapter 11.)

Don't delay. Have the conversation now. Face the tough ones and be courageous. Sit down and talk it through, no matter how difficult. If it helps you, plan what you want to say. No matter how difficult the situation, if you address it head on, you will resolve it—and that will be motivating and energizing for you and everyone else involved.

Take Charge

When people are down, times are tough, or things aren't going well, that's when leaders have to step up and take charge not just of the business but also of the emotional state of the organization. Your job as the leader is not only to make good decisions but also to make people believe in themselves. By taking charge of the emotional state of the team and communicating in a positive way, you can keep people focused and reconnect them with purpose. If you have ever done this, you know how your positive attitude can conquer challenges and energize the whole team.

By taking charge, I don't mean assuming command and control. Taking charge is owning your own emotional state and then communicating in a positive way with others. This attitude is contagious. What you communicate gets communicated; your mood affects others. They watch you, pick up cues, and act accordingly. Work through challenging times with purpose and help people to see the positive so that they believe in themselves. Whatever ups and downs you encounter, communicating positive messages with energy is powerful. People can work very well when the chips are down if they have an inspired leader and they believe they can overcome.

It may help you to think of leadership as Ellyn McColgan does—as a calling. When she realized that she saw it this way, it changed how she viewed her career. "I started a few years ago to see a spiritual integration of my life and work," she says. "If I was going to be a leader and have thousands of people pass through my care, then I had to think about what that meant and take responsibility for it."

Taking charge is taking ownership of how you see yourself and how you interact with others.

One Day at a Time

Many leaders whom I interviewed for this book say that it took several years to develop their communication skills and an approach to motivating people that worked for them. By taking one

> "If I was going to be a leader and have thousands of people pass through my care, then I had to think about what that meant and take responsibility for it," says McColgan.

idea at a time and incorporating it one day at a time, you start to develop new habits.

For example, each of these leaders took one step, one day to motivate others that set a tone for the way they would lead. They got up in the morning, saw an opportunity to connect, and took that step.

- Ranch Kimball, of the Joslin Diabetes Center, decided one day to walk down to the clinic and learn how to inject himself with a needle so that he could interact with the clinical team and learn how hard it was for them to teach their patients to do the same.
- Mike Daly, of Baystate Medical Center, stopped and listened to his nurses' complaints about interrupting patients to activate their TVs every day. He acknowledged on the spot that it was a hassle, and he dropped the policy, which demonstrated that he would walk his talk about respect.
- Greg Case got on an airplane and paid his first visit to Aon's offices—it was the first of several hundred visits that helped him to connect with a global organization.
- Evelyn Murphy changed out of her suit, put on casual clothes, and went to a picnic where she could campaign by just talking to voters instead of giving a stump speech, and it got her elected to the office of lieutenant governor.

One day, one decision at a time, you change the way you lead and find new ways to connect with people and engage them.

Move Out of Your Comfort Zone

Many of the skills we've talked about take you outside your comfort zone. For example, a lot of people want to improve their executive presence on stage or make their talks more inspirational. They may not think that they're good at it, so they don't know how to start. It's important to move out of your comfort zone and challenge yourself to try things that seem hard.

Matt Davis, of Dow Chemical, says, "As people move up, they have to leave behind their operational excellence and stop doing things that come naturally to them. They have to leave that baggage on the side of the road, say goodbye to the tactical work, and go upward to motivate, inspire, and deliver passion to the organization."

Maureen McGurl, a long-time human resources executive with Stop and Shop and other corporations, says that every leader needs to do the hard work of moving out of his or her comfort zone of doing. A leader needs to get comfortable, for example, with the idea that it is his or her role to develop a vision and communicate it. "A clear vision is essential." McGurl has guided and overseen professional development for hundreds of executives and knows that many need to be prodded to do the work of developing vision and values. They don't always take it on themselves.

Moving out of your comfort zone may mean taking time to ask big questions that are hard to answer. What kind of leader do I want to be? Where do I want to take the organization? What are the values that are important to me? "The first thing I ask is, 'What the heck do you stand for?'" says Matt Davis. "You can't convey passion until you know yourself." Look at Howard Schultz of Starbucks, Ellen Parker of Project Bread, David Woods of LIFE, and others. They took the long but rewarding road to discover what leadership is for them.

> *"The first thing I ask is, 'What the heck do you stand for?'" says Matt Davis.*

Believe in Yourself

You have what it takes to be the leader you want to be and to take your organization where you want to go. But sometimes you lose faith, and when you lose faith, you can't motivate and inspire others.

We all lose faith in ourselves from time to time. Not long ago it happened to me. At a meeting of my chapter of the Women Presidents Association, the cofacilitator, Mindy Goodfriend, asked each woman business owner in our group to share our three-year revenue targets. This was not an unusual topic because the group signs confidentiality agreements so that we can have an open forum and really help each other grow our businesses.

One by one, each member put a target revenue number on the table—some didn't have to think about it—others struggled. Only one other member and I "passed" the first time around. I couldn't come up with a number. The second time around, even she committed, but I held back. "How do I know?" I asked the group. "Is there a tool I can use to calculate this?" This is when the other facilitator, Lisa Matthews, realized it wasn't a calculator I needed—it was a boost. She gently reminded me that several months earlier I had not hesitated to share a revenue goal. What was happening? Somehow, I had lost my belief.

When you feel this happening, be aware of it and respect it, but don't allow it to control you or creep into your communication with others. Remember what has made you successful. Think about how you've done it before. Those same skills will see you through again. Believe in yourself, and you'll be a persuasive, influential leader. Don't just talk to yourself either. Surround yourself with people who believe in you. And then talk about it—take a leap of faith when you speak about your business ideal. As Mindy Goodfriend reminded me that day, "We hit the targets we aim for."

> *Think about what you really want for your business, not just what is possible.*

Do It Now

In the words of the great Duke Ellington, "I don't need more time. . . . I need a deadline!" It's easy to put things off, but as a coach, I've witnessed that a "do it now" approach serves you best. By just doing what you can today, you feel instantly energized and ready to take on the next task tomorrow.

You may be someone who tends to procrastinate, and if so, this technique will be difficult for you. It's tempting to wait until next week, next month, or next quarter to take on a big project. Yet you know that when you do it now, you position yourself and your company to take advantage of opportunities when they come along. Everyone on your team will be motivated to keep moving forward if you've at least started and can see what's next.

By "doing it now" I don't mean doing the work of others—you need to be the leader who encourages and motivates other people to take action. So don't take "do it now" too literally—what I mean is becoming a leader who sets the pace and expectation that people will take action. "One of the fundamental flaws with execs," says Beth Webster, a former human resources leader for Fidelity

> *"I don't need more time. . . . I need a deadline!"*

Investments, "is they are too busy doing and not leading." Disengage from the "doing," and communicate the expectations, ownership, and outcomes so that other people get things done.

Raise Your Game

It's important to look at the development of these skills as a lifelong pursuit. If you're part of the human resources or leadership development team, you know that leaders at every level who raise their game keep moving up in their organizations. Raising your game means developing what many people refer to as "soft skills" (a true misnomer) to improve your performance and help you to become a motivational leader.

Communication and related skills are not specifically spelled out in many professional development plans. They are often hidden in other skills, but if you look closely, many areas for development are really about communication. "If a leader doesn't report to someone who emphasizes the importance of communication skills," says Maureen McGurl, "it is the rare executive who will learn how and do it well. Unless it is valued and asked for and focused on, it's probably not going to happen."

Brian Johnson, a Fidelity Investments human resources leader specializing in succession planning, says that by the time you get to the top, you are expected to have a vision and to know how to *communicate* that vision. "There are people who won't make it because they are not strategic enough . . . they are either too tactical, too operational, too narrow minded, or too conservative. Then there are some people who are brilliant at developing a point of view but can't articulate it even with all the help in the world."

It's often too late when executives find out that communication skills are as important as they are. By the time they are told, they may not be seriously considered for top jobs. Or they have one chance in a high-stakes setting to get it right. I've had companies call me and tell me that an executive has to ace a board presentation or immediately start communicating differently with his or her staff or he or she will be out. So much time has gone by and so little has been done to support the executive's development in this area that there is no room for error. I'll hear, "He or she just can't blow it this time." This is the equivalent of emergency surgery on a critically ill patient—all you're really going to do is stop the bleeding.

> "One of the fundamental flaws with execs," says Beth Webster, a seasoned human resources leader, "is they are too busy doing and not leading."

It is impossible to learn these skills in a crash course. If the organization is asking, "How can we raise this issue with the executive?" my answer is always, "Do it now."

Practice the Art of Deliberate Practice

Deliberate practice is a term I learned about while reading about the work of three British researchers, Howe, Davidson, and Sluboda, who studied peak performance for ten years. These researchers found that peak performers in science, medicine, research, sales, sports, the arts, business, politics, or any profession put the most hours into deliberate practice. Deliberate practice is not just practice; it's practice with a specific goal in mind. For example, deliberate practice is not "going out and hitting a bucket of golf balls," they say. "It's hitting a golf ball 300 times with the goal of getting within 20 feet of the pin 80 percent of the time."

The great golfer Gary Player was for many years an awesome competitor in national and international golf tournaments. People constantly told him, "I'd give anything if I could hit a golf ball like you." On hearing this comment one too many times, the story goes, Player responded impatiently: "No, you wouldn't. You'd do anything to hit a golf ball like me . . . if it were easy! Do you know what you have to do to hit a golf ball like me? You've got to get up at 5, go out to the golf course, and hit a thousand golf balls! You walk to the clubhouse to wash the blood off your hands, slap a bandage on, and go out and hit another thousand golf balls! That is what it takes to hit a golf ball like me!"

Player's story dramatically illustrates the commitment that champions make to winning through deliberate practice. It is a conscious choice to go the extra mile. What separates winners from the rest of the pack is deliberate practice. It's how they achieve excellence.

> *It is impossible to learn everything you need to know in a crash course.*

Evelyn Murphy describes learning to speak well as a direct result of deliberate practice. She worked every day to improve her speaking skills. "I had no communication skills when I started running for office; I learned it all campaigning," says Murphy. Day after day on the campaign trail she improved and then discovered that she loved doing it! "Learning to connect with people was a tremendous experience," she says. "Businesspeople should run for office just once because it is humbling. You learn so much about the essentials of communication."

Never Stop—Keep Going

As CEO of Dow Chemical Company, Andrew Liveris has become an exceptional communicator and an inspiring leader. As good as he is at communicating a message though, he never rests on his laurels. He could probably "wing it" now and do well enough, but he never stops. He always prepares and practices. He meets with his speechwriter, reviews the text, edits, and practices many times. A talented communications team is assembled to help him (and the rest of the senior leaders) be the best they can be. The communications team knows how Liveris thinks. Team members are fully apprised of the strategy. The entire organization spends long hours, nights and weekends if necessary, to make sure that the message is communicated.

This is one of the best corporate models I've seen that illustrates the mantra, "Never stop." And it pays off. Never stop working toward your goals, and never stop trying to improve, incrementally, every day.

As we close in on the final thoughts of this book, I urge you to look at the opportunities you have right now. You have an organization that is waiting and hoping for great leaders. Imagine what you can achieve. Keep going, one day at a time, and have faith. Just remember the mantra, "Never stop."

Summary

- Just start. Take the first small step, and you'll soon discover that you feel motivated and energized. Even small investments of time and resources in the early stages will pay off.
- Believe in yourself. You have what it takes to be the leader you want to be, one who communicates, motivates, and inspires.
- The little things can make a big difference. Whenever you spend time with people and connect, you make an impact that reverberates around the organization.

Deliberate practice is the single most important factor in achieving excellence in anything. Most people underestimate how much experience they need to excel.

15

Final Thoughts on Becoming a Leader Who Motivates People

If your actions inspire others to dream more, learn more, do more and become more, you are a leader.

—John Quincy Adams

WE BEGAN BY LOOKING at what it takes to motivate and inspire people—having a strong purpose, connecting others to that purpose, and doing so with passion. We've looked at the principles of motivating and inspiring people, too, and how to connect the dots—align the organization, create the story, show passion, make the time, and practice new habits of motivational leaders.

Through all this, I hope that you see that becoming a leader who motivates people isn't mysterious and isn't even that hard. It's simply a matter of embracing your role as a motivational leader and getting in touch with that purpose. While I don't think a single one of the leaders I've talked about here would call themselves motivating leaders, they all have been able in their own way to connect people with purpose and achieve great things.

When you are looking to connect with a purpose, I think it's important to constantly be on the lookout for inspiration. Read books, go to movies, and stop and watch programs about people who are doing great things. When you see someone who is working with purpose and passion, it will reconnect you with your own passion and help you to find ways to express it.

Recently, I watched a story on ABC about an 18-year-old woman named Kristen Elliott who, at age 16, was diagnosed with a rare form of cancer—she had a tumor in her leg. Chances of survival of this aggressive form of cancer were low, but Kristen remained active. She played volleyball on the high school varsity team and even traveled to Zimbabwe with a school group to work with children living in poverty.

When the cancer spread to her lungs, the Make-a-Wish Foundation, which grants wishes to young patients with life-threatening illnesses, asked Kristen if she had a wish she wanted fulfilled. The most common request is a trip to Disney World, but Kristen had another idea. She wanted to build a home for orphaned children infected with AIDS in Zimbabwe.

Although her family and the foundation were skeptical at first, she insisted that this was her only wish. The foundation granted her $2,600, which she used as seed money to raise more. At the time the story aired on ABC, Kristen had raised $8,000. Her goal was $60,000, and I imagine that after that story, the donations poured in.

Now that is an inspiring story, one that puts things into perspective. If Kristen could find a positive sense of purpose out of this tremendous personal challenge, then each of us can learn from her. Some of us, like Kristen, are confronted with these types of challenges all too early in life, and they make the most of them by finding meaning in them. While Kristen's stunningly selfless act at such a young age is a compelling example of purpose, I would hope that each of us might take a page from her book.

As leaders, we are fortunate to have the opportunity to guide people toward a common goal. We should believe in what we do, the services and products our companies make, and the value we offer to others. Having a strong sense of our own purpose attracts others and allows us to build great organizations where people can express their talents.

When you work with purpose and foster an environment where people get excited and enthusiastic about what they are doing, everything you want to achieve is possible. You are the person who starts this in motion by motivating and inspiring others. To do this within the framework of business is a worthy pursuit because we spend so much of our time, energy, and talent at work. Our businesses are the engine that drives the economy, creates opportunity, and gives people a place to discover and exercise their talents and earn the money they need to fuel their lives and pursue their dreams. My hope for you is that you will discover and nurture a purpose that motivates you and others.

I hope that what you've read here has provoked you to think about leadership in a new way. The journey to becoming a leader who motivates and inspires others is a path worth taking. It is an inner journey to know yourself and an outer journey to share it with the world. After all, true leadership is not so much about what is in your head as about what is in your heart and how you use that to inspire others to greatness.

16

A List of Ideas to Get Started

HERE ARE SOME IDEAS that support some of the strategies in this book. Glance at these ideas, and put a few of them on your to-do list.

- Schedule four quarterly brown bag lunches for employees. Find out how things are going from their perspective, and share your vision and strategy.
- Make every Friday a walk-around day to visit people you don't see all the time.
- Go on a 90-day listening tour and gather information to help you develop a project plan that is supported by others and helps you achieve a long-range objective.
- Put a stack of note cards on your desk, and send at least three notes of thanks and congratulations each week.
- Every Thursday, schedule 30 minutes to write a positive, inspiring e-mail to the entire organization.
- Ask each person on your team to tell you a success story; capture it in story form, and share it with everyone.

- Schedule a one-hour meeting with a communications advisor, and talk about vision and strategy. Record the session on audiotape, and have it transcribed. Use the written remarks to develop a presentation.
- Videotape a presentation, and play it back with the specific purpose of evaluating how well you motivate and inspire others with your words. Pay attention to the message and how you deliver it. Ask a trusted advisor to offer suggestions.
- Look at the calendar for your next major business meeting and back-time several weeks or months—put time and resources into making it the best, most inspiring meeting ever.
- Take three to four hours over the next month to review your strategic plan, and write a communications plan to complement it. If you have a communications advisor, have that person also prepare a tactical plan to implement it.
- Answer the questionnaire in Chapter 3 on how to discover purpose. Talk with a trusted advisor about what you've learned from the exercise and what next steps you should take.
- Hire a coach for you and your team to help you improve communications in the organization. Find someone who can advise you on strategy as well as guide you in developing your communications skills.
- Hire a survey company or develop your own survey on how your customers or clients feel about your organization.
- Survey your employees, too. Do it this quarter, review the findings, and determine how you can make improvements. Then schedule a follow-up survey next year.
- If you have a challenge and need to communicate directly and clearly to alter the course, don't delay. Schedule the meeting now, and prepare for it.
- Take a creative approach to your next presentation. Schedule time right now to brainstorm with a creative person. Start way ahead of time.
- Before the presentation, lay out pieces of paper on the floor, and imagine that you can illustrate your points through pictures, photos, and powerful single-word visuals.

Recommended Reading

Carnegie, Dale. *The Leader in You: How to Win Friends, Influence People and Succeed in a Changing World.* New York: Simon and Schuster, March 31, 1994.

Coelho, Paul. *The Pilgrimage.* New York: HarperCollins, Sept. 2, 2008.

Drucker, Peter. *The Effective Executive: The Definitive Guide to Getting the Right Things Done.* New York: HarperBusiness Essentials, Jan. 3, 2006.

Dyer, Wayne. *The Power of Intention: Learning to Co-Create Your World Your Way.* New York: Hay House, Dec. 15, 2005.

Goldsmith, Marshall. *What Got You Here Won't Get You There: How Successful People Become Even More Successful.* New York: Hyperion, Jan. 9, 2007.

Green, Charles H. *Trust Based Selling: Using Customer Focus and Collaboration to Build Long Term Relationships.* New York: McGraw-Hill, Nov. 17, 2005.

Green, Thad B., and Raymond T. Butkus. *Motivation, Beliefs and Organizational Transformation.* New York: Quorum Books, June 30, 1999.

Hallowell, Edward M. *Crazy Busy: Overstretched, Overbooked, and About to Snap! Strategies for Handling Your Fast-Paced Life.* New York: Ballantine Books, 2006.

Kielburger, Craig, and Marc Kielburger. *Me to We: Finding Meaning in a Material World.* New York: Fireside Books, March 25, 2008.

Lizotte, Ken. *The Expert's Edge: Become the Go-To Authority People Turn to Every Time.* New York: McGraw-Hill, Dec. 26, 2007.

Lane, Bill. *Jacked UP, The Inside Story of How Jack Welch Talked GE into Becoming the World's Greatest Company.* New York: McGraw-Hill, Dec. 17, 2007.

Marston, Cam. *Motivating the 'What's In It for Me' Workforce: Manage Across the Generational Divide and Increase Profits.* Hoboken: Wiley, May 18, 2007.

Peale, Norman Vincent. *The Power of Positive Thinking.* Fireside, May 18, 2007.

Richardson, Cheryl. *Life Makeovers: 52 Practical and Inspiring Ways to Improve Your Life One Week at a Time.* New York: Broadway Books, Dec. 24, 2002.

Robinson, Lynn. *Divine Intuition: Your Guide to Creating the Life You Love.* DK Adult, Jan. 2001.

Sanborn, Mark. The Encore Effect: *How to Achieve Remarkable Performance in Anything You do.* New York: Doubleday, Sep. 2, 2008.

Schultz, Howard. *Pour Your Heart into It: How Starbucks Built a Company One Cup at a Time.* New York: Hyperion Books, Jan 6, 1999.

Shapiro, Steve. *Goal Free Living: How to Have the Life You Want NOW.* New York, Wiley, Jan. 3, 2006.

Tolle, Eckhart. *A New Earth: Awakening to Your Life's Purpose.* New York: Penguin Books, Jan. 30, 2008.

Warren, Rick. *The Purpose-Driven Life: What on Earth Am I Here For?* New York: Zondrvan, March 13, 2007.

Weiss, Alan. *Best-Laid Plans: Turning Strategy into Action Throughout Your Organization.* New York: Brisas Research Press, 1994.

Index